Alan Clark

Alan Clark

DK

KNOWLEDGE ENCYCLOPEDIA

ANIMAL!

Written by John Woodward
Consultant Dr Kim Dennis-Bryan

Illustrators Val @ Advocate-Art, Andrew Beckett @ Illustration Ltd, Adam Benton,
Peter Bull, Dynamo Ltd, Andrew Kerr, Jon @ KJA,
Arran Lewis, Peter Minister, Stuart Jackson-Carter – SJC Illustration

DK UK:
Senior Editor Jenny Sich
Senior Art Editor Stefan Podhorodecki
Editors Scarlett O'Hara, Rona Skene
Editorial Assistant Vicky Richards
Jacket Design Development Manager Sophia MTT
Jacket Editor Claire Gell
Producers (Pre-Production) Dragana Puvacic, Gillian Reid
Producer Sarah Burke
Managing Editor Francesca Baines
Managing Art Editor Philip Letsu
Publisher Andrew Macintyre
Associate Publishing Director Liz Wheeler
Art Director Karen Self
Design Director Philip Ormerod
Publishing Director Jonathan Metcalf

Special Sales and Custom Publishing Manager Michelle Baxter

DK India:
Senior Editor Rupa Rao
Senior Art Editor Anjana Nair
Art Editors Amit Varma, Alpana Aditya, Tanvi Sahu
Assistant Editor Charvi Arora
Senior DTP Designers Shanker Prasad, Vishal Bhatia, Harish Aggarwal
DTP Designers Ashok Kumar, Anita Yadav
Senior Picture Researcher Sumedha Chopra
Illustrator Arun Pottirayil
Jacket Designer Dhirendra Singh
Managing Jackets Editor Saloni Singh
Pre-Production Manager Balwant Singh
Production Manager Pankaj Sharma
Picture Research Manager Taiyaba Khatoon
Managing Editor Kingshuk Ghoshal
Managing Art Editor Govind Mittal

This abridged edition published in 2017

First published in Great Britain in 2016 by
Dorling Kindersley Limited
80 Strand, London WC2R 0RL

Copyright © 2016 Dorling Kindersley Limited
A Penguin Random House Company
10 9 8 7 6 5 4 3 2 1
001–308661–September/2017

ISBN: 978-0-2413-2132-4

Printed and bound in China

A WORLD OF IDEAS:
SEE ALL THERE IS TO KNOW

www.dk.com

CONTENTS

INVERTEBRATES

FISH

AMPHIBIANS

REPTILES

BIRDS

MAMMALS

Scales and sizes

The sizes given in this book are **average maximums**. For scale, animals are shown next to an average-height adult man, an adult human hand, or half a thumb. Where the length of an animal is given, this refers to: for fish, amphibians, and reptiles, the measurement from head to tail; for birds, the measurement from beak to tail; for mammals, the head-body length (excluding tail).

1.8 m (6 ft)

18 cm (7 in)

2 cm (3/4 in)

INVERTEBRATES

Most of the animals on Earth are not furry mammals, scaly reptiles, or feathery birds. They are invertebrates – animals that do not have an internal jointed skeleton. Many live in the oceans, but many more live on land. They include the most numerous, successful animals of all – the insects.

WHAT IS AN INVERTEBRATE?

An invertebrate is any animal that does not have an internal jointed skeleton. The term includes a wide diversity of animals, ranging from microscopic worms to giant squid, with little in common except the lack of a vertebrate skeleton. Some have soft bodies and many others have protective shells. But the most abundant are the amazing variety of crustaceans, insects, spiders, and similar animals that have hard, jointed external skeletons – the arthropods.

Outnumbered

Altogether, the invertebrates make up at least 97 per cent of all the animal species on Earth. The vertebrates include most of the biggest animals, but they are hugely outnumbered.

3% Vertebrates

97% Invertebrates

TYPES OF INVERTEBRATE

There are 35 major groups of species in the animal kingdom, each called a phylum. The vertebrates form part of just one phylum; all the other 34 phylae are made up of invertebrates. Shown below are some of these.

Sponges
These aquatic organisms are the simplest animals. They consist of many cells, but do not have specialized organs. They gather food by filtering it from the water.

Segmented worms
Also known as annelid worms, these include the earthworm and many marine species. Their bodies are made up of many identical, soft-skinned segments.

Molluscs
This large phylum consists of the snails and clams, as well as octopuses and similar animals. Most live in the sea, and many have chalky, protective shells.

Echinoderms
The word echinoderm means "spiny skin" – an apt name for a phylum that includes the spiny sea urchins. It also includes the starfish and sea cucumbers.

Comb jellies
These ocean drifters snare other animals and draw them into their transparent bodies. They swim by beating rows of comb-like structures on their skin.

Cnidarians
These include the sea anemones, corals, and jellyfish. They all live in the water where they extend their stinging tentacles to catch small animals.

Arthropods
The largest phylum consists of animals that have tough external skeletons with jointed legs. Their strong skeletons allow them to live on land as well as in water.

ARTHROPODS

More than 80 per cent of all known animal species are arthropods, and most of them are insects. They also include crustaceans, millipedes and other myriapods, and arachnids such as scorpions and spiders.

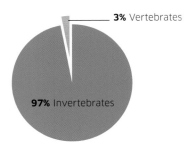

INSECTS

CRUSTACEANS

MYRIAPODS

ARACHNIDS

Inside an arthropod

An arthropod has many body segments, each supported by tough skin that acts as a skeleton. The skin may be thickened or reinforced with chalky minerals to form protective armour. Thin, flexible skin between the segments allows movement.

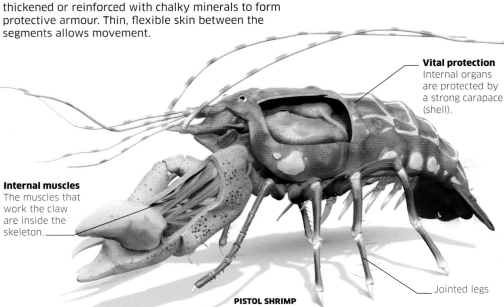
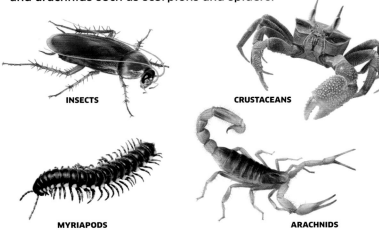

Vital protection
Internal organs are protected by a strong carapace (shell).

Internal muscles
The muscles that work the claw are inside the skeleton.

Jointed legs

PISTOL SHRIMP

HEADS AND TAILS

Invertebrates display a huge variety of body shapes. Many have the familiar body plan of a head, containing a brain and well-developed sense organs, a body equipped with legs, and a tail end. These animals often display bilateral symmetry, in which the right and left sides of the body are mirror images. But many other invertebrates either have a very different type of symmetry, while sponges have none at all.

Insect
This ladybird has bilateral symmetry. It has a distinct head, and a body made up of a thorax, bearing three pairs of legs, and an abdomen.

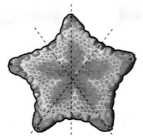

Sea star
Starfish and related animals have radial symmetry. Their bodies are arranged around a central point.

Octopus
Squid, octopuses, and their relatives have a strange body plan. The tentacles are attached directly to the head and their organs are contained in the bag-shaped mantle.

Clam
Inside its shell, a clam or similar bivalve mollusc has no clear body plan. It has no head, no brain, and only very basic sense organs.

BODIES AND SHELLS

Many invertebrates have soft bodies and do not need supportive skeletons. They maintain their shape using their muscles and body fluids. But soft bodies are vulnerable, so some have protective shells. The tough exoskeletons of arthropods provide both support and protection.

Soft body
This earthworm's body is supported by the soil, so it does not need a strong skeleton. The bodies of many aquatic invertebrates are supported by water in a similar way. The worm can move by stretching its head end forwards, then contracting to pull its tail forward too.

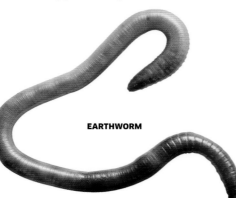

EARTHWORM

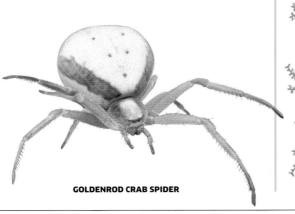

GARDEN SNAIL

Protective shell
A land snail has a soft body, but it also has a strong shell. If it feels threatened, it can draw its entire body into the shell. This also helps it survive dry weather, because the shell stops it losing body moisture.

Hard exoskeleton
The external skeleton of this spider supports its body, and also forms its venomous fangs. But the skeleton stops the spider growing, so at intervals it has to be shed and replaced. The soft new skeleton takes time to harden, leaving the spider very vulnerable.

GOLDENROD CRAB SPIDER

AQUATIC INVERTEBRATES

Many invertebrates live in the oceans. The water supports their bodies and gives them a steady supply of food. Land animals must search for things to eat, but aquatic invertebrates can wait for food to come to them.

BLUE MUSSELS

Rich pickings
Coastal seas are so rich in food that huge numbers of invertebrates can live in colonies on the rocks. These mussels feed by filtering the water through their bodies to gather edible particles. There is plenty for all.

SNAKELOCK'S ANEMONE

Rooted to the spot
This sea anemone spends most of its life attached to a rock. It does not need to move around, because water flowing around it carries small animals that it can catch with its long tentacles.

ORANGE TREE GORGONIAN

Shells close tight at low tide

Each bud is a polyp

Linked colonies
Many colonies of invertebrates are made up of separate animals. But others consist of animals that are linked together like buds on the branches of a tree. This sea fan is made up of many tiny feeding polyps that all share the same skeleton.

8 invertebrates ○ **CNIDARIANS**

A **Portuguese man o' war** can give **serious stings** even when washed up **dead on a beach**.

24 The number of **eyes** a **box jellyfish has**.

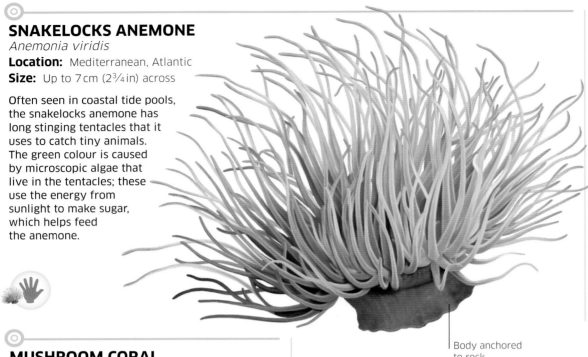

SNAKELOCKS ANEMONE
Anemonia viridis
Location: Mediterranean, Atlantic
Size: Up to 7 cm (2¾ in) across

Often seen in coastal tide pools, the snakelocks anemone has long stinging tentacles that it uses to catch tiny animals. The green colour is caused by microscopic algae that live in the tentacles; these use the energy from sunlight to make sugar, which helps feed the anemone.

Body anchored to rock

STRAWBERRY ANEMONE
Actinia fragacea
Location: N.E. Atlantic Ocean
Size: Up to 10 cm (4 in) across

Like several other sea anemones, this lives on rocky shores where the falling tide leaves it exposed out of water twice a day. It survives by retracting its tentacles into its body cavity, where they stay moist until the tide rises again and they can extend back out to catch food.

Tentacles retracted at low tide

MUSHROOM CORAL
Ctenactis echinata
Location: Indo-Pacific region
Size: Up to 25 cm (9¾ in) across

Solitary corals are similar to sea anemones, with cylindrical or oval bodies crowned by small tentacles surrounding a central mouth. This species is one of the stony, reef-building corals, with a limestone skeleton made from minerals absorbed from the seawater that it lives in.

Cnidarians

Jellyfish, corals, sea anemones, and their relatives are all cnidarians – aquatic animals with soft bodies that are usually armed with stinging cells for catching prey. Many are very beautiful, but a few can be deadly.

A typical cnidarian has a body made of jelly enclosed by two layers of cells – one on the outside, and the other forming the animal's stomach lining. It may also have a crown of mobile tentacles. Some cnidarians are free-drifting medusae, or jellyfish, but many are polyps (hollow cylinders surrounded by tentacles) that spend their lives attached to rocks or the sea bed. Many corals and sea anemones form colonies of interconnected polyps that share nutrients they gather from the water.

BRAIN CORAL
Diploria labyrinthiformis
Location: Caribbean Sea
Size: Up to 2 m (6½ ft) across

Looking like a human brain, this is a colonial stony coral, formed from thousands of interconnected coral polyps. While each one has its own array of food-gathering tentacles, the polyps also benefit from microscopic algae in their tissues that use solar energy to make food.

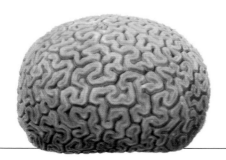

ORANGE TREE GORGONIAN
Swiftia exserta
Location: W. Atlantic Ocean
Height: Up to 2 m (6½ ft)

Also known as a sea fan, this is a colonial coral with many linked polyps attached to a skeleton of horny, flexible material. The colony grows in a flat, branching form, and gathers food from ocean currents that flow through the branches.

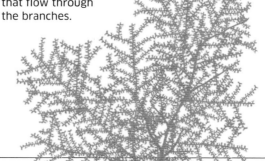

PURPLE SEA PEN
Virgularia sp.
Location: N. E. Atlantic, Mediterranean
Height: Up to 50 cm (19¾ in)

Made up of many feeding polyps attached to a much bigger central polyp that forms a stalk, sea pens gather food from the water in the same way as sea fans. The name comes from the way their feathery shape resembles a quill pen.

Colonial stony corals have formed the largest living structure on Earth – the Australian Great Barrier Reef, which is 2,300 km (1,430 miles) long.

100 years or more – the age some sea pens may reach.

9

GREEN HYDRA
Hydra viridissima

Location: Northern temperate regions

Height: Up to 3 cm (1¼ in)

Hydras are among the few cnidarians that live in freshwater. They gather tiny, drifting animals with their tentacles, but the green hydra also contains green algae that use light energy to make food. Buds that form on its body develop into new hydras.

New hydra forming as bud

PORTUGUESE MAN O' WAR
Physalia physalis

Location: Tropical and temperate seas worldwide

Size: Float up to 30 cm (11¾ in) across

This extraordinary organism is not a single animal, but a colony of polyps, each with a special role. One polyp forms a float that drifts on the ocean, supporting other polyps that gather food, digest it, or produce new polyps. The long, trailing tentacles deliver a dangerous sting.

Deadly tentacles
Tentacles can be up to 50 m (165 ft) long.

LION'S MANE JELLYFISH
Cyanea capillata

Location: Arctic Ocean

Size: Up to 2 m (6½ ft) across

One of the biggest of the true jellyfish, this ocean giant can swim slowly by contracting its broad, bell-shaped body, but normally drifts with the currents. It preys on fish, squid, and any other animals that it can trap in its long, stinging tentacles.

Stinging tentacles trail in the water

UPSIDE-DOWN JELLYFISH
Cassiopea andromeda

Location: Gulf of Mexico, Caribbean

Size: Up to 30 cm (11¾ in) across

Most jellyfish swim or drift in open water, but this unusual species lies upside down on the sea bed with its stinging tentacles extending upwards. This enables it to feed like a sea anemone, trapping animals carried past by the current.

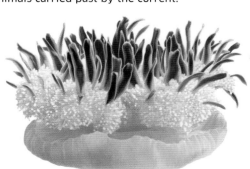

STALKED JELLYFISH
Haliclystus antarcticus

Location: Southern Ocean

Size: Up to 4 cm (1½ in) across

Recently discovered in shallow, near-freezing waters near Antarctica, this jellyfish has a central stalk and eight arms, each with a cluster of stinging tentacles. It clings to rocks and traps prey drifting in the cold but food-rich currents.

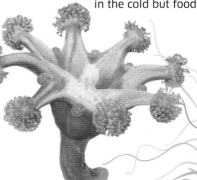

BOX JELLYFISH
Chironex fleckeri

Location: Indo-Pacific region

Size: Up to 25 cm (10 in) across

One of the most dangerous sea creatures, the box jellyfish is also known as the sea wasp because of its lethal sting. Each of its 60 long tentacles is armed with stinging cells that can cause serious and even fatal injuries to human swimmers.

INVERTEBRATES

GIANT CLAM

Tridacna gigas

Location: S. Pacific and Indian oceans

Size: Shell up to 1.4 m (4½ ft) across

Diet: Plankton

Water outlet
Water passing over the gills
is pumped out through an
opening in the mantle called
the exhalant siphon.

Sunlight energy
The mantle contains
transparent "windows",
through which sunlight
passes, allowing the
algae in the mantle
to make food.

Two halves
The giant clam is a bivalve
mollusc: its shell has two halves,
or valves, joined with a hinge.

Weighed down
Adult clams are held
in place by their great
weight. Young giant
clams are anchored
to the sea bed with a
muscular "foot" but
this shrinks with age.

Eggs and sperm
are pumped out of
the exhalant siphon

Spawning

Giant clams cannot move
around, so they reproduce
by all spawning at the same
time. Each clam can produce
both eggs and sperm, and
it releases them into the
water where they can be
fertilized by those of a
nearby clam. The sperm
is released first to reduce
the risk of self-fertilization.
Fertilized eggs hatch into
larvae that drift away in
the current.

Giant clam

**The magnificent giant clam is the heaviest living
mollusc – a colossal relative of cockles, mussels, and
oysters. It typically spends its life rooted in the sand
of a tropical coral reef, growing bigger each year.**

A giant clam spends its first few days of life as a free-drifting larva,
without a shell, in the tropical Indo-Pacific Ocean. But it soon turns
into a tiny replica of its parents, and settles on a coral reef. It feeds
on plankton strained from water pumped through its body, but up
to two-thirds of the nutrients it needs are supplied by millions of
microscopic, plant-like algae that live in its soft mantle tissue using
the energy of sunlight to make food.

Like many **bivalve molluscs**, the giant clam can **produce pearls** inside its shell.

100 years – the **age** a giant clam **can reach**.

6 billion The number of **eggs** an adult giant clam can **release during its lifetime**.

11

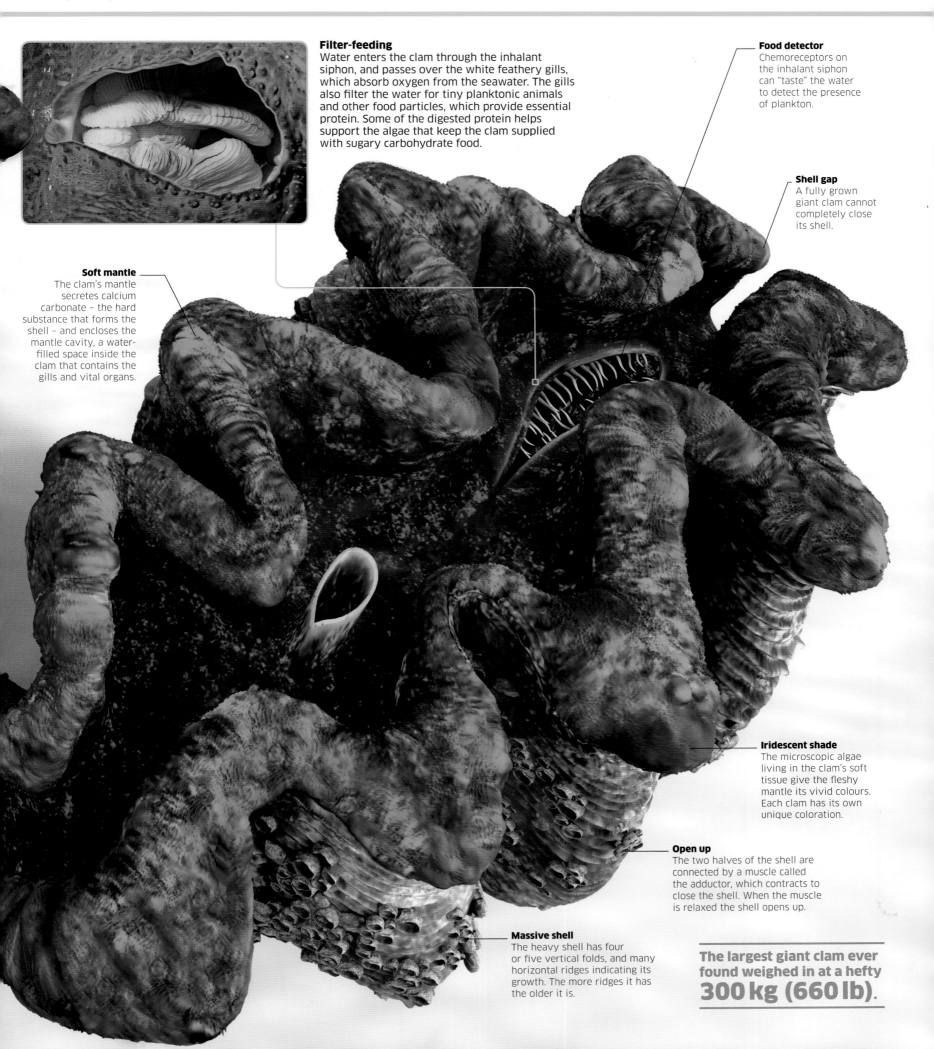

Filter-feeding
Water enters the clam through the inhalant siphon, and passes over the white feathery gills, which absorb oxygen from the seawater. The gills also filter the water for tiny planktonic animals and other food particles, which provide essential protein. Some of the digested protein helps support the algae that keep the clam supplied with sugary carbohydrate food.

Food detector
Chemoreceptors on the inhalant siphon can "taste" the water to detect the presence of plankton.

Shell gap
A fully grown giant clam cannot completely close its shell.

Soft mantle
The clam's mantle secretes calcium carbonate – the hard substance that forms the shell – and encloses the mantle cavity, a water-filled space inside the clam that contains the gills and vital organs.

Iridescent shade
The microscopic algae living in the clam's soft tissue give the fleshy mantle its vivid colours. Each clam has its own unique coloration.

Open up
The two halves of the shell are connected by a muscle called the adductor, which contracts to close the shell. When the muscle is relaxed the shell opens up.

Massive shell
The heavy shell has four or five vertical folds, and many horizontal ridges indicating its growth. The more ridges it has the older it is.

The largest giant clam ever found weighed in at a hefty 300 kg (660 lb).

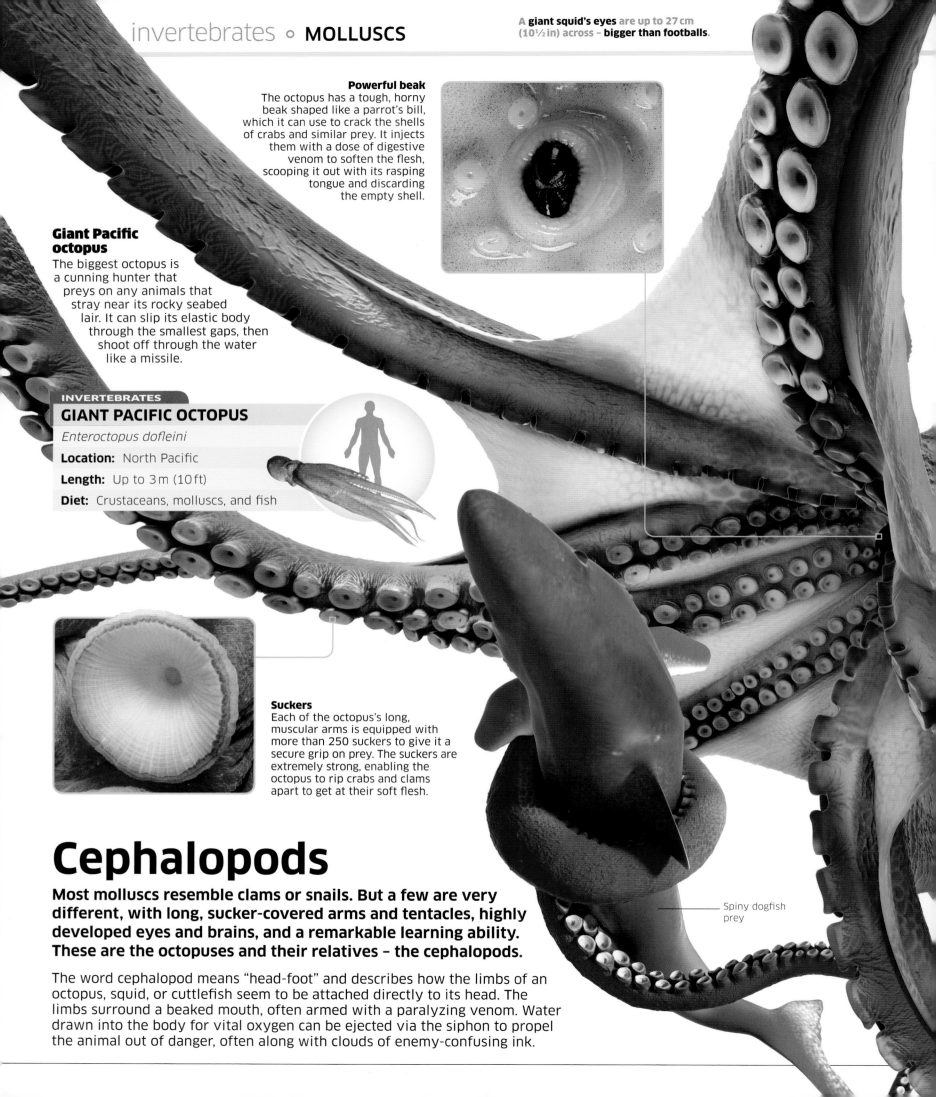

Powerful beak
The octopus has a tough, horny beak shaped like a parrot's bill, which it can use to crack the shells of crabs and similar prey. It injects them with a dose of digestive venom to soften the flesh, scooping it out with its rasping tongue and discarding the empty shell.

Giant Pacific octopus
The biggest octopus is a cunning hunter that preys on any animals that stray near its rocky seabed lair. It can slip its elastic body through the smallest gaps, then shoot off through the water like a missile.

INVERTEBRATES

GIANT PACIFIC OCTOPUS

Enteroctopus dofleini

Location: North Pacific

Length: Up to 3 m (10 ft)

Diet: Crustaceans, molluscs, and fish

Suckers
Each of the octopus's long, muscular arms is equipped with more than 250 suckers to give it a secure grip on prey. The suckers are extremely strong, enabling the octopus to rip crabs and clams apart to get at their soft flesh.

Spiny dogfish prey

Cephalopods

Most molluscs resemble clams or snails. But a few are very different, with long, sucker-covered arms and tentacles, highly developed eyes and brains, and a remarkable learning ability. These are the octopuses and their relatives – the cephalopods.

The word cephalopod means "head-foot" and describes how the limbs of an octopus, squid, or cuttlefish seem to be attached directly to its head. The limbs surround a beaked mouth, often armed with a paralyzing venom. Water drawn into the body for vital oxygen can be ejected via the siphon to propel the animal out of danger, often along with clouds of enemy-confusing ink.

A **vampire squid's body** is covered in **light-producing organs** that **glow in the dark**.

The **venom** of the **blue-ringed octopus** contains a neurotoxin 1,200 times **more toxic than cyanide**.

13

CHAMBERED NAUTILUS
Nautilus pompilius

Location: Western Pacific

Length: Up to 20 cm (7³⁄₄ in) across shell

Distinguished by its coiled, multi-chambered shell, the nautilus floats in mid-water where it regulates its buoyancy by adjusting the amount of gas in the shell chambers. It has 90 small tentacles, and pinhole eyes with no lenses.

COMMON CUTTLEFISH
Sepia officinalis

Location: Eastern Atlantic

Length: Up to 45 cm (17³⁄₄ in)

A cuttlefish is adapted for hunting on shallow sea beds, swimming slowly and seizing prey with two extendible tentacles. Its skin is peppered with nerve-controlled colour cells that can expand or contract to change its pattern, to express its mood, to hide, or to startle predators.

OPALESCENT INSHORE SQUID
Doryteuthis opalescens

Location: Eastern Pacific

Length: Up to 30 cm (11³⁄₄ in)

Similar to cuttlefish, squid have the same feeding technique and colour-changing abilities. But they are adapted for speed, shooting through the water by jet propulsion. This Pacific species preys on fish, crabs, and even other cephalopods.

GIANT SQUID
Architeuthis dux

Location: Deep Atlantic

Length: Up to 13 m (42¹⁄₂ ft)

This gigantic, elusive deep-ocean cephalopod is rarely seen alive, but has occasionally been found stranded on sea shores. It has the largest eyes of any animal, which it uses to target prey in the gloom of the oceanic twilight zone.

Mammal eyes
The big eyes are as sophisticated as the eyes of a mammal.

VAMPIRE SQUID
Vampyroteuthis infernalis

Location: Deep oceans worldwide

Length: Up to 28 cm (11 in)

The umbrella-like vampire squid is named for its blood-red coloration rather than its habits. It drifts in the dark zone of the deep ocean, eating edible debris and other invertebrates that it catches with the suckered tips of its arms.

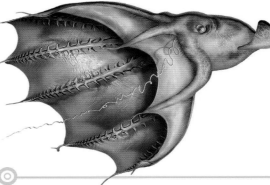

GREATER BLUE-RINGED OCTOPUS
Hapalochlaena lunulata

Location: Indo-Pacific coral reefs

Length: Up to 10 cm (4 in)

Like other octopuses this small, colourful species has a venomous bite for immobilizing small crabs, fish, and other prey. Its venom is incredibly toxic, making it one of the most deadly animals on Earth.

Siphon tube
Water is forced out of this opening to propel the animal along.

Inky opening
Near the base of the siphon tube is the opening to the ink sac. The octopus can shoot out an inky cloud to disorientate predators.

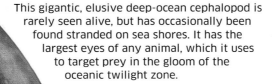

Elastic arms
The octopus has eight highly flexible arms.

14 invertebrates ∘ **MOLLUSCS**

80 per cent of molluscs are **gastropods** – snails, slugs, and their relatives.

LINED CHITON
Tonicella lineata
Location: North Pacific coasts
Length: Up to 5 cm (2 in)

Forming a group of their own, chitons crawl over rocks on a slimy foot, like snails do. Their shells are divided into eight interlocking plates. They have no eyes or tentacles but contain cells in their shells that react to light. This species feeds on marine algae.

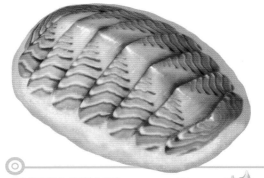

QUEEN CONCH
Lobatus gigas
Location: Caribbean Sea
Shell length: Up to 35 cm (13¾ in)

The queen conch is a giant marine snail that feeds on seagrasses and seaweeds in tropical seas. It is well known for its big, pinkish-tinged shell.

TEXTILE CONE SHELL
Conus textile
Location: Indo-Pacific region
Shell length: Up to 15 cm (6 in)

GARDEN SNAIL
Helix aspersa
Location: Worldwide
Shell length: Up to 4.5 cm (1¾ in)

Familiar in gardens throughout Europe and many other parts of the world, this typical snail glides over the ground or plants on its muscular foot, leaving a trail of slimy mucus. In dry weather it retreats into its coiled shell.

SPANISH SHAWL NUDIBRANCH
Flabellina iodinea
Location: Pacific Ocean
Length: Up to 7 cm (2¾ in)

A nudibranch is a type of sea slug – a gastropod with no shell. Many, including this Pacific species, prey on stinging animals and store the stinging cells in their tentacles for their own defence.

RED RAMSHORN SNAIL
Planorbis rubrum
Location: Europe, North Africa
Shell length: Up to 2 cm (¾ in)

Many snails live in ponds, lakes, and rivers. This species is one of the most colourful ramshorn snails – aquatic air-breathers that forage for food underwater, and return to the surface to breathe.

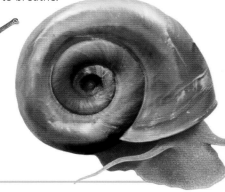

BLUE SEA SLUG
Glaucus atlanticus
Location: Pacific, Atlantic, and Indian oceans
Length: Up to 3 cm (1¼ in)

This sea slug floats upside down on the ocean surface, where it preys on other drifting animals – including venomous jellyfish.

Breathing tube
Siphon draws water into gill cavity.

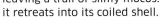

Fish prey
Paralyzed prey is swallowed whole.

Huge extendable mouth

The beautifully marked shell of this tropical sea snail conceals a deadly weapon – a tiny harpoon that injects a potent nerve poison. The cone shell uses it to paralyze its prey, but the venom is powerful enough to kill a human.

507 The **age** of a type of **edible clam** found in the **North Atlantic** in 2006. It was the **oldest-known living animal**.

110,000 living **species of molluscs** have been scientifically described and named.

15

Molluscs

These mainly marine animals include some of the most colourful and diverse of all invertebrates. Many have elaborate shells that protect their soft bodies, allowing some to survive exposure to the air on tidal shores.

Molluscs consist of three main groups. Cephalopods (see pp.24–25) include the octopuses and their relatives. Gastropods – snails and slugs – are mainly mobile animals that crawl on a muscular foot; many are hunters that track down and kill their prey. The two-shelled bivalves mostly live in burrows or attached to rocks, and filter the water for food.

TUSK SHELL
Antalis vulgaris
Location: North Atlantic Ocean
Length: Up to 5 cm (2 in)

Tusk shells form a distinctive group of molluscs that are not closely related to gastropods or bivalves. They burrow into soft, sandy, or muddy sea beds, using their tiny tentacles to gather fragments of food and small animals.

Small head
The head and tentacles burrow deep into the sediment.

Feeding tentacles
Long tentacles gather food particles.

FLAME SHELL
Limaria hians
Location: Northeast Atlantic coasts
Shell length: Up to 4 cm (1½ in)

Also known as the gaping file shell, this bivalve sports a host of flamboyant orange tentacles. These put off predators by producing a sticky, sour-tasting substance.

Shallow seas off western Scotland support reefs of up to 100 million flame shells.

COMMON MUSSEL
Mytilus edulis
Location: Atlantic and Pacific oceans
Shell length: Up to 10 cm (4 in)

Harvested and farmed in vast numbers for food, this bivalve mollusc attaches itself to rocks on tidal shores with strong, silk-like threads. It feeds by filtering the water for edible particles.

SPINY COCKLE
Acanthocardia aculeata
Location: Mediterranean Sea
Shell length: Up to 10.2 cm (4 in)

Like many bivalve molluscs, this small clam spends its life buried in soft sand. It draws water though its body to gather oxygen and filter out food particles. Its two hinged shells can be tightly closed for protection.

QUEEN SCALLOP
Aequipecten opercularis
Location: North Atlantic Ocean
Shell length: Up to 11 cm (4¼ in)

Scallops are unusual bivalves because they can swim. By clapping its hinged shells together to force water out, the scallop shoots backwards out of danger.

Eye spots
Tentacles have eye spots at their base.

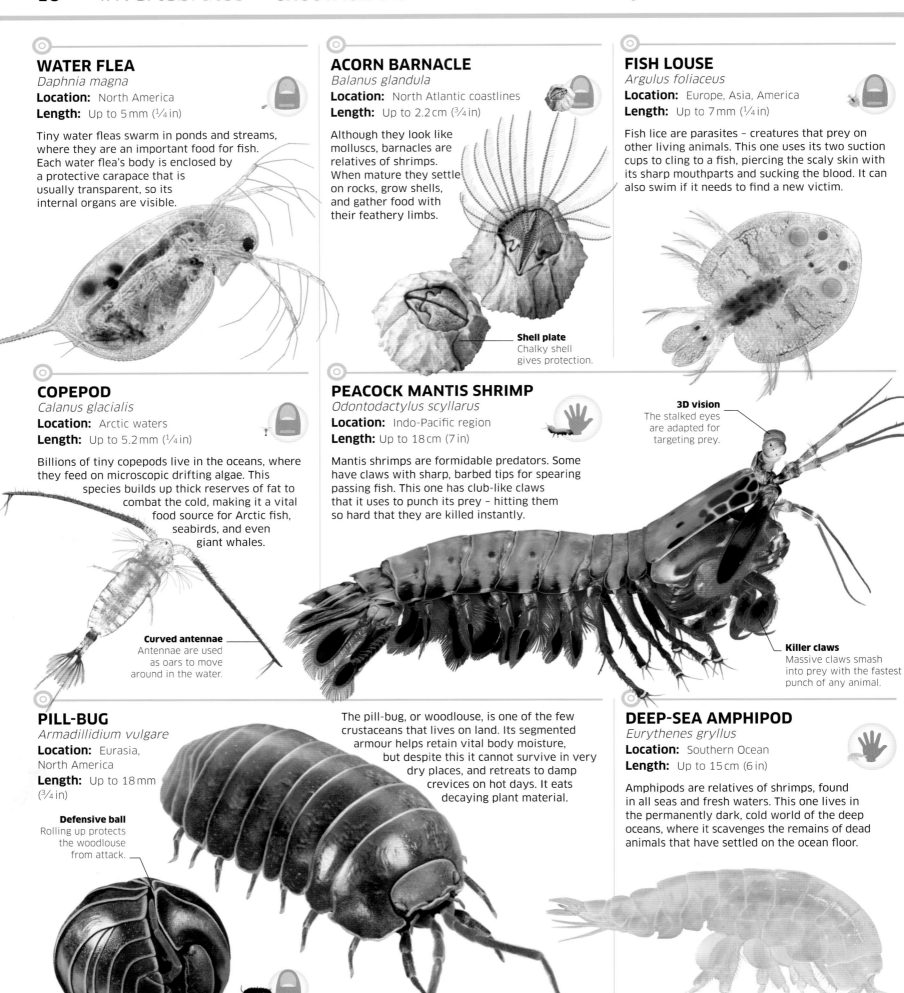

WATER FLEA
Daphnia magna
Location: North America
Length: Up to 5 mm (¼ in)

Tiny water fleas swarm in ponds and streams, where they are an important food for fish. Each water flea's body is enclosed by a protective carapace that is usually transparent, so its internal organs are visible.

ACORN BARNACLE
Balanus glandula
Location: North Atlantic coastlines
Length: Up to 2.2 cm (¾ in)

Although they look like molluscs, barnacles are relatives of shrimps. When mature they settle on rocks, grow shells, and gather food with their feathery limbs.

Shell plate
Chalky shell gives protection.

FISH LOUSE
Argulus foliaceus
Location: Europe, Asia, America
Length: Up to 7 mm (¼ in)

Fish lice are parasites – creatures that prey on other living animals. This one uses its two suction cups to cling to a fish, piercing the scaly skin with its sharp mouthparts and sucking the blood. It can also swim if it needs to find a new victim.

COPEPOD
Calanus glacialis
Location: Arctic waters
Length: Up to 5.2 mm (¼ in)

Billions of tiny copepods live in the oceans, where they feed on microscopic drifting algae. This species builds up thick reserves of fat to combat the cold, making it a vital food source for Arctic fish, seabirds, and even giant whales.

Curved antennae
Antennae are used as oars to move around in the water.

PEACOCK MANTIS SHRIMP
Odontodactylus scyllarus
Location: Indo-Pacific region
Length: Up to 18 cm (7 in)

Mantis shrimps are formidable predators. Some have claws with sharp, barbed tips for spearing passing fish. This one has club-like claws that it uses to punch its prey – hitting them so hard that they are killed instantly.

3D vision
The stalked eyes are adapted for targeting prey.

Killer claws
Massive claws smash into prey with the fastest punch of any animal.

PILL-BUG
Armadillidium vulgare
Location: Eurasia, North America
Length: Up to 18 mm (¾ in)

Defensive ball
Rolling up protects the woodlouse from attack.

The pill-bug, or woodlouse, is one of the few crustaceans that lives on land. Its segmented armour helps retain vital body moisture, but despite this it cannot survive in very dry places, and retreats to damp crevices on hot days. It eats decaying plant material.

DEEP-SEA AMPHIPOD
Eurythenes gryllus
Location: Southern Ocean
Length: Up to 15 cm (6 in)

Amphipods are relatives of shrimps, found in all seas and fresh waters. This one lives in the permanently dark, cold world of the deep oceans, where it scavenges the remains of dead animals that have settled on the ocean floor.

70,000 The approximate number of **crustacean species**.

The **largest-known crustacean** is the **Japanese spider crab**. Its **claws** can span up to **4 m (13 ft)**.

17

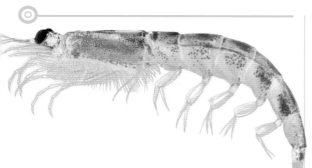

BANDED CORAL SHRIMP
Stenopus hispidus
Location: Indo-Pacific region
Length: Up to 6 cm (2¼ in)

The extraordinary cleaner shrimp feeds by picking parasites and flakes of dead skin from the bodies of fish. The fish could easily eat the shrimp, but they value its services too highly to do it any harm.

ANTARCTIC KRILL
Euphausia superba
Location: Southern Ocean
Length: Up to 6 cm (2¼ in)

Shrimp-like krill live in vast swarms, drifting with the ocean currents and feeding on microscopic plankton. The Antarctic krill is the most abundant species, and is the main food of most Antarctic penguins, seals, and whales – including the largest of all animals, the colossal blue whale.

SIGNAL CRAYFISH
Pacifastacus leniusculus
Location: North America
Length: Up to 18 cm (7 in)

This lobster-like crustacean lives in rivers and lakes, where it eats any animal and plant material it can find. Native to North America, it has been introduced to Europe where it is now widespread, and considered a pest.

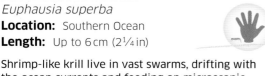

Crustaceans

Crabs, prawns, and lobsters are some of the most familiar crustaceans – invertebrates with armoured bodies and jointed limbs. Most of them live in the sea, but a few are adapted for life on land.

The crustaceans are part of the huge group of animals known as arthropods. Their boneless bodies are protected and supported by hardened skins that act as external skeletons. The rigid sections are linked by flexible joints that allow them to move.

Eyes on stalks
The big, horned eyes fold down into slots in the shell when the crab is inactive.

Eight legs
The crab uses its legs to run sideways.

COMMON HERMIT CRAB
Pagurus bernhardus
Location: N. W. Europe
Size: Host shell up to 35 cm (13¾ in) across

Instead of relying on its own tough armour for protection, the hermit crab moves into the empty shell of a mollusc such as a whelk. As it grows, it keeps swapping the shell for a bigger one.

HORNED GHOST CRAB
Ocypode ceratophthalma
Location: Indo-Pacific region
Size: Up to 8 cm (3¼ in) across carapace

A crab has gills, like a fish, but by keeping them wet with seawater, the ghost crab can breathe air and scavenge for food on beaches at low tide. It can run very fast, and since its colour often matches the sand it seems to vanish like a ghost when it stops moving.

Safe refuge
If it is attacked, the crab retreats into the shell.

Pincer power
Big claws rip food apart.

Desert locust

Although it is notorious for flying in huge, hungry swarms that destroy every green leaf and edible plant they encounter, the desert locust may spend its entire life in a solitary and harmless state.

Desert locusts are a type of grasshopper and like other grasshoppers they normally feed quietly on grass and similar plants. But if food gets scarce and the locusts are forced to crowd together, their behaviour and their colour change and they turn into a ravenous army, eventually taking off in a gigantic swarm in search of any food they can find.

Big appetite
The locust's sharp chewing mouthparts are adapted for eating leaves, grass, seeds, and other tough vegetable foods. Each insect eats its body weight in food every day, so a vast swarm can soon strip a farmer's field of every plant.

Big compound eye

Growing up
Locusts are insects, with tough skins that act as external skeletons. They shed their skins five times as they grow, getting bigger each time. The first five stages are flightless "hoppers", but the final stage is a winged adult that can fly. In their solitary state, the hoppers are green.

Developing wings

HOPPER

Jointed legs
The strong legs are formed of rigid sections linked by flexible joints.

Clawed feet

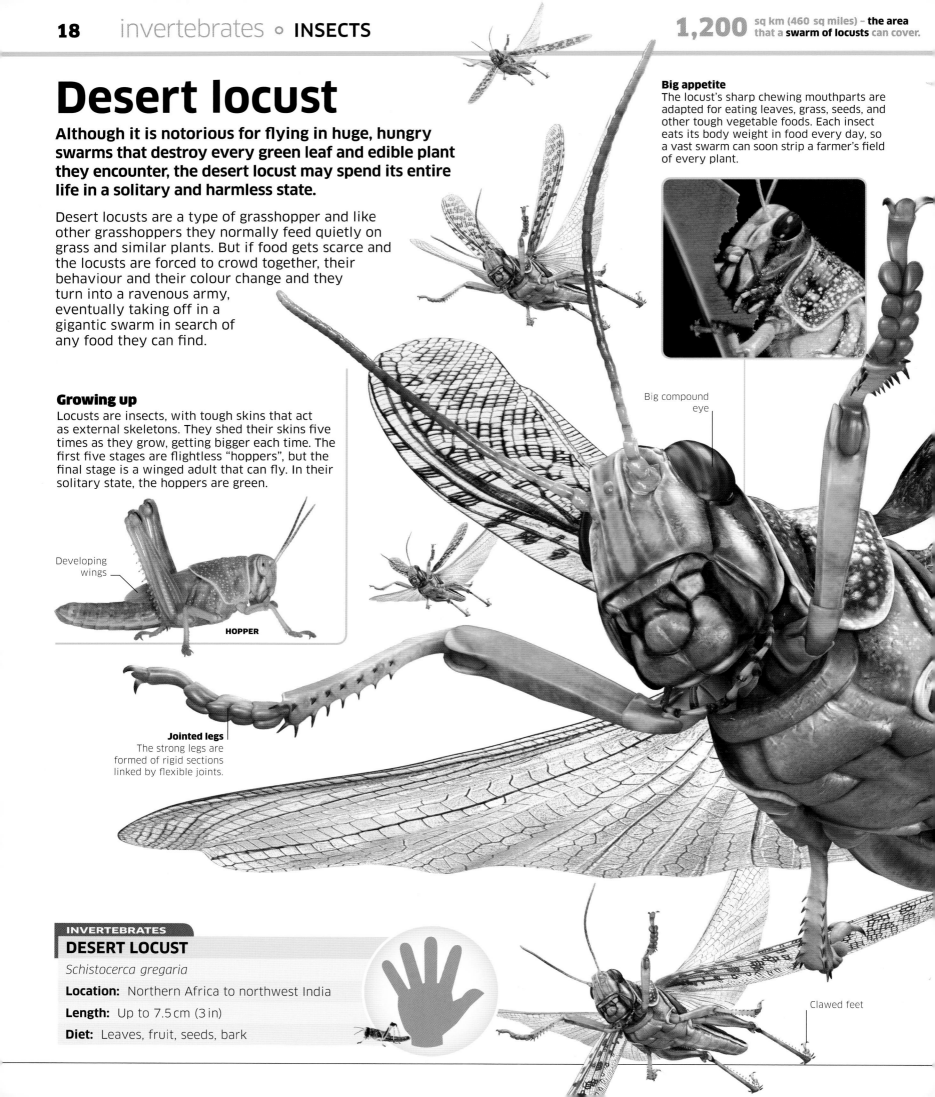

INVERTEBRATES

DESERT LOCUST

Schistocerca gregaria

Location: Northern Africa to northwest India

Length: Up to 7.5 cm (3 in)

Diet: Leaves, fruit, seeds, bark

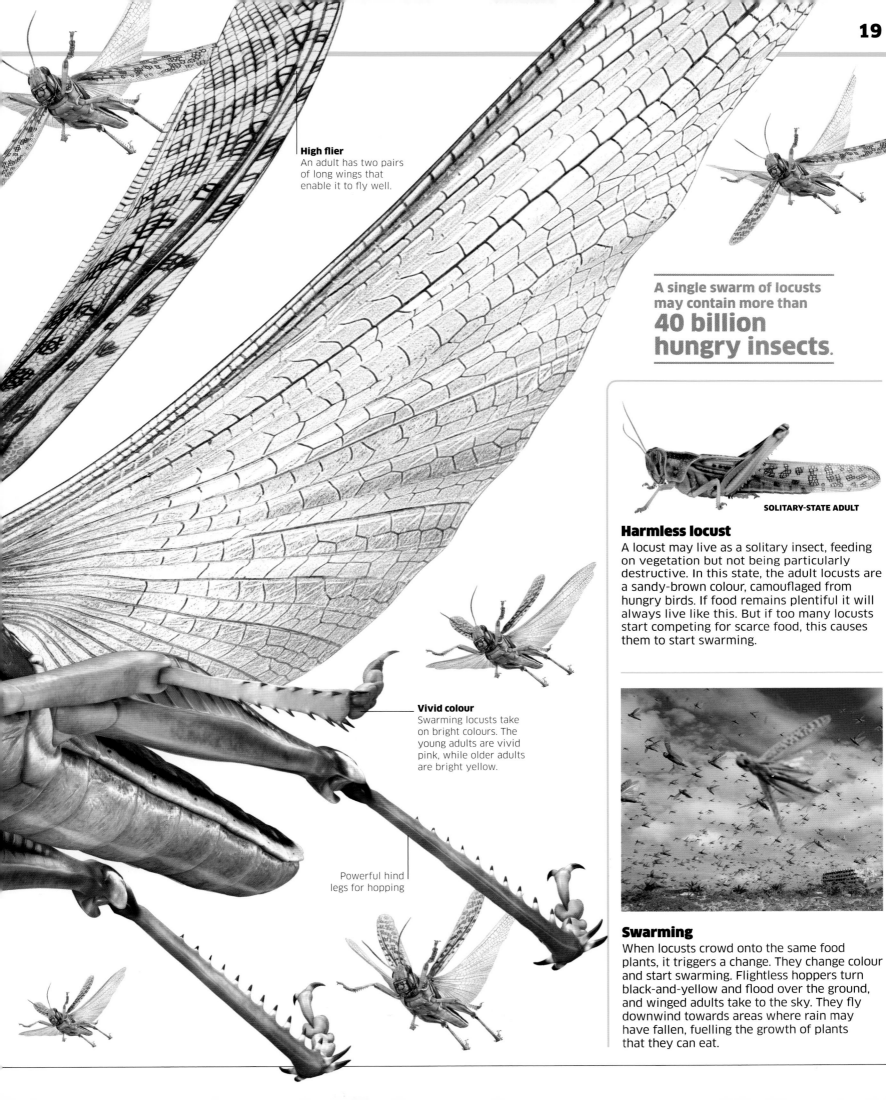

High flier
An adult has two pairs of long wings that enable it to fly well.

A single swarm of locusts may contain more than **40 billion hungry insects**.

SOLITARY-STATE ADULT

Harmless locust
A locust may live as a solitary insect, feeding on vegetation but not being particularly destructive. In this state, the adult locusts are a sandy-brown colour, camouflaged from hungry birds. If food remains plentiful it will always live like this. But if too many locusts start competing for scarce food, this causes them to start swarming.

Vivid colour
Swarming locusts take on bright colours. The young adults are vivid pink, while older adults are bright yellow.

Powerful hind legs for hopping

Swarming
When locusts crowd onto the same food plants, it triggers a change. They change colour and start swarming. Flightless hoppers turn black-and-yellow and flood over the ground, and winged adults take to the sky. They fly downwind towards areas where rain may have fallen, fuelling the growth of plants that they can eat.

30,000 The number of **lenses** in a **dragonfly's eye**.

Dragonflies have **existed on Earth** for at least **325 million years**.

Emperor dragonfly

Vividly coloured, amazingly fast, and spectacularly agile in the air, the emperor dragonfly is one of the most spellbinding of all insects. It is a deadly enemy of small flies such as mosquitoes, snatching them out of the air and even eating them on the wing.

Dragonflies, and their similar-looking relatives the damselflies, have long bodies and big eyes. The emperor dragonfly is one of the hawker or darner dragonflies – big, powerful insects that specialize in patrolling the air for prey rather than ambushing it from a perch. It usually hunts over ponds, lakes, and slow-flowing rivers, flying over the surface in search of airborne prey that it can seize in its specially adapted legs.

Huge eyes
A dragonfly has huge compound eyes, each made up of thousands of microscopic lenses. They are wrapped around its head like a helmet, giving it a virtually 360-degree view, so it can spot prey anywhere and is very difficult to take by surprise.

On the wing
Unlike other insects, dragonflies have two pairs of wings that beat independently. This is a feature of some of the earliest flying insects and it gives the emperor exceptional flexibility in the air. It can fly forwards at amazing speeds, hover on the spot, and even fly backwards or sideways.

INVERTEBRATES

EMPEROR DRAGONFLY

Anax imperator

Location: Europe, central Asia, north Africa

Length: Up to 7.8 cm (3¼ in)

Diet: Flying insects

Get a grip
A pair of sharp, curved claws at the end of each leg helps to grip prey.

Transparent wings
Each wing is a thin sheet of skeletal material – chitin – supported by slender struts.

Transformation

Dragonflies lay their eggs in water, where they hatch as aquatic nymphs. These fierce underwater hunters grow for two or three years. Each then climbs out of the water and its skin splits, allowing a crumpled, pale adult dragonfly to emerge. It pumps up its wings, waits for them to dry, and flies off.

Sky blue
A male's abdomen is bright blue with black markings. A female's is greener.

Prey snare
The dragonfly's spiny legs are so specialized for seizing prey that it cannot walk.

Aerial attack

As it darts over the water at speed, the emperor watches for any hint of an airborne victim. Swerving into the attack, it thrusts its bristly legs forwards to scoop its prey out of the air. If the victim is small enough the emperor will eat it in flight, but it carries larger prey to a perch before mashing it up with its powerful, serrated jaws.

Secure grip
The male has claspers on the tip of his abdomen for gripping females.

Beetles

Almost a quarter of all known animal species are beetles. This makes them the most successful animals on the planet. Most of them are instantly recognizable by their tough, shiny wing cases.

Known to scientists as elytra, the wing cases are modified, hardened forewings, which cover and protect the beetle's delicate, folded hindwings when they are not needed. This allows many beetles to scramble through dense plant foliage, burrow underground, or even swim underwater without putting their flying ability at risk. As a result, they can live in an amazingly wide variety of habitats, where they eat all kinds of food ranging from flower nectar to the remains of dead animals.

Sharp claws
Curved claws on each foot give the beetle a good grip on smooth plant stems.

Open wide
The wing cases hinge open for flight, and may help by providing extra lift.

Reflex bleeding
If attacked, the ladybird oozes a noxious yellow fluid from its body joints – a tactic known as reflex bleeding. The vivid pattern on its wing cases warns birds and other enemies that it tastes bad.

Black spots
This ladybird has seven black spots. Other species may have 21 or more.

An adult ladybird can eat as many as
75 aphids
in just one day.

Folded wings
Long, delicate wings have to be quickly unfurled for flight.

INVERTEBRATES
SEVEN-SPOT LADYBIRD

Coccinella septempunctata

Location: Europe, North America

Length: Up to 1 cm (½ in)

Diet: Aphids

ACTUAL SIZE

The **earliest fossil beetle** dates back more than **300 million years**.

The **heaviest beetle in the world** is the **Goliath beetle**. It can **weigh** 100 g (3½ oz).

370,000 The number of **known species** of beetles.

23

Seven-spot ladybird

This small, colourful beetle lives in grassland and woodland where it is a voracious predator. Both the adult beetle and its wingless young hunt small, soft-bodied insects, especially sap-sucking aphids such as greenfly.

Antennae
Short antennae detect scents and air movements.

NUT WEEVIL
Curculio nucum
Location: Europe
Length: Up to 9 mm (¼ in)

The nut weevil's amazingly long snout has a pair of tiny jaws at the tip. The female uses them to drill into a hazel nut, where she lays an egg. When it hatches, the weevil grub eats the nut.

SIX-SPOTTED TIGER BEETLE
Cicindela sexguttata
Location: North America
Length: Up to 1.4 cm (½ in)

Relative to its size, this ferocious hunter runs faster than any other animal. It can cover 125 times its own body length in a second as it chases after insect prey in the broad-leaved woodland where it lives.

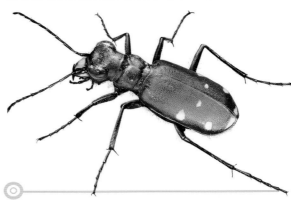

GOLDEN CHAFER
Chrysina resplendens
Location: Central America
Length: Up to 2 cm (¾ in)

The armoured body of this tropical American scarab beetle reflects light in a way that makes it look metallic. Also called the golden scarab beetle, it inhabits tropical rainforest.

AMERICAN BURYING BEETLE
Nicrophorus americanus
Location: USA
Length: Up to 3.8 cm (1½ in)

This is one of many similar beetles that seek out the dead bodies of larger animals, in grassland or scrubland, and bury them by digging away the ground below. The female then lays her eggs on the carcass, and helps her young feed when they hatch.

STAG BEETLE
Lucanus cervus
Location: Europe
Length: Up to 7.5 cm (3 in)

Grappling hooks
Hooked claws on the feet help the beetles climb tree bark in the woodland where they live.

All show
Despite their size, the male's jaws do not have a powerful bite.

Hidden wings
Wing cases conceal long wings used to fly in search of females.

The alarmingly big jaws of the male stag beetle are not for hunting, but for wrestling with rival males. They are also used during courtship displays to the normal-jawed females.

GREAT DIVING BEETLE
Dytiscus marginalis
Location: Europe, Northern Asia
Length: Up to 3.5 cm (1½ in)

Living in ponds, lakes, and rivers, this underwater hunter chases small fish and other prey by driving itself along with its hair-fringed legs. It carries an air supply of bubbles beneath its wing cases so it can breathe.

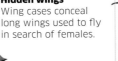

Malaria mosquito

The most deadly animal on Earth is not a killer shark or a venomous snake, but a small fly with a bloodsucking bite – the malaria mosquito. The parasites that it carries in its body are responsible for at least a million human deaths every year.

Mosquitoes are slender two-winged flies with an irritating habit. The females suck the blood of larger animals to get the nutrients they need to make their eggs. Mosquitoes are found all over the world and most are nothing more than a nuisance. But certain tropical species in the genus *Anopheles* can pass on some serious diseases, the most deadly of which is malaria. The malarial parasite infects a victim's red blood cells, causing a fever that can be fatal.

Bloodsucker

The female flies mainly by night, and finds her victims by detecting their breath and body heat. She can often land and bite without being detected, allowing her to drink her fill of a victim's blood. After a blood meal the abdomen fills with eggs over two to three days. The eggs are then laid in water.

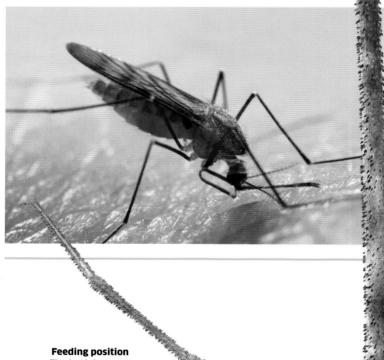

Scutum
A tough shield called the scutum covers the mosquito's thorax.

Wings

Feeding position
The back legs are raised when the mosquito is feeding.

Swollen abdomen
The body can swell to hold three times the mosquito's weight in blood.

Sensory hairs
Fine hairs on the body detect air movements and warn of danger. Nerve endings at the base of the hairs are stimulated by the movement.

INVERTEBRATES
MALARIA MOSQUITO

Anopheles gambiae

Location: Africa

Length: Up to 8 mm (¼ in)

Diet: Nectar and blood

ACTUAL SIZE

200 million people are **infected with malaria** each year **worldwide**.

An **adult** female mosquito **lives** for just **two weeks**, at most.

There are **3,500 known species** of mosquito but only about **30 carry malaria**.

25

Slender antennae
This female has thread-like antennae. Harmless males have more sensitive feathery antennae, which they use to detect females.

Sensitive palps
Long palps have sensors that detect the breath of nearby victims.

Some species of tropical mosquitoes pass on other serious diseases such as **yellow fever, West Nile virus, and dengue fever.**

Modified eyes
Scientists have tried to modify certain mosquitoes' genes so they cannot spread malaria. To track which insects they have modified, they turn their eyes green.

Slim legs
Like all adult insects, the mosquito has six legs.

Protective sheath
When the mosquito pierces a host's skin to feed, the sheath bends back out of the way.

Long proboscis
A mosquito's straw-like mouthparts are used to suck up blood, or the sugary nectar of flowers.

Precision tool
This false-colour image reveals the cluster of sharp stylets (probes) at the tip of the mosquito's long proboscis, emerging from their protective sheath. The sensitive tip of the sheath can detect a vein beneath the victim's skin.

The **largest butterfly**, Queen Alexandra's birdwing, has a **wingspan** of up to 27.3 cm (10¾ in).

GLASSWING BUTTERFLY
Greta oto
Location: Central America
Wingspan: Up to 6.1 cm (2½ in)

The wings of most butterflies are covered with coloured scales. But this butterfly, found in the tropical rainforest of Central America, only has scales on the edges of each wing; the rest is transparent, like glass. This makes it almost invisible to its predators.

MONARCH BUTTERFLY
Danaus plexippus
Location: Europe, Americas, Australasia
Wingspan: Up to 11 cm (4¼ in)

The big, powerful monarch is renowned for its long migration flights. In North America, the butterflies gradually work their way northeast across the continent in summer, then fly all the way back to California and Mexico, where they spend the winter.

Warning coloration
Bright orange colour warns birds that the butterflies are toxic.

LUNA MOTH
Actias luna
Location: North America
Wingspan: Up to 11.5 cm (4½ in)

Like several other butterflies and moths, the luna moth has an amazingly brief adult lifespan. It spends most of its time as a caterpillar, and the beautiful, winged adult lives for only a week – just long enough to mate and lay eggs. It does not eat but lives on the nutrients it took in as a caterpillar.

Butterflies and moths

With their big, often brightly coloured wings and dancing flight, butterflies are among the most attractive insects. But they are rivalled by some moths – close relatives that share the same nectar-feeding lifestyle of most butterflies.

Though very similar, butterflies are active by day, unlike typical moths, which fly by night and spend the day concealed by their camouflage from hungry birds. They all start life as soft-bodied caterpillars that eat voraciously before turning into short-lived, winged adults.

HUMMINGBIRD HAWKMOTH
Macroglossum stellatarum
Location: Eurasia, North America
Wingspan: Up to 4.5 cm (1¾ in)

The hummingbird hawkmoth lives in woodland and grassland and is unusual because it flies by day. Its name refers to the way it hovers on whirring wings to sip sweet nectar, just like a tropical hummingbird. It is a powerful flier, making long journeys to find food.

Nectar probe
Extra-long tongue (proboscis) probes deep into flowers.

RED UNDERWING
Catocala nupta
Location: Europe
Wingspan: Up to 8 cm (3¼ in)

Most moths fly at night, and are camouflaged by day. This moth is the same, but when it flies it reveals red hindwings. These may confuse birds, which cannot find the moth when its red wings are hidden again.

Long antennae

There are **165,000** described species of **butterflies and moths**.

80 The **number of times** a hummingbird hawkmoth **beats its wings per second**.

27

CAIRNS BIRDWING
Ornithoptera euphorion
Location: Australasia
Wingspan: Up to 15 cm (6 in)

The tropical birdwings are the biggest of all butterflies, with very long wings; they even fly rather like birds. They are a spectacular, frequent visitor to gardens in tropical northeastern Australia, where they often sip nectar from hibiscus flowers.

Wing scales
The patterns on the painted lady's wings are made up of very small, coloured scales that overlap like tiles on a roof. Over time the scales fall away, so the longer the butterfly lives, the less colourful it becomes. All butterflies and moths have wing scales of this type.

Clubbed antennae
Like most butterflies the painted lady has long, club-ended antennae.

Wing speed
Butterflies beat their wings steadily when they fly. Moths, in comparison, move their wings so fast that they are a blur.

Nectar feeding
The butterfly uses a long, hollow proboscis to sip sugary, energy-rich nectar from flowers, coiling it up like a spring when it is not needed.

Painted lady
Many butterflies have a very restricted range, but the painted lady is widespread in dry, open areas. It can also fly long distances, making mass migrations in search of good breeding grounds. The butterfly has six legs, but keeps the front pair tightly folded against its body.

INVERTEBRATES
PAINTED LADY
Vanessa cardui

Location: Europe, Asia, N. America, Africa

Wingspan: Up to 7.5 cm (3 in)

Diet: Adult drinks nectar

Honeybee

Named for the way they use sweet flower nectar to make fragrant honey, honeybees also provide a vital service by carrying pollen from plant to plant in order for cross-pollination to occur. Without bees, some plants might struggle to survive.

Bees are vegetarian wasps. Instead of hunting other insects, they gather sugary nectar and protein-rich pollen, which they take back and store in the hive. Many live solitary lives, but honeybees form big colonies centred on a single breeding queen. She is the mother of thousands of worker bees that build the nest, gather nectar and pollen, and make honey from regurgitated nectar to feed the colony during the winter.

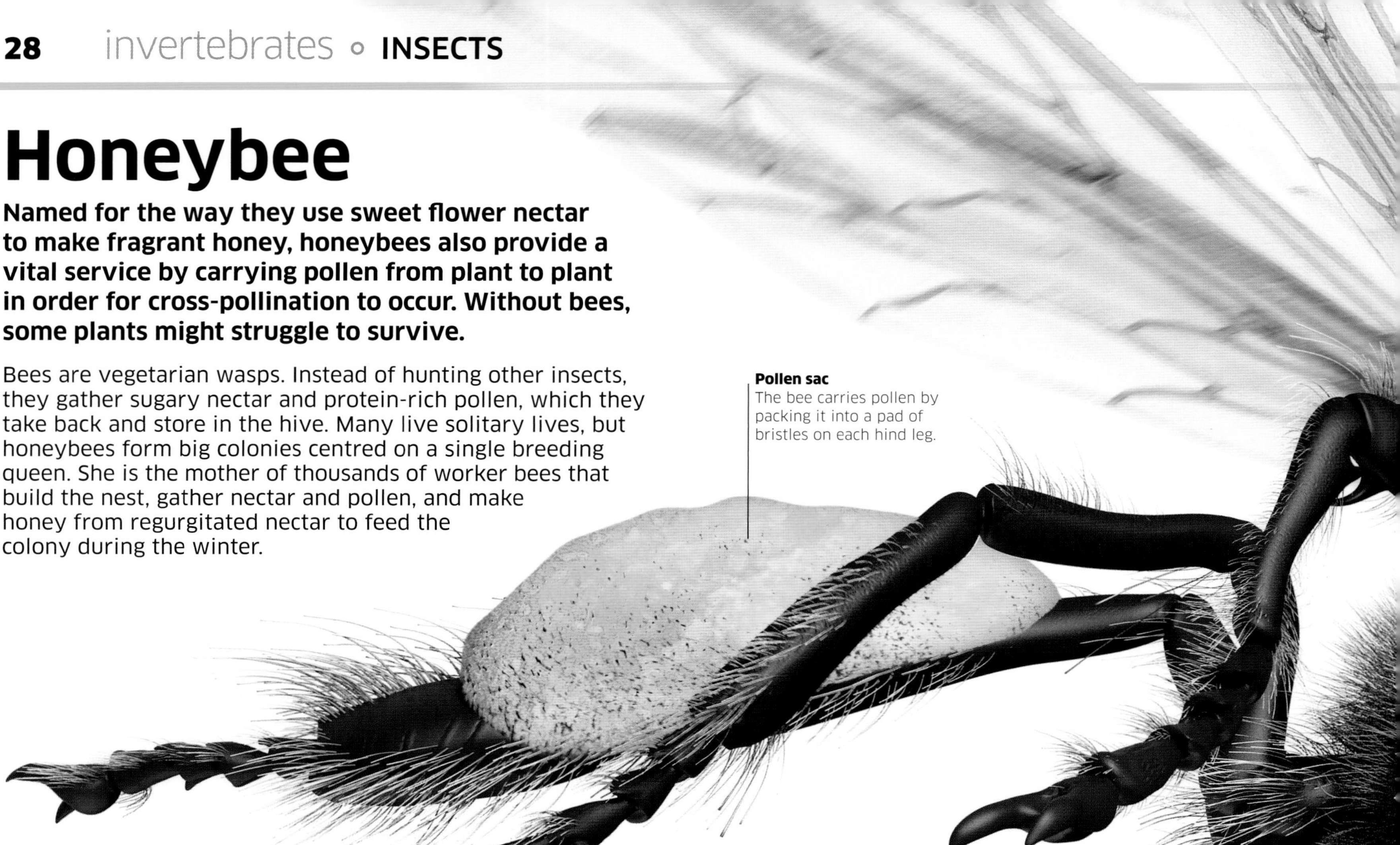

Pollen sac
The bee carries pollen by packing it into a pad of bristles on each hind leg.

Clawed feet
Each foot has sharp claws for clinging to flower petals.

Barbed sting
A worker bee is armed with a sting – a sharp, barbed blade linked to a gland that produces a painful venom – for defending the colony. If the bee stings a mammal, the barbs catch in the victim's skin. When the bee pulls away, this rips the sting out of its body, and it dies.

QUEEN

DRONE

WORKER

Bee colony
Although the queen is not much bigger than the other bees, she may lay thousands of eggs in a day. Each egg is placed into a honeycomb cell where it hatches as a legless larva. Some of these larvae develop into new queens or male "drones", but most become sterile female workers. The function of the drone is to mate with the queen from another colony.

250 The number of times a bee **beats its wings every second**. This creates the bee's **buzz**.

2,000 The **number of eggs** a queen honeybee may **lay per day** in spring.

29

Compound eyes
Made up of many tiny lenses, compound eyes see colour well to help the bee find nectar-rich flowers.

INVERTEBRATES

HONEYBEE

Apis mellifera

Location: Worldwide

Length: Up to 1.5 cm (½ in) (worker)

Diet: Nectar and pollen

ACTUAL SIZE

Sensitive antennae
Each antenna has thousands of scent detectors for finding fragrant flowers.

Hair trap
Hairs all over the bee's body pick up pollen from flowers.

Proboscis
When a honeybee lands on a flower it unrolls a long, tubular proboscis that acts like a drinking straw. The bee uses it to suck sugar-rich nectar into a part of its digestive system called the crop. When its crop is full it returns to the colony, where it passes the nectar to other bees. These then turn it into honey.

Wings
In flight, the two pairs of wings are joined by tiny hooks so they beat as one.

Bristly legs
The legs have bristly combs for brushing pollen off the bee's body and into the pollen sacs.

400 million years – the approximate length of time **insects** have **existed on Earth**.

There are **more than a million known species of insects**.

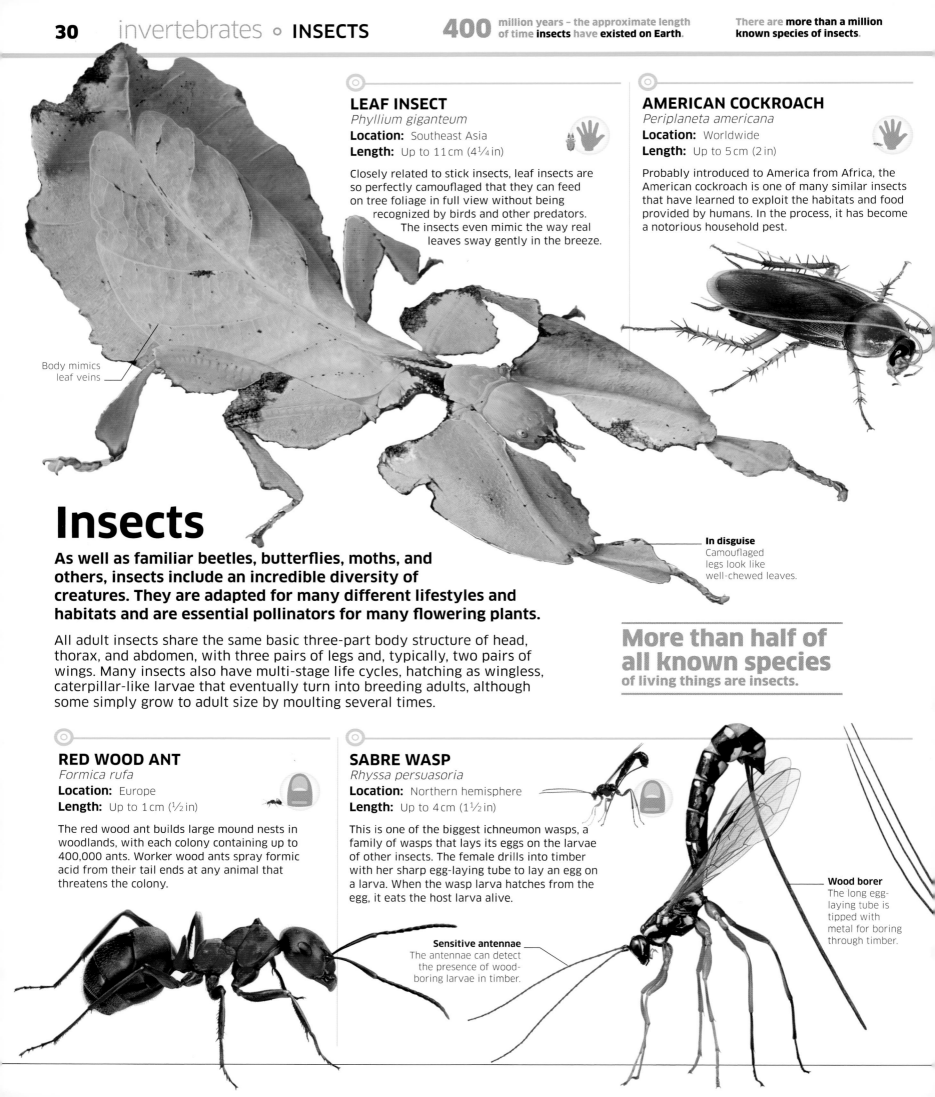

LEAF INSECT
Phyllium giganteum
Location: Southeast Asia
Length: Up to 11 cm (4¼ in)

Closely related to stick insects, leaf insects are so perfectly camouflaged that they can feed on tree foliage in full view without being recognized by birds and other predators. The insects even mimic the way real leaves sway gently in the breeze.

AMERICAN COCKROACH
Periplaneta americana
Location: Worldwide
Length: Up to 5 cm (2 in)

Probably introduced to America from Africa, the American cockroach is one of many similar insects that have learned to exploit the habitats and food provided by humans. In the process, it has become a notorious household pest.

Body mimics leaf veins

In disguise
Camouflaged legs look like well-chewed leaves.

Insects

As well as familiar beetles, butterflies, moths, and others, insects include an incredible diversity of creatures. They are adapted for many different lifestyles and habitats and are essential pollinators for many flowering plants.

All adult insects share the same basic three-part body structure of head, thorax, and abdomen, with three pairs of legs and, typically, two pairs of wings. Many insects also have multi-stage life cycles, hatching as wingless, caterpillar-like larvae that eventually turn into breeding adults, although some simply grow to adult size by moulting several times.

More than half of all known species
of living things are insects.

RED WOOD ANT
Formica rufa
Location: Europe
Length: Up to 1 cm (½ in)

The red wood ant builds large mound nests in woodlands, with each colony containing up to 400,000 ants. Worker wood ants spray formic acid from their tail ends at any animal that threatens the colony.

SABRE WASP
Rhyssa persuasoria
Location: Northern hemisphere
Length: Up to 4 cm (1½ in)

This is one of the biggest ichneumon wasps, a family of wasps that lays its eggs on the larvae of other insects. The female drills into timber with her sharp egg-laying tube to lay an egg on a larva. When the wasp larva hatches from the egg, it eats the host larva alive.

Wood borer
The long egg-laying tube is tipped with metal for boring through timber.

Sensitive antennae
The antennae can detect the presence of wood-boring larvae in timber.

Insects were the **first animals to fly**. The oldest-known flying insect lived 300 million years ago.

Although **insects** live in **every type** of land and freshwater habitat, **very few** live in **seas and oceans**.

31

RABBIT FLEA
Spilopsyllus cuniculi
Location: Northern hemisphere
Length: Up to 1 mm ($^1/_{16}$ in)

Fleas are parasites that feed on the blood of other animals. Some species are adapted for attacking a particular host, and this one favours rabbits. It has powerful hind legs for leaping onto its victims, and sharp mouthparts for piercing their skin.

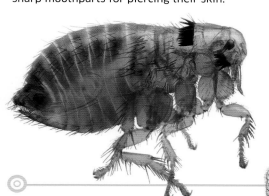

SPECKLED BUSH CRICKET
Leptophyes punctatissima
Location: Europe
Length: Up to 3 cm (1¼ in)

Also known as katydids, the bush crickets are relatives of grasshoppers. They have long hind legs for leaping, but rarely do so, preferring to climb slowly through bushes looking for food. This species cannot fly. The female, seen here, has a curved, blade-like, egg-laying organ.

AFRICAN TERMITE
Macrotermes bellicosus
Location: Africa
Length: Soldier up to 2.5 cm (1 in)

This termite lives in vast colonies, each centred on a single breeding queen. It builds tall, tower-like nests of mud, defended by big-jawed soldiers. The smaller workers gather grass and use it as compost for growing edible fungus inside the nest.

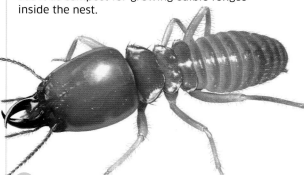

HOVER FLY
Syrphus ribesii
Location: Europe
Length: Up to 1.3 cm ($^1/_2$ in)

One of many hover fly species, this skilled flier can dart forwards or back in the air, fly sideways, or hover on the spot. It is a harmless nectar-feeder, but has warning stripes that mimic those of wasps to deter birds and other predators.

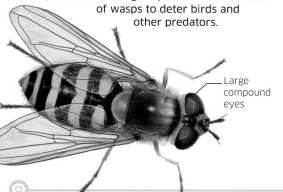

Large compound eyes

GREEN LACEWING
Chrysopa perla
Location: Europe
Length: Up to 1.3 cm ($^1/_2$ in)

Named for the delicate-looking lacy veining of its long wings, the green lacewing is a fierce predator that preys on smaller insects. Its caterpillar-like larvae do the same, and are important controllers of plant pests such as sap-sucking aphids.

PERIODICAL CICADA
Magicicada septendecim
Location: USA
Length: Up to 4 cm (1½ in)

Cicadas spend most of their lives as burrowing nymphs, then emerge briefly as winged adults to breed. Most cicadas do this each year, but American periodical cicadas emerge every 13 or 17 years, then vanish until the next mass emergence.

MAYFLY
Ephemera danica
Location: Europe
Length: Up to 2.5 cm (1 in)

Mayflies are famous for their short adult lifespans. This species survives for only a few days – just long enough to find a mate and breed. However, it has a much longer life as a larva, feeding underwater for up to three years before it takes to the air.

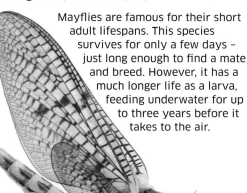

Binocular vision
Widely spaced eyes allow the mantis to strike with deadly accuracy.

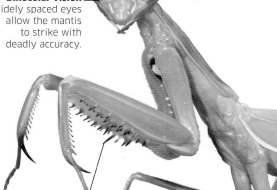

Deathtrap
Spines on the forelegs make escape almost impossible for prey.

PRAYING MANTIS
Mantis religiosa
Location: Central and Southern Europe
Length: Up to 7.4 cm (3 in)

The most well known of many similar mantids, this fearsome predator seizes other insects with its powerful, spiny forelegs, bites off their heads, and eats them. It perches motionless waiting for prey to come within range, then ambushes its victim with a split-second strike.

The **giant centipede** can dangle from a cave ceiling to **snatch passing bats**.

The mother centipede **coils around her eggs** to **protect them** from predators.

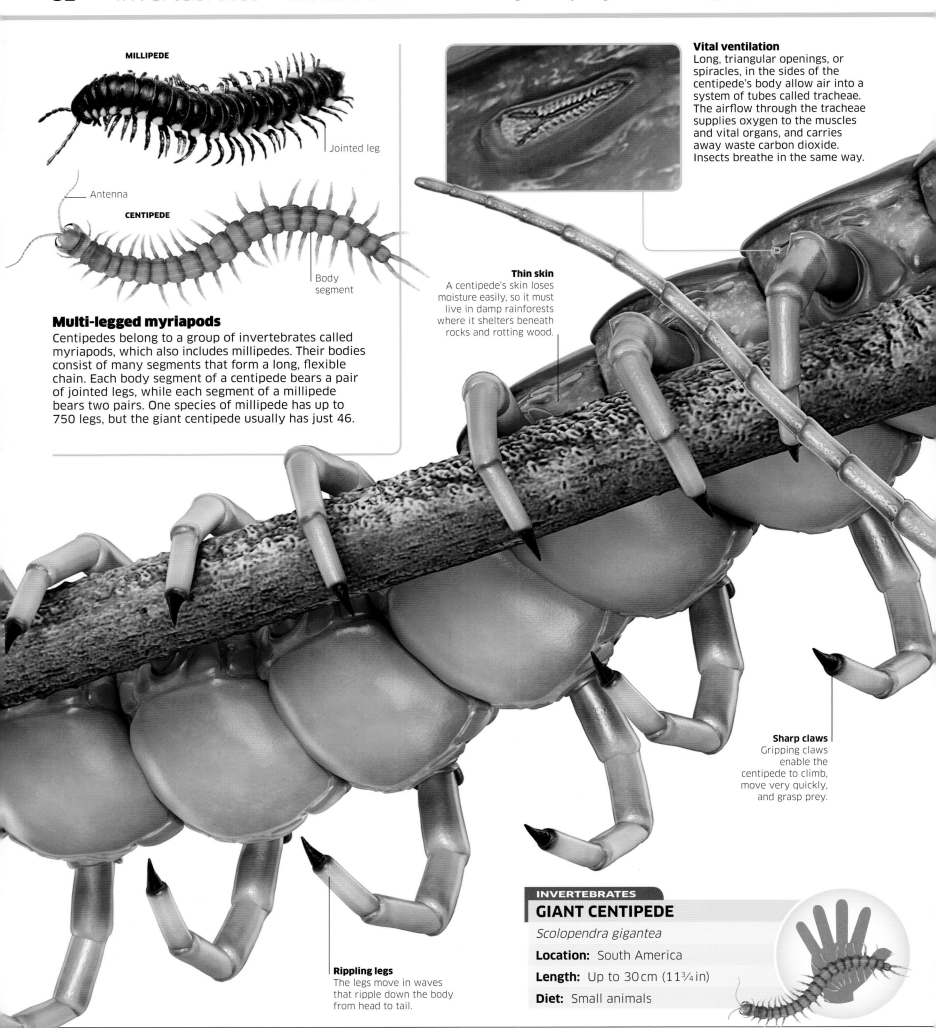

MILLIPEDE

Jointed leg

Antenna

CENTIPEDE

Body segment

Multi-legged myriapods

Centipedes belong to a group of invertebrates called myriapods, which also includes millipedes. Their bodies consist of many segments that form a long, flexible chain. Each body segment of a centipede bears a pair of jointed legs, while each segment of a millipede bears two pairs. One species of millipede has up to 750 legs, but the giant centipede usually has just 46.

Vital ventilation
Long, triangular openings, or spiracles, in the sides of the centipede's body allow air into a system of tubes called tracheae. The airflow through the tracheae supplies oxygen to the muscles and vital organs, and carries away waste carbon dioxide. Insects breathe in the same way.

Thin skin
A centipede's skin loses moisture easily, so it must live in damp rainforests where it shelters beneath rocks and rotting wood.

Sharp claws
Gripping claws enable the centipede to climb, move very quickly, and grasp prey.

Rippling legs
The legs move in waves that ripple down the body from head to tail.

INVERTEBRATES
GIANT CENTIPEDE

Scolopendra gigantea

Location: South America

Length: Up to 30 cm (11¾ in)

Diet: Small animals

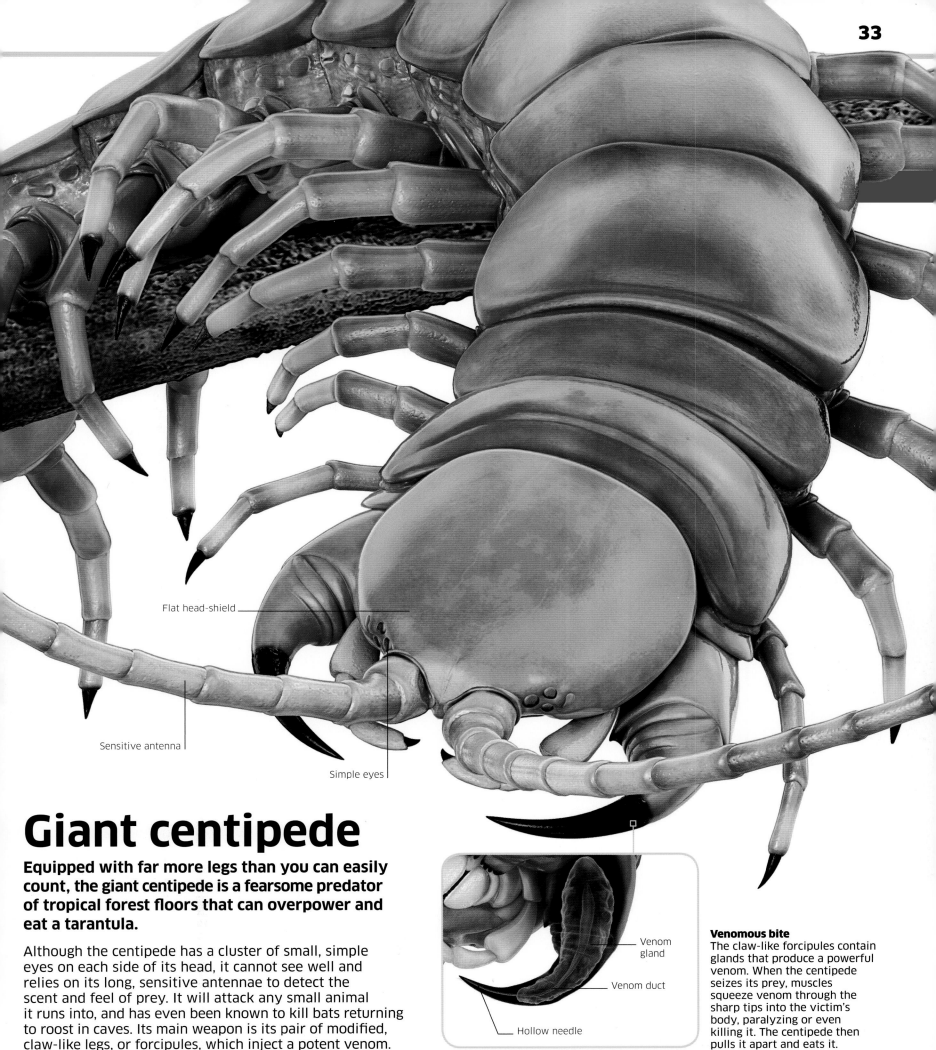

Flat head-shield

Sensitive antenna

Simple eyes

Giant centipede

Equipped with far more legs than you can easily count, the giant centipede is a fearsome predator of tropical forest floors that can overpower and eat a tarantula.

Although the centipede has a cluster of small, simple eyes on each side of its head, it cannot see well and relies on its long, sensitive antennae to detect the scent and feel of prey. It will attack any small animal it runs into, and has even been known to kill bats returning to roost in caves. Its main weapon is its pair of modified, claw-like legs, or forcipules, which inject a potent venom.

Venom gland

Venom duct

Hollow needle

Venomous bite
The claw-like forcipules contain glands that produce a powerful venom. When the centipede seizes its prey, muscles squeeze venom through the sharp tips into the victim's body, paralyzing or even killing it. The centipede then pulls it apart and eats it.

Hitching a ride

Scorpions give birth to live young that are like tiny, pale-skinned replicas of their parents, complete with stings. As they are born, they crawl up their mother's pincers and legs onto her back. She carries them around until they can fend for themselves.

Strange glow

The hard cuticle, or exoskeleton, of a scorpion contains fluorescent chemicals that make it glow a bright green-blue under ultraviolet light. No one really knows the reason for this, but it helps scientists to locate them in the dark.

The emperor scorpion's sting is no worse than a bee's, but the sting of some other scorpions can be **deadly to humans**.

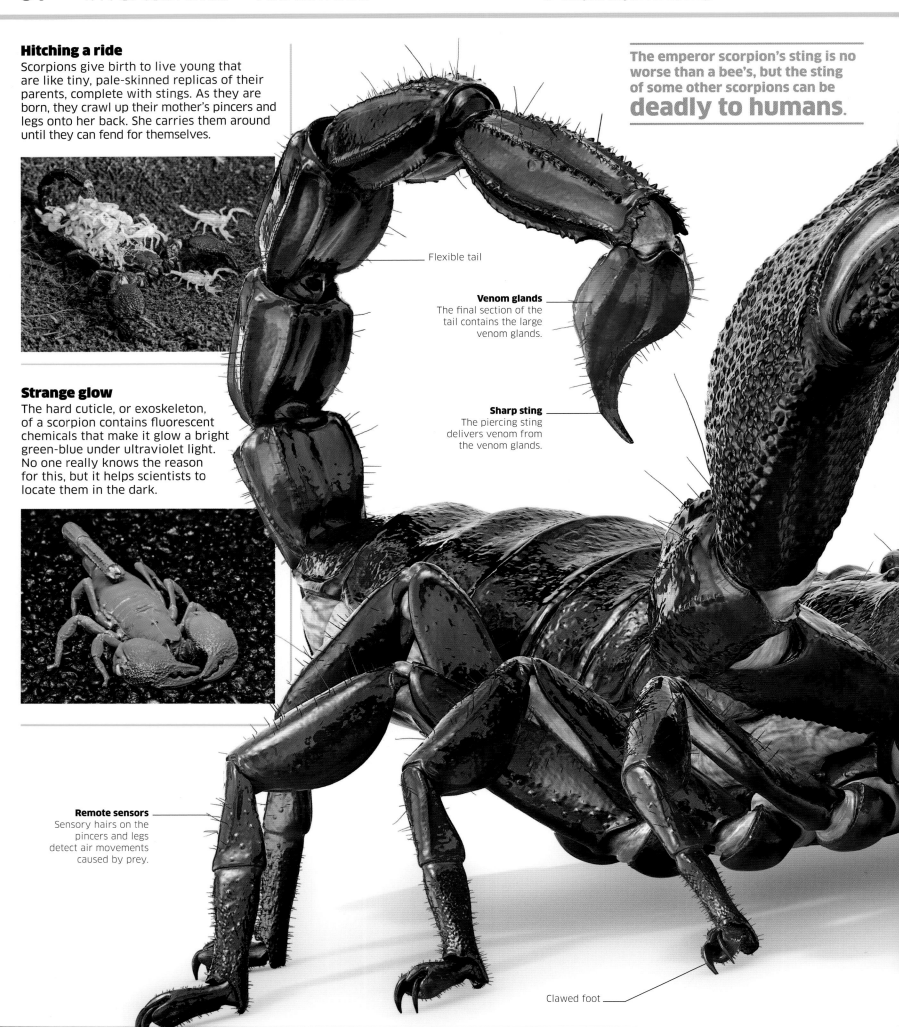

Flexible tail

Venom glands
The final section of the tail contains the large venom glands.

Sharp sting
The piercing sting delivers venom from the venom glands.

Remote sensors
Sensory hairs on the pincers and legs detect air movements caused by prey.

Clawed foot

28 grams (1 oz) – the **weight** that a **pregnant scorpion** can reach.

A **mother emperor scorpion** may carry **up to 30 babies** on her back.

35

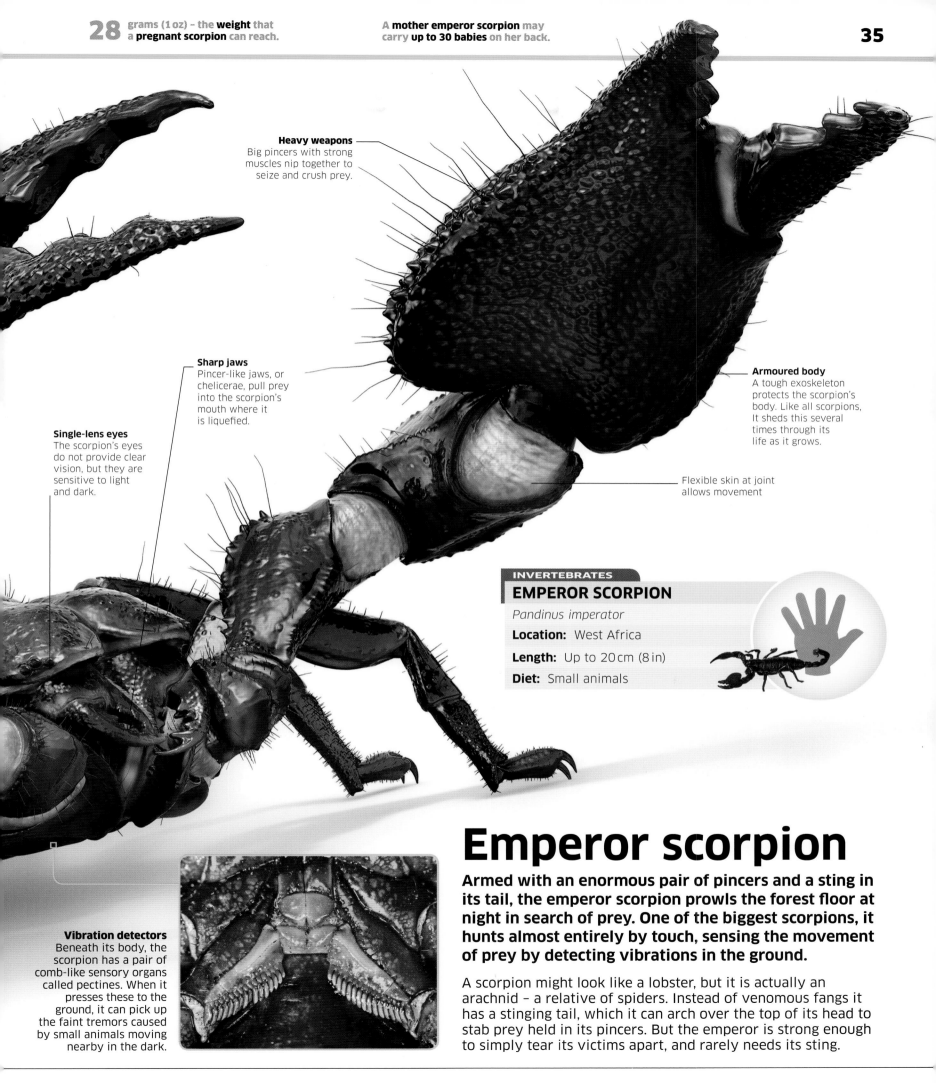

Heavy weapons
Big pincers with strong muscles nip together to seize and crush prey.

Sharp jaws
Pincer-like jaws, or chelicerae, pull prey into the scorpion's mouth where it is liquefied.

Single-lens eyes
The scorpion's eyes do not provide clear vision, but they are sensitive to light and dark.

Armoured body
A tough exoskeleton protects the scorpion's body. Like all scorpions, it sheds this several times through its life as it grows.

Flexible skin at joint allows movement

INVERTEBRATES
EMPEROR SCORPION
Pandinus imperator
Location: West Africa
Length: Up to 20 cm (8 in)
Diet: Small animals

Vibration detectors
Beneath its body, the scorpion has a pair of comb-like sensory organs called pectines. When it presses these to the ground, it can pick up the faint tremors caused by small animals moving nearby in the dark.

Emperor scorpion

Armed with an enormous pair of pincers and a sting in its tail, the emperor scorpion prowls the forest floor at night in search of prey. One of the biggest scorpions, it hunts almost entirely by touch, sensing the movement of prey by detecting vibrations in the ground.

A scorpion might look like a lobster, but it is actually an arachnid – a relative of spiders. Instead of venomous fangs it has a stinging tail, which it can arch over the top of its head to stab prey held in its pincers. But the emperor is strong enough to simply tear its victims apart, and rarely needs its sting.

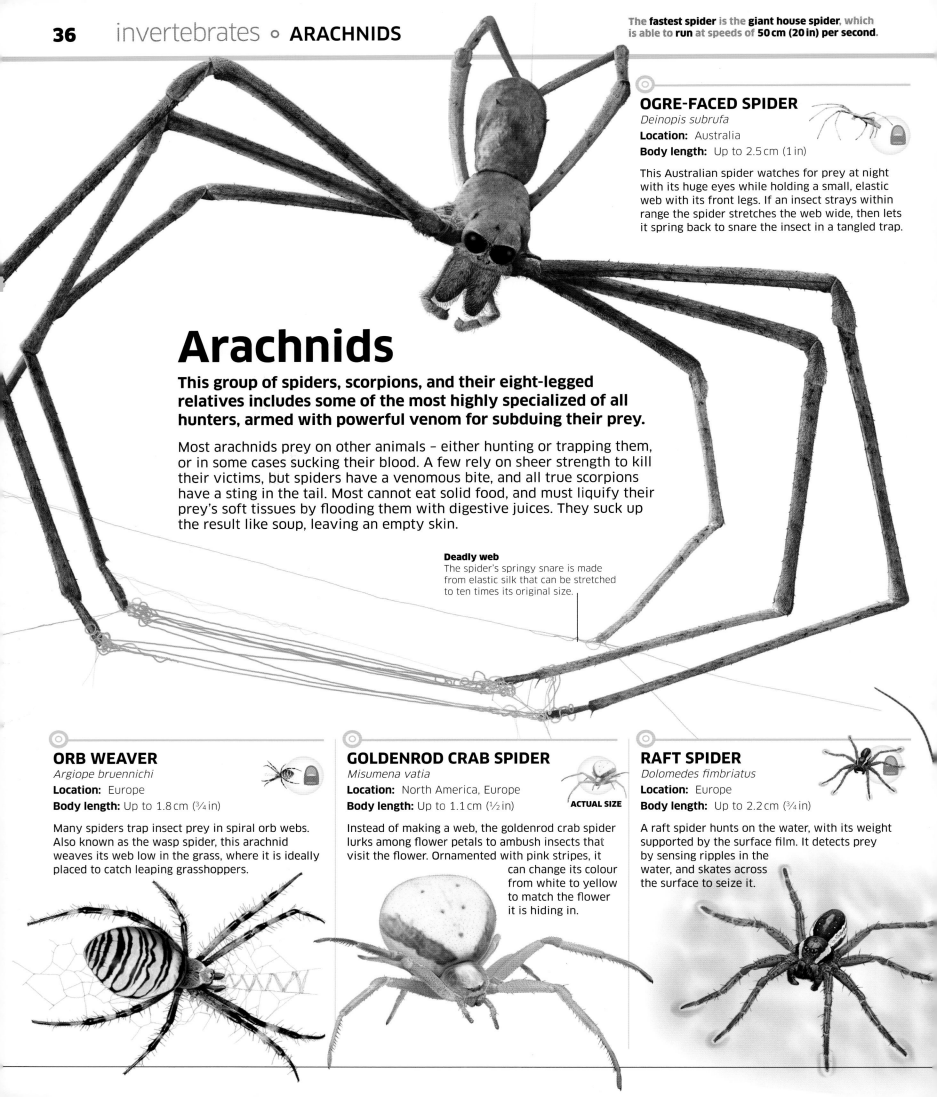

OGRE-FACED SPIDER

Deinopis subrufa

Location: Australia

Body length: Up to 2.5 cm (1 in)

This Australian spider watches for prey at night with its huge eyes while holding a small, elastic web with its front legs. If an insect strays within range the spider stretches the web wide, then lets it spring back to snare the insect in a tangled trap.

Arachnids

This group of spiders, scorpions, and their eight-legged relatives includes some of the most highly specialized of all hunters, armed with powerful venom for subduing their prey.

Most arachnids prey on other animals – either hunting or trapping them, or in some cases sucking their blood. A few rely on sheer strength to kill their victims, but spiders have a venomous bite, and all true scorpions have a sting in the tail. Most cannot eat solid food, and must liquify their prey's soft tissues by flooding them with digestive juices. They suck up the result like soup, leaving an empty skin.

Deadly web
The spider's springy snare is made from elastic silk that can be stretched to ten times its original size.

ORB WEAVER

Argiope bruennichi

Location: Europe

Body length: Up to 1.8 cm (¾ in)

Many spiders trap insect prey in spiral orb webs. Also known as the wasp spider, this arachnid weaves its web low in the grass, where it is ideally placed to catch leaping grasshoppers.

GOLDENROD CRAB SPIDER

Misumena vatia

Location: North America, Europe

Body length: Up to 1.1 cm (½ in)

ACTUAL SIZE

Instead of making a web, the goldenrod crab spider lurks among flower petals to ambush insects that visit the flower. Ornamented with pink stripes, it can change its colour from white to yellow to match the flower it is hiding in.

RAFT SPIDER

Dolomedes fimbriatus

Location: Europe

Body length: Up to 2.2 cm (¾ in)

A raft spider hunts on the water, with its weight supported by the surface film. It detects prey by sensing ripples in the water, and skates across the surface to seize it.

3,250 The number of people reportedly **killed** by scorpion stings worldwide **each year**.

30 cm (12 in) – the legspan of the **giant huntsman** spider, the **biggest legspan** of any spider.

37

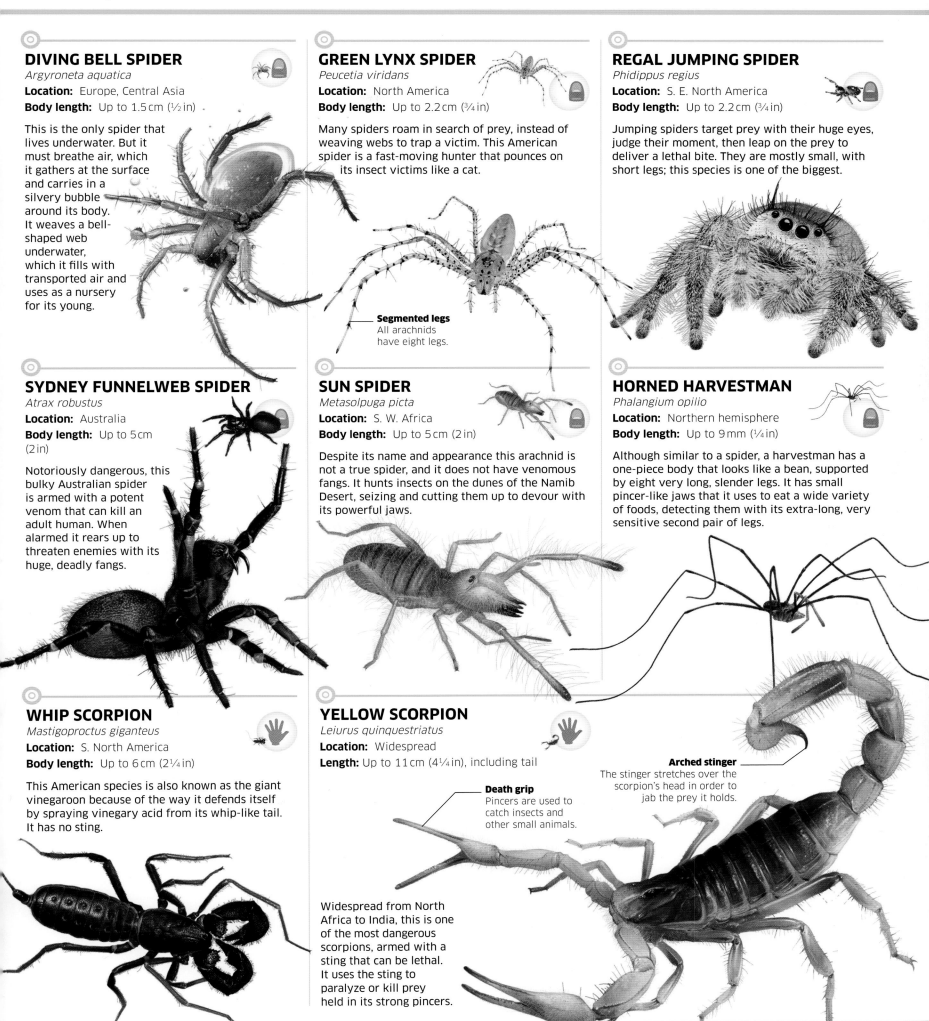

DIVING BELL SPIDER
Argyroneta aquatica
Location: Europe, Central Asia
Body length: Up to 1.5 cm (½ in)

This is the only spider that lives underwater. But it must breathe air, which it gathers at the surface and carries in a silvery bubble around its body. It weaves a bell-shaped web underwater, which it fills with transported air and uses as a nursery for its young.

GREEN LYNX SPIDER
Peucetia viridans
Location: North America
Body length: Up to 2.2 cm (¾ in)

Many spiders roam in search of prey, instead of weaving webs to trap a victim. This American spider is a fast-moving hunter that pounces on its insect victims like a cat.

Segmented legs
All arachnids have eight legs.

REGAL JUMPING SPIDER
Phidippus regius
Location: S. E. North America
Body length: Up to 2.2 cm (¾ in)

Jumping spiders target prey with their huge eyes, judge their moment, then leap on the prey to deliver a lethal bite. They are mostly small, with short legs; this species is one of the biggest.

SYDNEY FUNNELWEB SPIDER
Atrax robustus
Location: Australia
Body length: Up to 5 cm (2 in)

Notoriously dangerous, this bulky Australian spider is armed with a potent venom that can kill an adult human. When alarmed it rears up to threaten enemies with its huge, deadly fangs.

SUN SPIDER
Metasolpuga picta
Location: S. W. Africa
Body length: Up to 5 cm (2 in)

Despite its name and appearance this arachnid is not a true spider, and it does not have venomous fangs. It hunts insects on the dunes of the Namib Desert, seizing and cutting them up to devour with its powerful jaws.

HORNED HARVESTMAN
Phalangium opilio
Location: Northern hemisphere
Body length: Up to 9 mm (¼ in)

Although similar to a spider, a harvestman has a one-piece body that looks like a bean, supported by eight very long, slender legs. It has small pincer-like jaws that it uses to eat a wide variety of foods, detecting them with its extra-long, very sensitive second pair of legs.

WHIP SCORPION
Mastigoproctus giganteus
Location: S. North America
Body length: Up to 6 cm (2¼ in)

This American species is also known as the giant vinegaroon because of the way it defends itself by spraying vinegary acid from its whip-like tail. It has no sting.

YELLOW SCORPION
Leiurus quinquestriatus
Location: Widespread
Length: Up to 11 cm (4¼ in), including tail

Death grip
Pincers are used to catch insects and other small animals.

Arched stinger
The stinger stretches over the scorpion's head in order to jab the prey it holds.

Widespread from North Africa to India, this is one of the most dangerous scorpions, armed with a sting that can be lethal. It uses the sting to paralyze or kill prey held in its strong pincers.

Common starfish

Gliding over the sea bed towards a clam, on hundreds of flexible feet, the common starfish creeps up on its victim and launches an attack. It pulls the clam's shell apart so it can consume the soft flesh within.

A starfish may not look like a hunter, but to other marine animals it is a voracious predator, prepared to eat anything – even other starfish – that cannot escape its clutches. It hunts by scent, following the chemical trail until its victim is within reach. Gripping the prey animal with the suckers of its tiny tube feet, the starfish forces out part of its stomach lining through its central mouth and smothers the soft parts of its victim with digestive juices. The juices break down the prey's soft tissues, so the starfish can suck them into its body.

When spawning, a female common starfish releases up to **2.5 million eggs**.

Smell sensors
The spiny skin contains sensitive chemical receptors that detect the faintest scent of prey.

Spiny skin
Rows of short white spines are flanked by bumpy skin. Soft structures called papulae (orange in this image) protrude through gaps in the skin. These act in the same way as gills, absorbing oxygen from the water and releasing carbon dioxide.

Simple eye
An eyespot at the end of each arm can detect light and shade.

Tube feet
Beneath each arm are rows of flexible tube feet, moved by small muscles and hydraulic pressure, as fluid-filled sacs in the arms squeeze water into the tube feet to make them move. Each foot ends in a sucker that can grip the sea bed, so the starfish can crawl around.

Five-rayed star
The starfish has five tapering arms. Its skin is usually orange but can be shades of purple or brown.

The **surface of a starfish** is dotted with **hundreds of minuscule pincers** that keep it **free of dirt** and **stop other animals settling on its skin**.

39

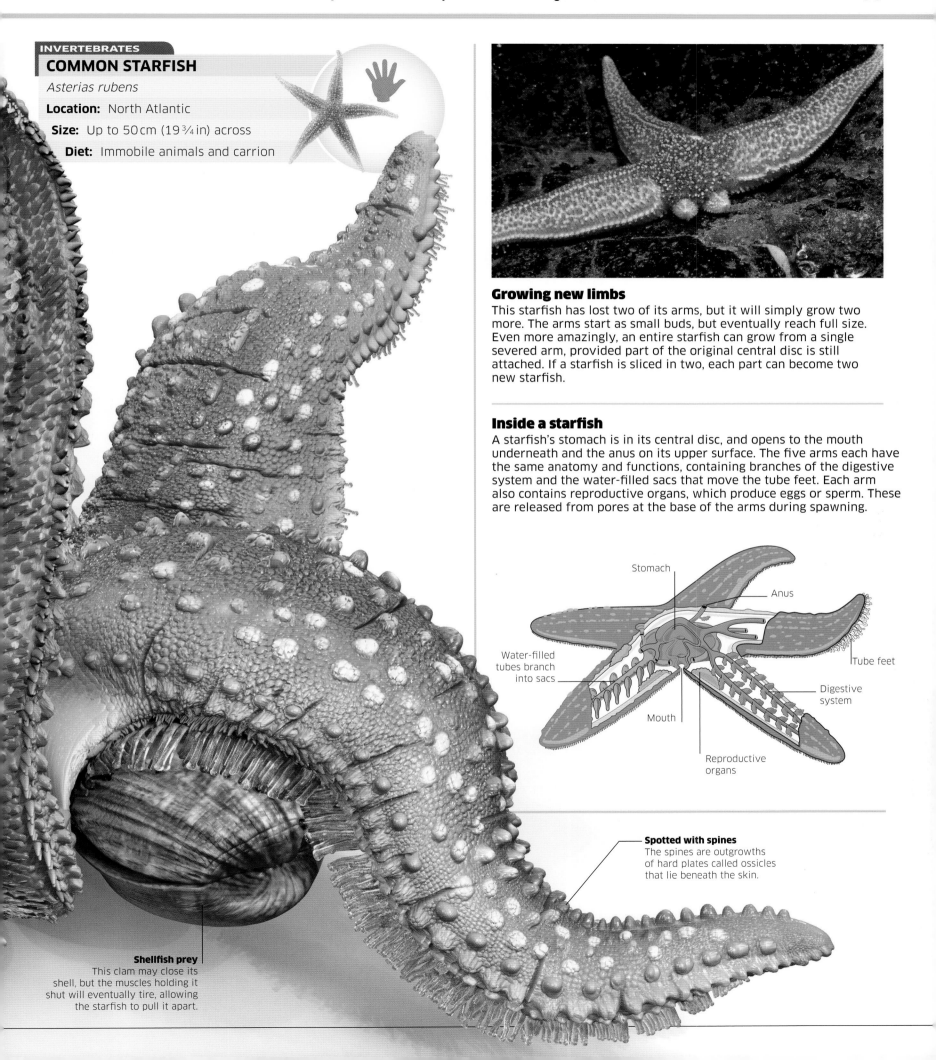

COMMON STARFISH

Asterias rubens

Location: North Atlantic

Size: Up to 50 cm (19 ¾ in) across

Diet: Immobile animals and carrion

Growing new limbs

This starfish has lost two of its arms, but it will simply grow two more. The arms start as small buds, but eventually reach full size. Even more amazingly, an entire starfish can grow from a single severed arm, provided part of the original central disc is still attached. If a starfish is sliced in two, each part can become two new starfish.

Inside a starfish

A starfish's stomach is in its central disc, and opens to the mouth underneath and the anus on its upper surface. The five arms each have the same anatomy and functions, containing branches of the digestive system and the water-filled sacs that move the tube feet. Each arm also contains reproductive organs, which produce eggs or sperm. These are released from pores at the base of the arms during spawning.

Stomach

Anus

Water-filled tubes branch into sacs

Tube feet

Digestive system

Mouth

Reproductive organs

Spotted with spines
The spines are outgrowths of hard plates called ossicles that lie beneath the skin.

Shellfish prey
This clam may close its shell, but the muscles holding it shut will eventually tire, allowing the starfish to pull it apart.

Echinoderms are among the few animals that **do not have heads**.

Some **sea urchins** can use their spines to **burrow into solid rock**.

Echinoderms

Starfish, sea urchins, and their relatives are known as echinoderms, which means "spiny-skinned". The spines are very obvious on some sea urchins, which are the prickliest creatures on the planet.

Other echinoderms are studded with hard plates, or have flexible but tough skins. All sea-dwelling creatures, they have bodies that are built on a radial plan, with a mouth and stomach in the centre and segments extending outwards like a flower.

CROWN-OF-THORNS STARFISH
Acanthaster planci
Location: Indo-Pacific region
Width: Up to 35 cm (13¾ in)

One of the biggest, spiniest sea stars, this is a notorious predator of reef-building corals. Armies of them swarm over the reefs, and devour the coral by smothering it with digestive juices and soaking up the result, leaving a skeleton of bare rock.

Toxic spines
The stiff spines are laced with a toxin that inflicts a painful sting.

Arms
Up to 21 spiny arms radiate from the broad central disc.

BLUE STARFISH
Linckia laevigata
Location: Indo-Pacific region
Width: Up to 30 cm (11¾ in)

One of the most colourful echinoderms, this tropical starfish grazes on algae or the encrusting animals that cling to rocks and reefs. It has five arms but, like all starfish, has the ability to grow new ones if it loses any.

BISCUIT STAR
Tosia australis
Location: South Australian coastline
Width: Up to 10 cm (4 in)

Starfish come in many shapes and sizes. This south Australian biscuit star has a typical five-sided form, but very short arms. Like all starfish it creeps over the sea bed on many small, tube feet with suckers at the tips.

Plate armour
Body is fringed with tough plates.

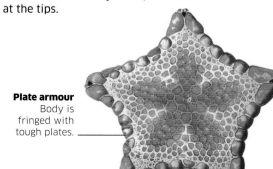

CELTIC FEATHER STAR
Leptometra celtica
Location: Coasts of N. W. Europe
Width: Up to 30 cm (11¾ in)

Feather stars are built like starfish, but live upside down attached to rocks, and filter food from the water with their feathery arms. Their bodies are mostly made up of hard, chalky plates and spines.

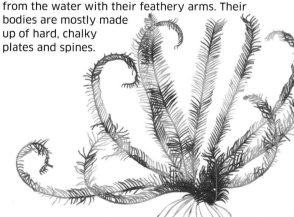

7,000 The approximate number of **echinoderm species**.

As a defence mechanism, **sea cucumbers** can **expel some of their own organs**, which become **long and sticky** and can **entangle predators**.

41

PURPLE URCHIN
Strongylocentrotus purpuratus
Location: North American coastline
Width: Up to 10 cm (4 in), excluding spines

A sea urchin body's is made up of five "radial segments", a bit like the segments of an orange, enclosed in a spiny skeleton. This species feeds on giant kelp seaweed in the coastal Pacific.

THORNY SEA URCHIN
Goniocidaris tubaria
Location: Australian coastline
Width: Up to 4.5 cm (1¾ in), excluding spines

Typical sea urchins have slender, sharp-tipped spines, but this south Australian species has very stout spines armed with thorns. Like other sea urchins it has a set of central jaws that it uses to eat a wide variety of foods.

LONG-SPINED SEA URCHIN
Diadema antillarum
Location: Western Atlantic Ocean
Width: Up to 10 cm (4 in), excluding spines

The extremely long spines of this tropical urchin make it a prickly mouthful for predators, but despite this it is still eaten by some fish. It feeds at night on algae and coral, retreating to dark crevices by day.

Sharp spines
The sharp, brittle black spines can be up to 30 cm (12 in) long.

WESTERN SAND DOLLAR
Dendraster excentricus
Location: Pacific North American coast
Width: Up to 7.5 cm (3 in)

Some urchins are adapted for burrowing in sand. They are covered in tiny bristly spines, and often have distinct front and back ends. This American species has an unusually flattened body.

Petal-shaped structure on surface

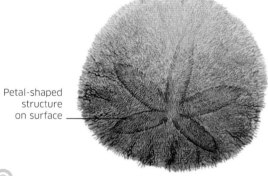

BASKET STAR
Astroboa nuda
Location: Indo-Pacific region
Width: Up to 1 m (3¼ ft)

Similar to feather stars, basket stars cling to rocks or corals in places with strong currents, and use their multi-branched arms to gather food from the water. They are closely related to brittle stars, with the same bony, yet flexible structure.

RETICULATED BRITTLE STAR
Ophionereis reticulata
Location: N. and S. American coastline
Width: Up to 25 cm (9¾ in)

A brittle star has a small central disc and five slender, very mobile arms, each supported by a flexible chain of bony plates. It uses its arms to cling to corals and rocks, or crawl across the sea bed in search of edible debris.

Spiny arms
Each flexible arm is fringed with rows of spines.

FLORIDA SEA CUCUMBER
Holothuria floridana
Location: Caribbean Sea, Gulf of Mexico, Florida coast
Length: Up to 20 cm (8 in)

The body of a sea cucumber is formed of five radial segments like a typical sea urchin, but elongated. The animal's mouth is at one end, surrounded by a ring of tentacles used for gathering particles of food.

Knobbly skin
Leathery skin is dotted with conical studs.

SEA APPLE
Pseudocolochirus violaceus
Location: Tropical waters of the Indo-Pacific
Length: Up to 18 cm (7 in)

Unlike most sea cucumbers, which roam over the sea bed in search of food, a sea apple stays in one place and uses its tentacles to filter edible plankton from the water. This coral reef species is particularly colourful.

Tube feet
Hydraulic tube feet with suckers on the end allow the sea apple to attach itself to rocks.

FISH

Fish were the first animals to have bony internal skeletons, and therefore the first vertebrates. Since their appearance in the seas and oceans more than 500 million years ago, they have evolved into a dazzling diversity of forms, ranging from delicate seahorses to huge, powerful, predatory sharks.

WHAT IS A FISH?

Fish are easy to recognize, but harder to define. They include three distinct groups of animals, most of which breathe through gills but are otherwise quite different. But a typical fish is a streamlined swimmer that propels itself through the water using strong muscles anchored to a flexible backbone.

Spiny fin
The first dorsal fin is supported by slender, bony spines.

Scales
Each scale is a thin plate. Scales overlap like roof tiles.

Eyes
These have thick lenses adapted for underwater vision.

TYPES OF FISH

The first fish to evolve were jawless fish, which flourished in the distant past but have now been reduced to a few species. The cartilaginous sharks and rays are more numerous, but the vast majority of fish belong to the large group of bony fish.

SEA LAMPREY

Jawless fish
As their name indicates, the jawless fish do not have hinged jaws. The group consists of fewer than 40 species of eel-like lampreys, and may also include the slimy hagfishes.

EUROPEAN ANCHOVY

Bony fish
With some 32,000 species, the bony fish make up most of the fish on the planet. Nearly all of them are ray-finned fish (with fins supported by bony struts or spines), but they also include lobe-finned fish related to the ancestors of all land vertebrates.

SCALLOPED HAMMERHEAD SHARK

Cartilaginous fish
The sharks, rays, and their relatives have skeletons made from gristly, pliable cartilage instead of bone. There are about 1,200 species, which include the largest, most powerful fish in the sea.

Brain

Heart

Pelvic fin

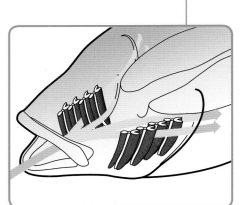

Gills
The gills are rows of very fine, thin-walled tubes filled with blood that is pumped around the body. The blood contains waste carbon dioxide produced by muscles and organs. Water flowing into the fish's mouth and through the gills carries away the carbon dioxide, replacing it with oxygen absorbed from the water. The fish uses this oxygen to turn its food into energy.

KEY FEATURES

All fish share a number of key features, although the nature of those features varies. They are all vertebrates, with internal skeletons based on spinal vertebrae. Their skin is usually protected by scales, and almost all have gills that gather oxygen from the water. Mainly cold-blooded, they all live primarily in the water of oceans, seas, lakes, and rivers.

Vertebrates
A typical fish's skeleton consists of the spine, skull and jaws, ribs, and fin supports.

Cold-blooded
The body of a typical fish is the same temperature as the water in which it lives.

Breathe with gills
Blood in the gills absorbs oxygen from the water, but a few fish can breathe air.

Live in water
All fish live in either fresh water or salty seawater. A few can move between the two.

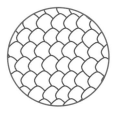

Scaly skin
Tough, overlapping scales cover the skin of most fish, but some types have no scales.

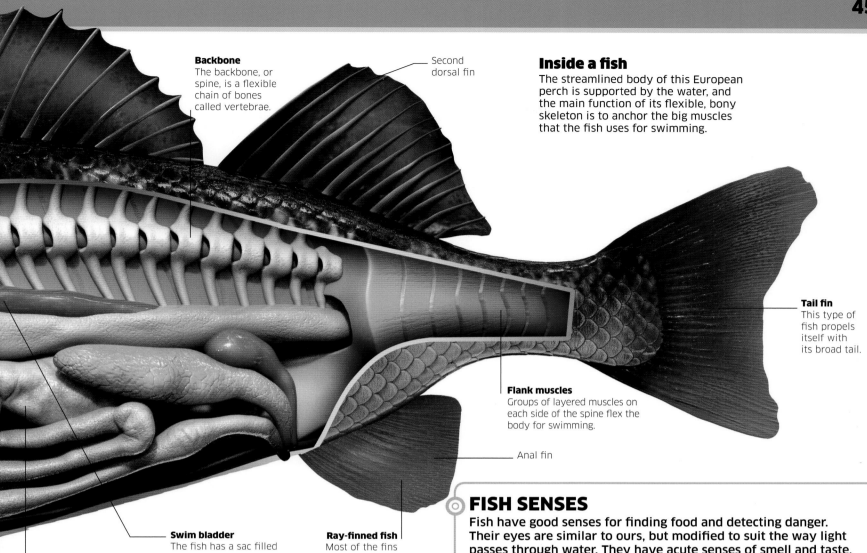

Backbone
The backbone, or spine, is a flexible chain of bones called vertebrae.

Second dorsal fin

Inside a fish
The streamlined body of this European perch is supported by the water, and the main function of its flexible, bony skeleton is to anchor the big muscles that the fish uses for swimming.

Tail fin
This type of fish propels itself with its broad tail.

Flank muscles
Groups of layered muscles on each side of the spine flex the body for swimming.

Anal fin

Stomach

Swim bladder
The fish has a sac filled with gas that acts as an adjustable float.

Ray-finned fish
Most of the fins are supported by flexible rays.

FISH SENSES

Fish have good senses for finding food and detecting danger. Their eyes are similar to ours, but modified to suit the way light passes through water. They have acute senses of smell and taste, and most can pick up sound waves. More importantly they detect pressure changes using a network of sensors called the lateral line. These sensors alert the fish to nearby movements and allow them to swim in perfectly coordinated shoals.

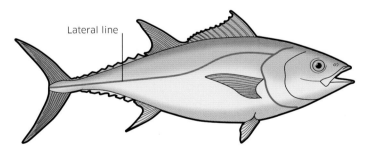

Lateral line

SWIMMING LIKE A FISH

Eels swim by flexing their bodies like snakes, creating rippling waves that push them through the water. Many other fish swim in a similar way, using the massive flank muscles on each side of their backbones, with the greatest movement at the tail. Some make greater movements of their bodies than others. The fastest fish – which include tuna, some sharks, and the sailfish – hold their bodies straight and use their flank muscles to flick their tail fins from side to side.

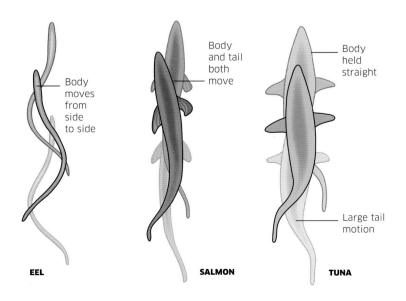

Body moves from side to side

Body and tail both move

Body held straight

Large tail motion

EEL

SALMON

TUNA

EGGS AND YOUNG

A female shark's eggs are fertilized internally, and many sharks bear live young that develop inside the mother. But most female fish produce large numbers of eggs and release them into the water to be fertilized by the male. The eggs usually drift in open water where most of them are eaten by other fish, but this mouth-brooding fish protects its eggs in its mouth.

Vampire attack

When a fish is attacked by a sea lamprey, it has few defences. The lamprey clings tightly with its sucker, and is not easy to dislodge. As it bores into its victim's flesh, its saliva stops the blood clotting, so the lamprey can drink its fill. Its prey will be lucky to survive the attack.

Inside view

A lamprey's skull and skeleton are made of pliable cartilage, like those of a shark, but unlike a shark the lamprey does not have a hinged jaw. The mouth is surrounded by a disc of tough, flexible tissue studded with teeth made of keratin – the substance that forms our fingernails. The mouth and respiratory tube are separate, so the lamprey can draw water over its gills while its mouth is clamped to a victim.

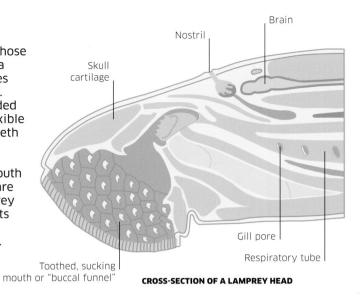

Skull cartilage

Nostril

Brain

Gill pore

Respiratory tube

Toothed, sucking mouth or "buccal funnel"

CROSS-SECTION OF A LAMPREY HEAD

Dorsal fin
The only fins are the tail and dorsal fins, which are supported by stiff fin rays. There are no pectoral fins.

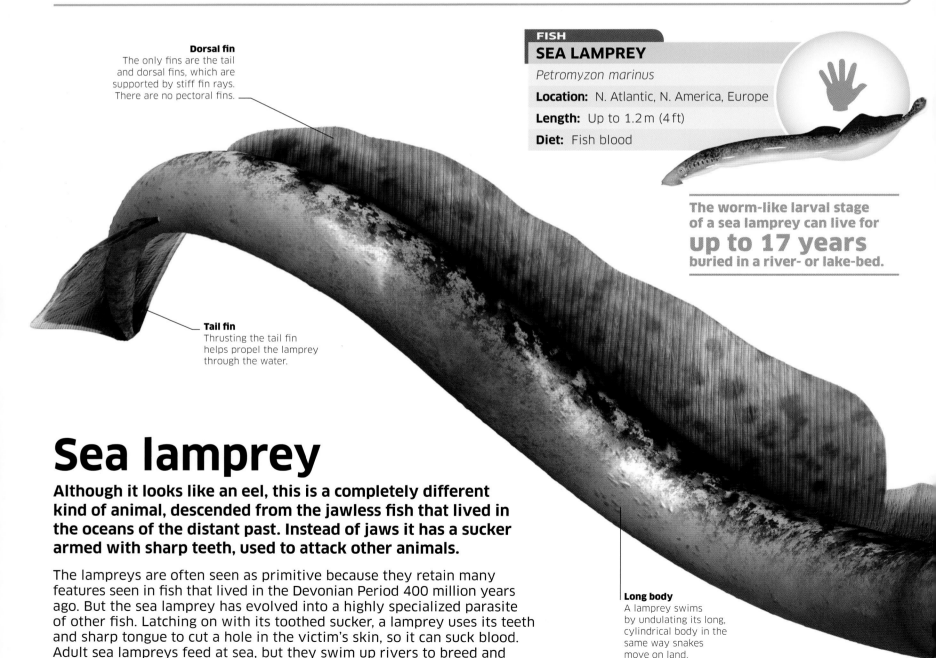

FISH

SEA LAMPREY

Petromyzon marinus

Location: N. Atlantic, N. America, Europe

Length: Up to 1.2 m (4 ft)

Diet: Fish blood

The worm-like larval stage of a sea lamprey can live for
up to 17 years
buried in a river- or lake-bed.

Tail fin
Thrusting the tail fin helps propel the lamprey through the water.

Sea lamprey

Although it looks like an eel, this is a completely different kind of animal, descended from the jawless fish that lived in the oceans of the distant past. Instead of jaws it has a sucker armed with sharp teeth, used to attack other animals.

The lampreys are often seen as primitive because they retain many features seen in fish that lived in the Devonian Period 400 million years ago. But the sea lamprey has evolved into a highly specialized parasite of other fish. Latching on with its toothed sucker, a lamprey uses its teeth and sharp tongue to cut a hole in the victim's skin, so it can suck blood. Adult sea lampreys feed at sea, but they swim up rivers to breed and spend their early lives in fresh water.

Long body
A lamprey swims by undulating its long, cylindrical body in the same way snakes move on land.

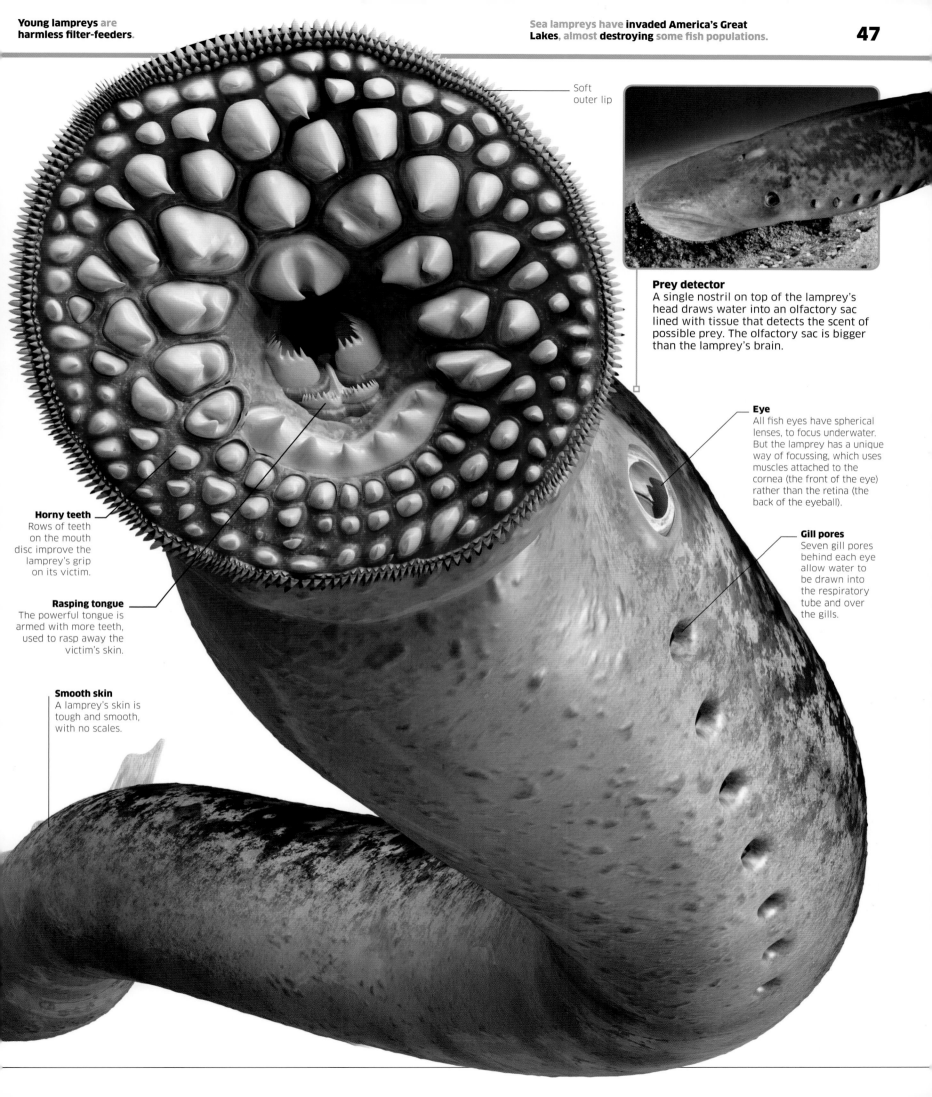

Young lampreys are harmless filter-feeders.

Sea lampreys have invaded America's Great Lakes, almost destroying some fish populations.

47

Soft outer lip

Prey detector
A single nostril on top of the lamprey's head draws water into an olfactory sac lined with tissue that detects the scent of possible prey. The olfactory sac is bigger than the lamprey's brain.

Eye
All fish eyes have spherical lenses, to focus underwater. But the lamprey has a unique way of focussing, which uses muscles attached to the cornea (the front of the eye) rather than the retina (the back of the eyeball).

Horny teeth
Rows of teeth on the mouth disc improve the lamprey's grip on its victim.

Gill pores
Seven gill pores behind each eye allow water to be drawn into the respiratory tube and over the gills.

Rasping tongue
The powerful tongue is armed with more teeth, used to rasp away the victim's skin.

Smooth skin
A lamprey's skin is tough and smooth, with no scales.

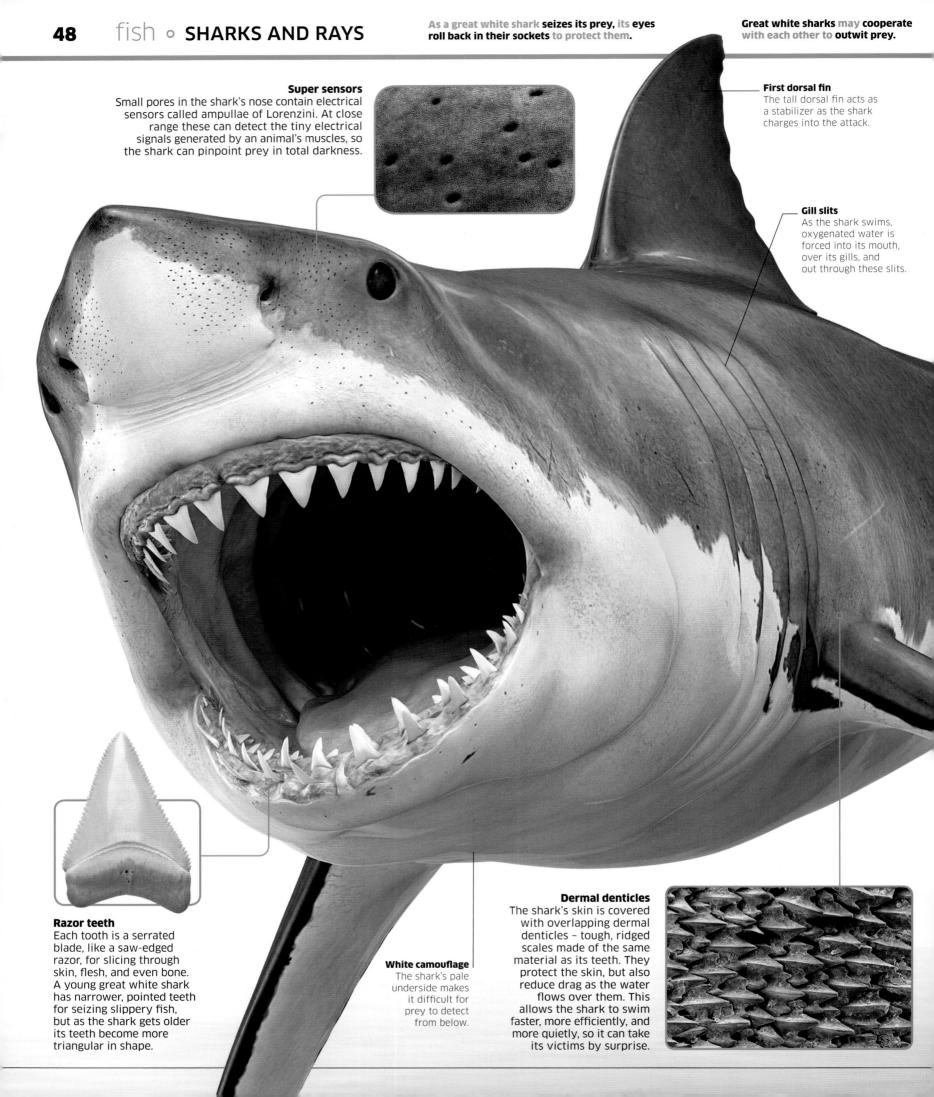

As a great white shark **seizes its prey,** its eyes roll back in their sockets **to protect them.**

Great white sharks may cooperate with each other to **outwit prey.**

Super sensors
Small pores in the shark's nose contain electrical sensors called ampullae of Lorenzini. At close range these can detect the tiny electrical signals generated by an animal's muscles, so the shark can pinpoint prey in total darkness.

First dorsal fin
The tall dorsal fin acts as a stabilizer as the shark charges into the attack.

Gill slits
As the shark swims, oxygenated water is forced into its mouth, over its gills, and out through these slits.

Razor teeth
Each tooth is a serrated blade, like a saw-edged razor, for slicing through skin, flesh, and even bone. A young great white shark has narrower, pointed teeth for seizing slippery fish, but as the shark gets older its teeth become more triangular in shape.

White camouflage
The shark's pale underside makes it difficult for prey to detect from below.

Dermal denticles
The shark's skin is covered with overlapping dermal denticles – tough, ridged scales made of the same material as its teeth. They protect the skin, but also reduce drag as the water flows over them. This allows the shark to swim faster, more efficiently, and more quietly, so it can take its victims by surprise.

56 km/h (35 mph) – **the speed** at which a great white shark **can swim**.

A **hungry great white** may **raise its head from the water** to sniff out prey.

70 years – **the age** a great white can **live to** in the wild.

49

Great white shark

Notorious as the most deadly of all sharks, the great white is specialized for hunting big, warm-blooded animals such as seals, dolphins, and even whales.

Few creatures have such a murderous reputation as the great white shark. Hugely powerful and fast, it is equipped with a devastatingly efficient array of senses for detecting its prey, and a set of ripsaw teeth that can slice its victims in half with a single bite. Capable of killing and eating almost anything it runs into – including people – its only enemies are orcas and human hunters.

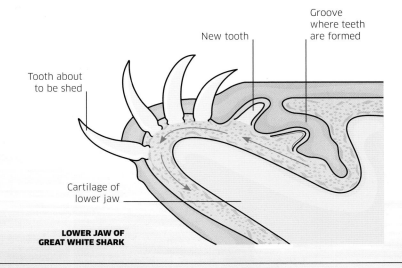

Solid muscle
Massively powerful muscles flank the shark's body.

Second dorsal fin

Built for speed
The crescent-shaped tail provides propulsion. As with fast-swimming tuna, the body and tail are connected by a slim joint – this allows the tail to be flipped rapidly from side to side while the body stays relatively rigid.

The great white shark's nostrils can sniff out blood in the water from well over

1 km (½ mile) away.

Wing fins
Long pectoral fins act like wings as the shark swims forwards.

Conveyor-belt teeth

The great white shark never has to worry about losing its teeth, however old it gets. As with all sharks, teeth are shed and continuously replaced, with new teeth moving up from behind. The new teeth roll out from inside the jaws as if on a conveyor belt, while the old, blunt teeth drop off the outside.

New tooth

Groove where teeth are formed

Tooth about to be shed

Cartilage of lower jaw

LOWER JAW OF GREAT WHITE SHARK

FISH

GREAT WHITE SHARK

Carcharodon carcharias

Location: All warm oceans

Length: Up to 7.2 m (24 ft)

Diet: Fish, seals, and cetaceans

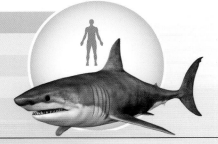

The **earliest-known** sharks **lived** more than **420 million years** ago.

Some rays **stun or kill** their prey by **electrocuting** them.

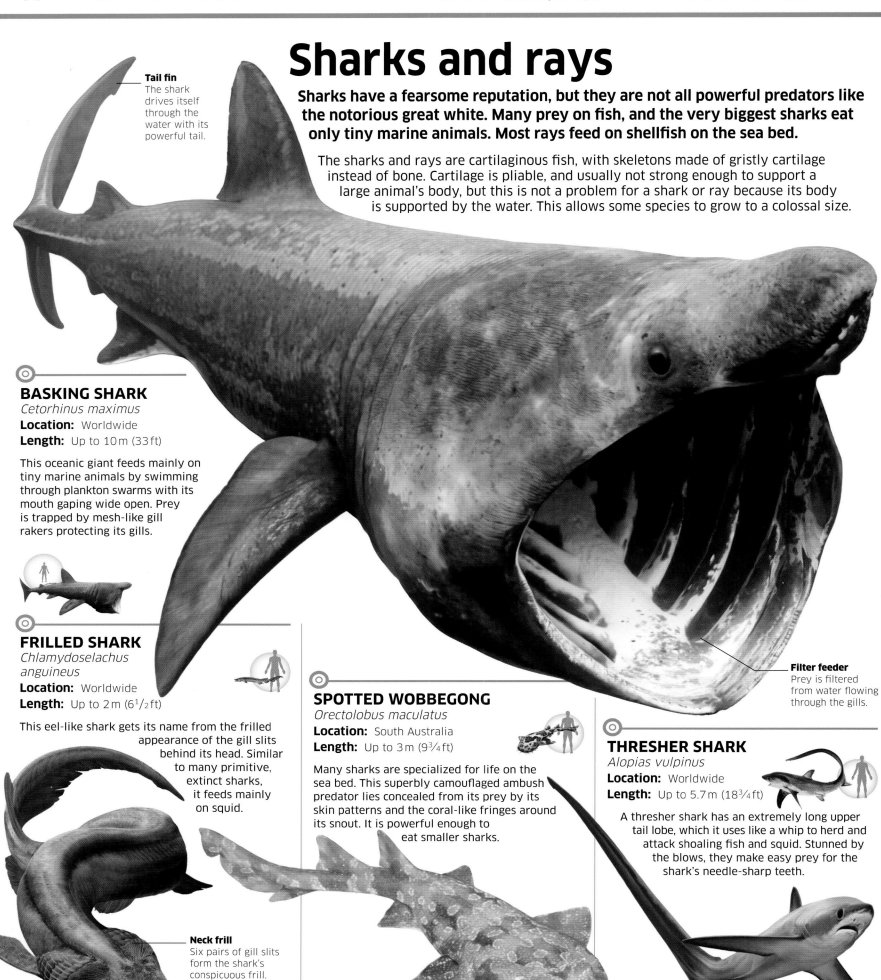

Sharks and rays

Sharks have a fearsome reputation, but they are not all powerful predators like the notorious great white. Many prey on fish, and the very biggest sharks eat only tiny marine animals. Most rays feed on shellfish on the sea bed.

The sharks and rays are cartilaginous fish, with skeletons made of gristly cartilage instead of bone. Cartilage is pliable, and usually not strong enough to support a large animal's body, but this is not a problem for a shark or ray because its body is supported by the water. This allows some species to grow to a colossal size.

Tail fin
The shark drives itself through the water with its powerful tail.

BASKING SHARK
Cetorhinus maximus

Location: Worldwide
Length: Up to 10 m (33 ft)

This oceanic giant feeds mainly on tiny marine animals by swimming through plankton swarms with its mouth gaping wide open. Prey is trapped by mesh-like gill rakers protecting its gills.

Filter feeder
Prey is filtered from water flowing through the gills.

FRILLED SHARK
Chlamydoselachus anguineus

Location: Worldwide
Length: Up to 2 m (6½ ft)

This eel-like shark gets its name from the frilled appearance of the gill slits behind its head. Similar to many primitive, extinct sharks, it feeds mainly on squid.

Neck frill
Six pairs of gill slits form the shark's conspicuous frill.

SPOTTED WOBBEGONG
Orectolobus maculatus

Location: South Australia
Length: Up to 3 m (9¾ ft)

Many sharks are specialized for life on the sea bed. This superbly camouflaged ambush predator lies concealed from its prey by its skin patterns and the coral-like fringes around its snout. It is powerful enough to eat smaller sharks.

THRESHER SHARK
Alopias vulpinus

Location: Worldwide
Length: Up to 5.7 m (18¾ ft)

A thresher shark has an extremely long upper tail lobe, which it uses like a whip to herd and attack shoaling fish and squid. Stunned by the blows, they make easy prey for the shark's needle-sharp teeth.

12.5 m (41 ft) or more – the length of the **biggest shark**, the filter-feeding **whale shark**.

17 cm (6¾ in) – the length of the **smallest shark**, the deep-sea dwarf lanternshark.

51

SANDTIGER SHARK
Carcharias taurus
Location: Coastal waters worldwide
Length: Up to 3.2 m (10½ ft)

The ferocious-looking sandtiger shark is specialized for catching fish. Its ragged, spiky teeth are ideally adapted for seizing and gripping slippery, struggling prey, which it then swallows whole or in large mouthfuls. It usually hunts by night, often near the sea bed.

BLUE SHARK
Prionace glauca
Location: Worldwide
Length: Up to 3.8 m (12½ ft)

Sleek and elegant, the blue shark gets its name from its metallic blue back. Its slender body and pointed snout make it superbly streamlined for cruising at speed in search of prey, which are mainly smaller fish and squid. It sometimes hunts in packs.

SCALLOPED HAMMERHEAD
Sphyrna lewini
Location: Worldwide
Length: Up to 4.2 m (13¾ ft)

A hammerhead shark has a bizarre plank-like head with its eyes and nostrils at each tip. This shape may help it make tight turns in the water, or it may provide space for extra electro-receptors for detecting hidden prey.

ANGEL SHARK
Squatina squatina
Location: Northern Atlantic Ocean, Mediterranean Sea, Black Sea
Length: Up to 2.4 m (7¾ ft)

The broad, flattened body of the angel shark is more like that of a ray than a typical shark. Its shape enables it to lie concealed on the sea bed, waiting for fish to swim within ambush range.

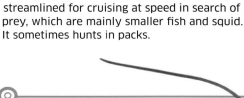

GIANT MANTA RAY
Manta birostris
Location: Worldwide
Length: Up to 7.6 m (25 ft)

The biggest of the rays, the giant manta is a filter-feeder like the basking shark. It cruises tropical oceans searching for swarms of planktonic animals, and feeds by straining the water through its gills to trap prey.

SPOTTED EAGLE RAY
Aetobatus narinari
Location: Worldwide
Length: Up to 5 m (16½ ft)

This elegant ray often swims in open water, sometimes in groups of 10 or more. Despite this, it feeds mainly on the sea bed by digging into the sand with its shovel-shaped snout for clams, crabs, and other shellfish. It has very strong, flattened teeth for crushing shells.

THORNBACK RAY
Raja clavata
Location: Eastern Atlantic, Mediterranean
Length: Up to 1 m (3¼ ft)

Although this ray has the kite-shaped body typical of many rays, its back is covered in sharp, thorny spines that extend down its long tail. Its mouth is beneath its head, so it can scoop buried prey off the sea bed.

LONGCOMB SAWFISH
Pristis zijsron
Location: Indo-Pacific region
Length: Up to 4.3 m (14 ft)

The extraordinary snout of this sawfish is a long, slender blade fringed with rows of triangular teeth. The fish uses it to strike and stun fish prey, and to rake burrowing animals from the sea bed.

Saw blade
Toothed snout can be more than 1.5 m (5 ft) long.

6 mm (¼ in) – **the length** of a spotted seahorse **at birth**.

Spotted seahorses **pair up for life**, renewing their bond each morning with a **courtship dance**.

Chameleon colour

The spotted seahorse is typically yellowish with darker spots and blotches. But like most seahorses it is able to change its skin colour, by making colour cells in its skin expand or contract. The seahorse can then blend with its surroundings for protective camouflage. It often turns very dark to conceal itself from both enemies and prey. But it may also glow a deep red, especially during its courtship displays.

Planktonic prey

The seahorse's prey are small shrimp-like animals that drift in open water and make up plankton. Watching intently with its big, mobile eyes, the seahorse targets a victim and swivels its snout towards it. Using its flexible neck, it lunges at the animal and sucks it into its toothless mouth, swallowing it whole.

Spotted seahorse

Named for their horse-like head shape, seahorses are highly specialized fish with a unique swimming technique and one of the most extraordinary breeding systems in the entire animal kingdom.

Widespread in the Indo-Pacific regions the spotted seahorse lives in shallow coastal waters where it feeds on small, drifting animals. It can swim slowly in a vertical position, propelled by its beating dorsal fin, but prefers to use its prehensile (grasping) tail to cling to corals, seagrasses, and seaweed and watch for prey. As with all seahorses, the female passes her eggs to the male, who holds them in a pouch on his belly, fertilizing and nurturing them until they become miniature seahorses.

FISH

SPOTTED SEAHORSE

Hippocampus kuda

Location: Indian and Pacific Oceans

Length: Up to 35 cm (13¾ in)

Diet: Small planktonic animals

Bony rings

Thin skin is stretched over bony plates that form ring-shaped ridges.

Prehensile tail

Coiling its tail around seaweed stops the seahorse drifting in the current.

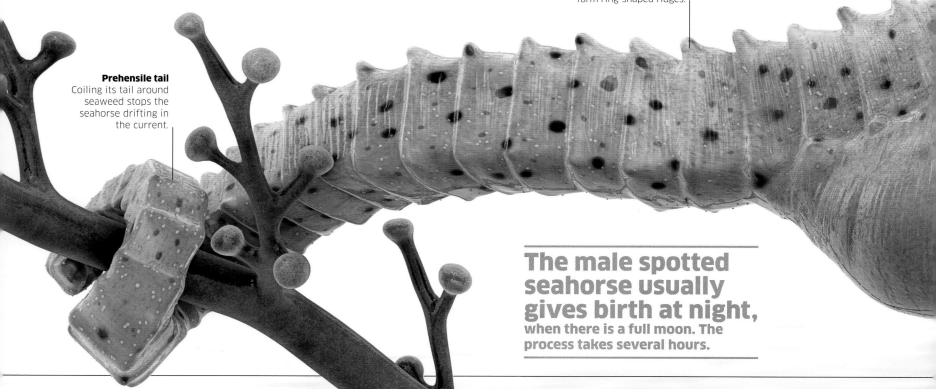

The male spotted seahorse usually gives birth at night, when there is a full moon. The process takes several hours.

200 The number of **baby seahorses** that the **male seahorse may give birth to**.

As soon as his young are born, the **male** starts **brooding another batch of eggs**.

53

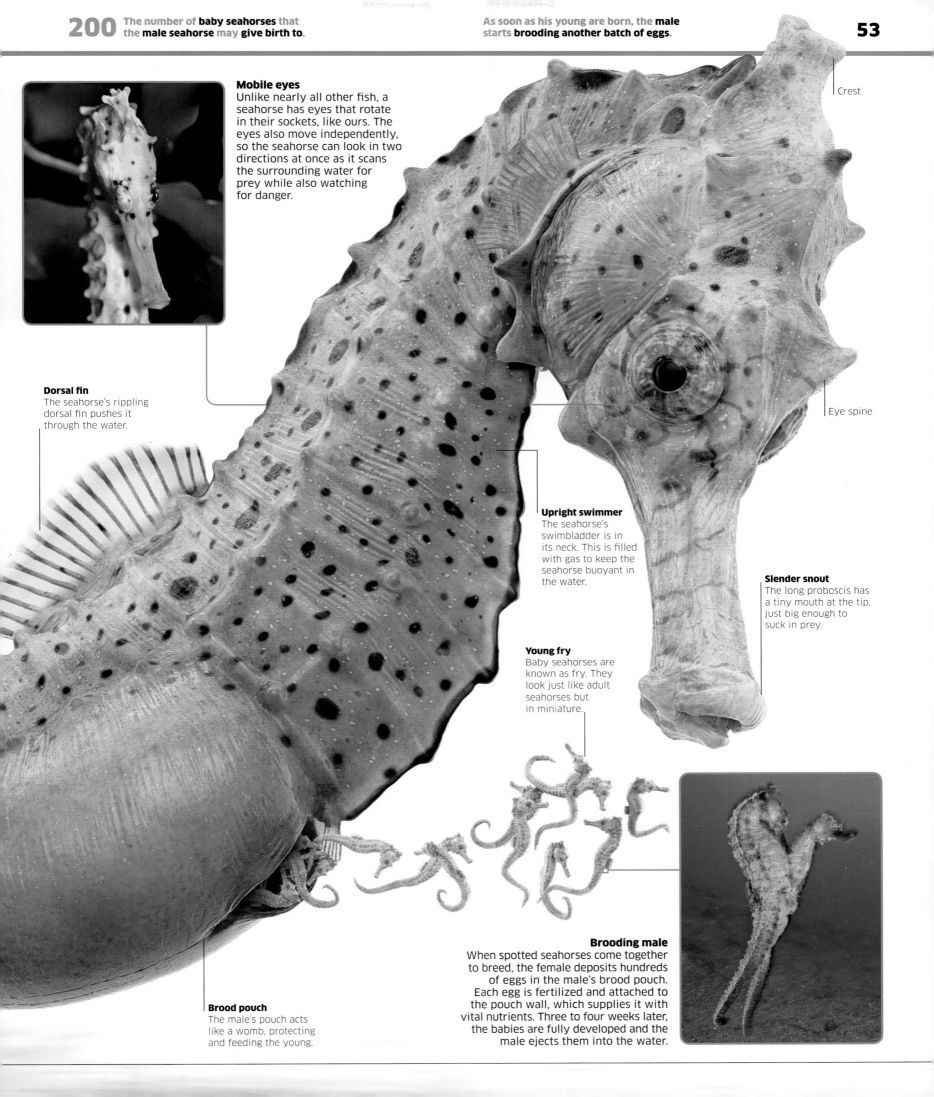

Mobile eyes
Unlike nearly all other fish, a seahorse has eyes that rotate in their sockets, like ours. The eyes also move independently, so the seahorse can look in two directions at once as it scans the surrounding water for prey while also watching for danger.

Crest

Dorsal fin
The seahorse's rippling dorsal fin pushes it through the water.

Eye spine

Upright swimmer
The seahorse's swimbladder is in its neck. This is filled with gas to keep the seahorse buoyant in the water.

Slender snout
The long proboscis has a tiny mouth at the tip, just big enough to suck in prey.

Young fry
Baby seahorses are known as fry. They look just like adult seahorses but in miniature.

Brood pouch
The male's pouch acts like a womb, protecting and feeding the young.

Brooding male
When spotted seahorses come together to breed, the female deposits hundreds of eggs in the male's brood pouch. Each egg is fertilized and attached to the pouch wall, which supplies it with vital nutrients. Three to four weeks later, the babies are fully developed and the male ejects them into the water.

Red lionfish

This spectacular sea fish is a resident of tropical coral reefs, where it creeps up on smaller fish that it can seize and swallow whole. Venomous spines ensure that it rarely suffers the same fate itself.

The lionfish's candy-striped pattern and feathery fans of spiny finlets create a dazzling impression, designed to warn bigger fish that it is dangerous to eat. Its flamboyant fins slow it down, but this is not a problem for a fish that lives in the food-rich waters of the coral reef. Surrounded by prey, it uses its superb mobility to work its way into position for a lightning-fast strike, snapping up each victim before it has a chance to escape.

Head tentacles
A strange feature of the lionfish is the pair of tentacles that sprouts from its head. These vary in form across different populations: some are spiky (below) while others are feathery (left). They may help the fish win a mate, or might act as lures to attract inquisitive prey.

Outsized eyes
Large eyes, which maximize the amount of light captured, give the lionfish sharp vision.

Prey swallowed head-first

Their venomous spines mean that lionfish have **few predators**, though some sharks have been known to eat them.

Broad mouth
The wide mouth can extend forwards to create a suction tube for catching prey.

Defensive spines

Many of a lionfish's long spines are laced with venom, and the fish uses them to defend itself when threatened. When one of the spines pierces the skin of a victim, a loose sheath is pushed down to expose venomous tissue contained in three grooves running the length of the spine. Venom squeezed out of this tissue enters the wound, causing intense pain, sickness, and difficulty breathing.

Exposed spine

Venom flows into wound

Threatened lionfish lowers head to point spines at enemy

Sheath pushes down when spine enters skin

Groove containing venomous tissue

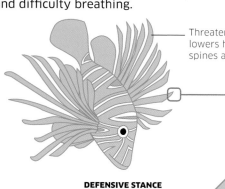

DEFENSIVE STANCE

VENOMOUS SPINE

Lionfish often use their **long pectoral fins** to **herd prey** into tight corners where they are **easier to catch**.

2 million – the **number of eggs** a female lionfish can produce in **one year**.

55

Bony spines
The red lionfish's spines are made of the same bony material as its skeleton, which is why they show up on this X-ray image. The spines are modified fin rays – structures that support the fish's fins. In most fish, fin rays are slender and flexible, but in lionfish they are more rigid and some carry a powerful venom.

Dorsal fin contains 13 venomous spines

Feathery finlets
The pectoral fin rays support fans of long, narrow finlets.

Pectoral fin
The thin, translucent membrane of the pectoral fin stretches between the spines.

RED LIONFISH

Pterois volitans

Location: Indo-Pacific region

Length: Up to 38 cm (15 in)

Diet: Small fish

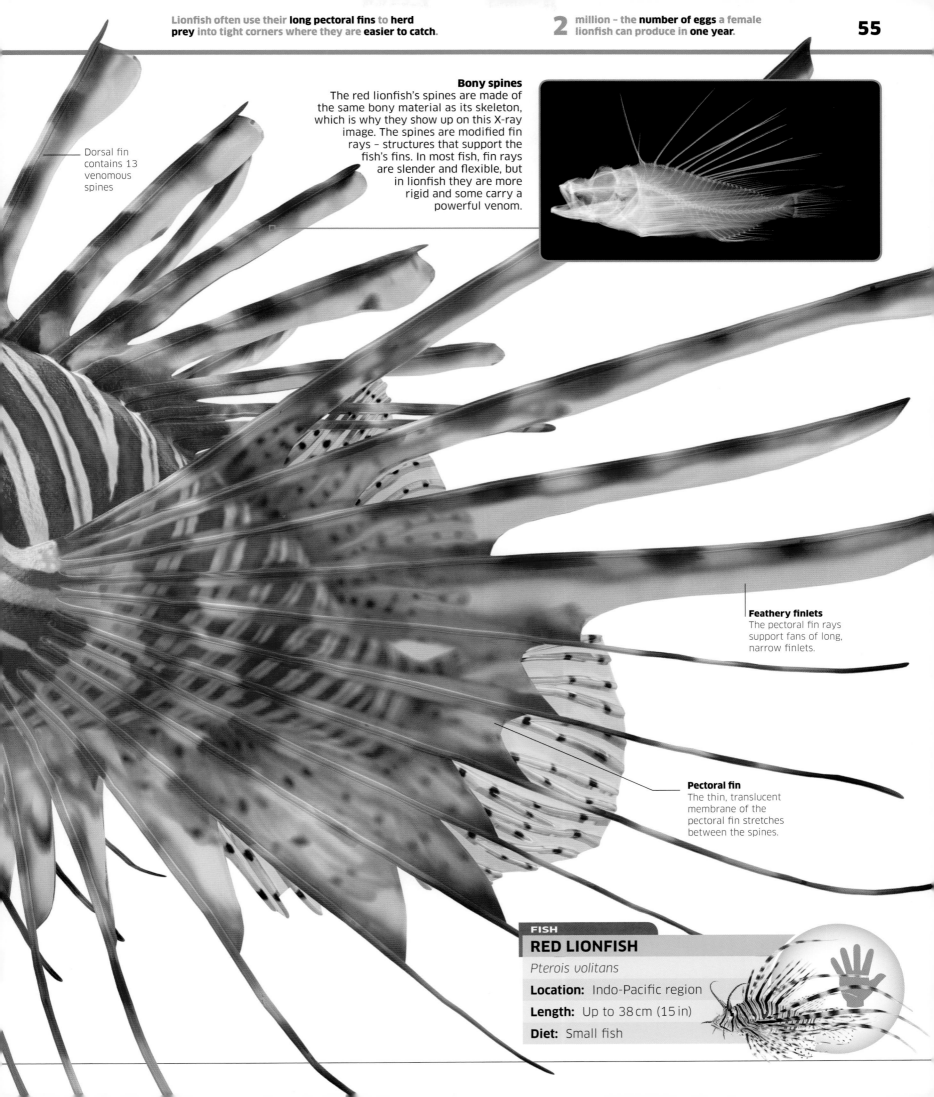

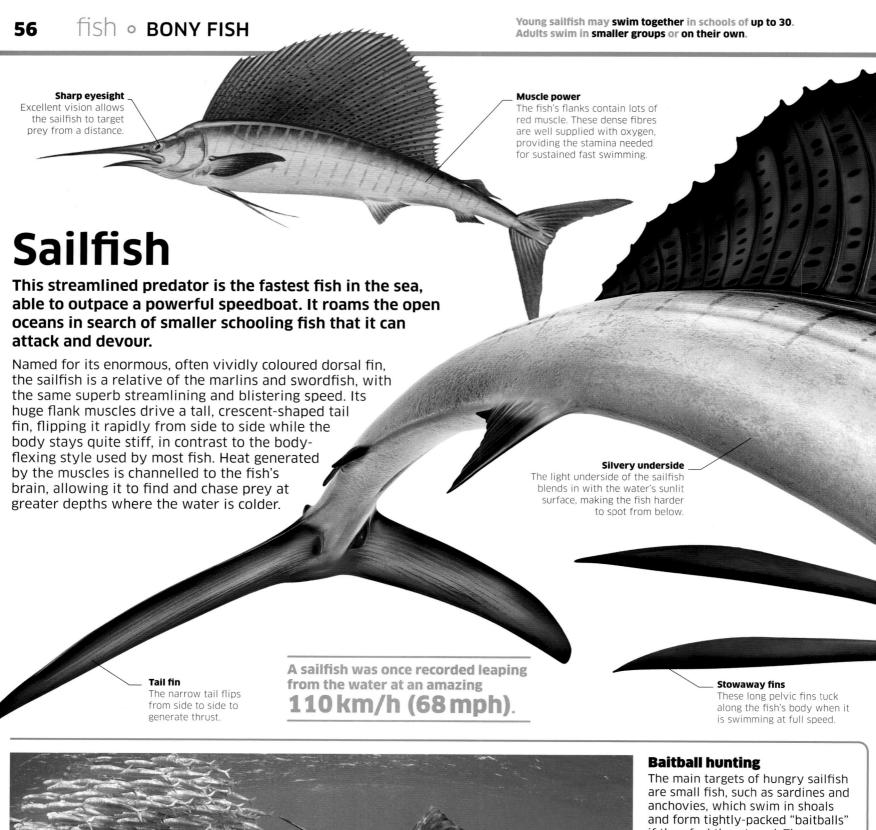

Sharp eyesight
Excellent vision allows the sailfish to target prey from a distance.

Muscle power
The fish's flanks contain lots of red muscle. These dense fibres are well supplied with oxygen, providing the stamina needed for sustained fast swimming.

Sailfish

This streamlined predator is the fastest fish in the sea, able to outpace a powerful speedboat. It roams the open oceans in search of smaller schooling fish that it can attack and devour.

Named for its enormous, often vividly coloured dorsal fin, the sailfish is a relative of the marlins and swordfish, with the same superb streamlining and blistering speed. Its huge flank muscles drive a tall, crescent-shaped tail fin, flipping it rapidly from side to side while the body stays quite stiff, in contrast to the body-flexing style used by most fish. Heat generated by the muscles is channelled to the fish's brain, allowing it to find and chase prey at greater depths where the water is colder.

Silvery underside
The light underside of the sailfish blends in with the water's sunlit surface, making the fish harder to spot from below.

Tail fin
The narrow tail flips from side to side to generate thrust.

A sailfish was once recorded leaping from the water at an amazing
110 km/h (68 mph).

Stowaway fins
These long pelvic fins tuck along the fish's body when it is swimming at full speed.

Baitball hunting

The main targets of hungry sailfish are small fish, such as sardines and anchovies, which swim in shoals and form tightly-packed "baitballs" if they feel threatened. Three or four sailfish may work together to herd the fish into a baitball, then dart through them to isolate small groups that the sailfish can attack more effectively. The sailfish slash their long bills from side to side, stunning or even crippling their prey to make the smaller fish easier to scoop up and swallow whole.

100 kg (220 lb) – the **weight** a big **sailfish** can reach.

A sailfish can **live** for up to **10 years**.

57

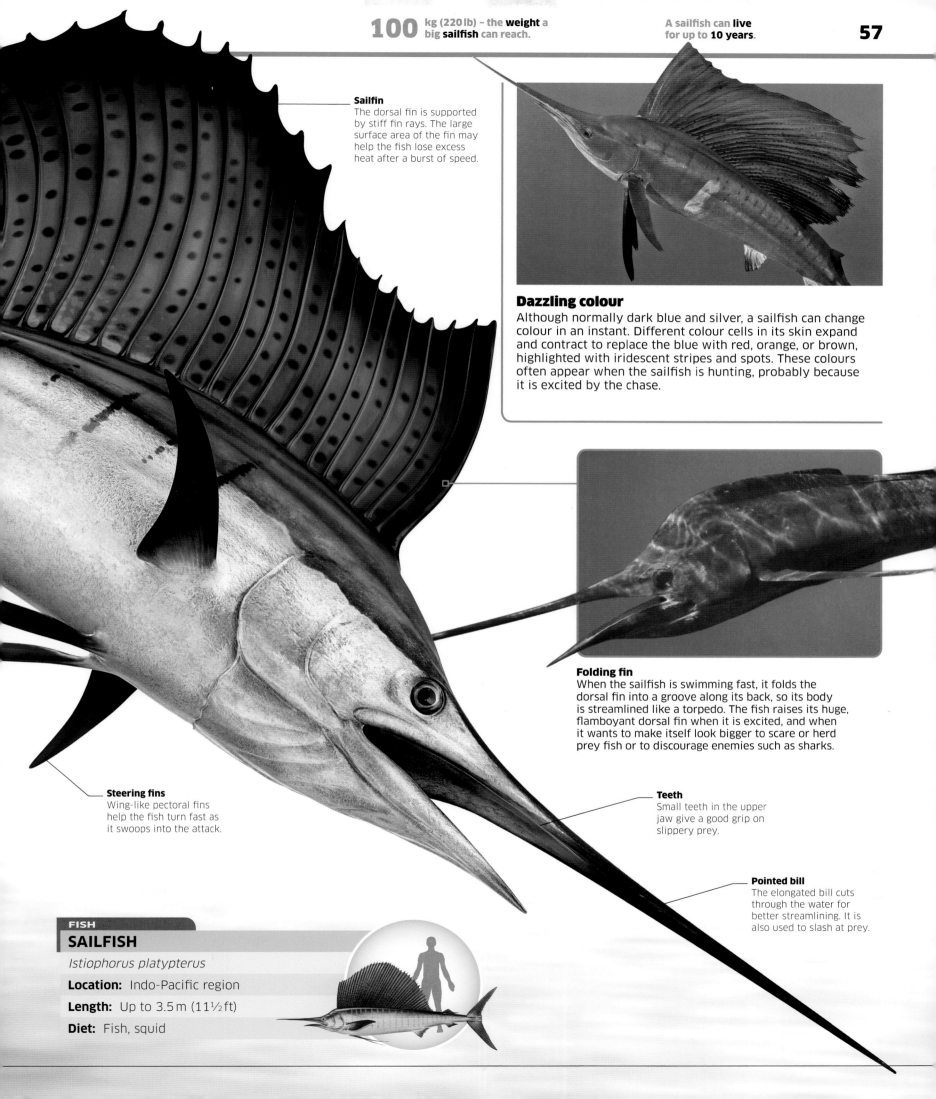

Sailfin
The dorsal fin is supported by stiff fin rays. The large surface area of the fin may help the fish lose excess heat after a burst of speed.

Dazzling colour
Although normally dark blue and silver, a sailfish can change colour in an instant. Different colour cells in its skin expand and contract to replace the blue with red, orange, or brown, highlighted with iridescent stripes and spots. These colours often appear when the sailfish is hunting, probably because it is excited by the chase.

Folding fin
When the sailfish is swimming fast, it folds the dorsal fin into a groove along its back, so its body is streamlined like a torpedo. The fish raises its huge, flamboyant dorsal fin when it is excited, and when it wants to make itself look bigger to scare or herd prey fish or to discourage enemies such as sharks.

Steering fins
Wing-like pectoral fins help the fish turn fast as it swoops into the attack.

Teeth
Small teeth in the upper jaw give a good grip on slippery prey.

Pointed bill
The elongated bill cuts through the water for better streamlining. It is also used to slash at prey.

FISH
SAILFISH
Istiophorus platypterus

Location: Indo-Pacific region

Length: Up to 3.5 m (11½ ft)

Diet: Fish, squid

Bony fish

The seas, lakes, and rivers of the world are home to a dazzling diversity of bony fish, adapted for a wide variety of aquatic habitats and lifestyles.

Most bony fish belong to the ray-finned group, with fins supported by slender bony struts and spines. But a few – the coelacanths and lungfish – have two pairs of fleshy lobed fins on the lower body containing strong bones. Similar lobe-finned fish were the ancestors of all four-legged vertebrate animals.

GREEN MORAY

Gymnothorax funebris

Location: Western Atlantic Ocean

Length: Up to 2.5 m (8¼ ft)

Morays are fiercely predatory eels that lurk in the crevices of rocky reefs. They detect prey mainly by scent, darting out to seize fish and other animals in their sharp, hooked teeth. The moray's vibrant colour comes from the thick protective layer of mucus that covers its skin.

Double jaw
Another set of teeth is hidden in the moray's throat. This "second jaw" snaps forward when the fish bites down, to help force struggling prey down the throat.

MEDITERRANEAN FLYINGFISH

Cheilopogon heterurus

Location: Northeastern Atlantic

Length: Up to 40 cm (15¾ in)

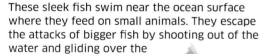

These sleek fish swim near the ocean surface where they feed on small animals. They escape the attacks of bigger fish by shooting out of the water and gliding over the waves on their long, wing-like pectoral fins.

STARRY FLOUNDER

Platichthys stellatus

Location: North Pacific Ocean

Length: Up to 91 cm (35¾ in)

Flatfish, such as the starry flounder, start life looking like normal juvenile fish. As the fish grows, one eye moves to other side of its head, so both eyes are on the same side. It spends the rest of its life lying flat on its other side on the sea bed.

SOCKEYE SALMON

Oncorhynchus nerka

Location: North Pacific Ocean

Length: Up to 84 cm (33 in)

Like other salmon, this species spends most of its adult life at sea, but swims up rivers to spawn in fresh water. Breeding males have a bright red body with a green head and tail.

8 mm (¼ in) – the size of *Paedocypris progenetica*, the **smallest** bony fish.

The **ocean sunfish** is the **biggest** of all bony fish, reaching a weight of **more than 2 tonnes**.

59

EUROPEAN ANCHOVY
Engraulis encrasicolus
Location: Eastern Atlantic Ocean
Length: Up to 20 cm (8 in)

Anchovies swim in huge schools, filtering water through their gills to trap tiny marine animals. Other schooling fish such as herring feed in the same way. The schools are preyed upon by oceanic hunters including tuna, sharks, seabirds, and even giant humpback whales.

EMPEROR ANGELFISH
Pomacanthus imperator
Location: Indo-Pacific region
Length: Up to 40 cm (15¾ in)

Tropical coral reefs glitter with colourful fish of many types, each with their own way of life. This angelfish lives in reef crevices, and the males defend patches of the reef as their own territories.

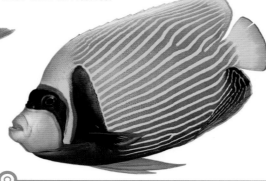

STURGEON
Acipenser sturio
Location: Eastern Atlantic
Length: Up to 6 m (19½ ft)

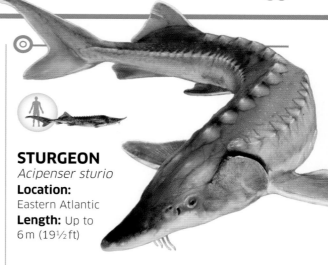

The sturgeons include some of the largest fish found in fresh water, and the longest-lived – this species may live for 100 years. It spends most of its life in coastal seas, where it feeds on molluscs, crabs, and similar animals on the sea bed, but swims upriver like a salmon to spawn.

COELACANTH
Latimeria chalumnae
Location: Indian Ocean
Length: Up to 2 m (6½ ft)

One of a group of lobe-finned fish once thought to have died out 65 million years ago, the coelacanth was discovered living in the Indian Ocean in 1938. It lives in deep tropical coastal waters, where it preys on fish and molluscs.

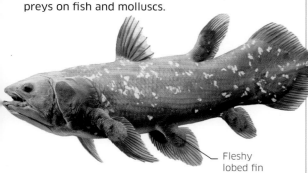

Fleshy lobed fin

SLOANE'S VIPERFISH
Chauliodus sloani
Location: All temperate oceans
Length: Up to 35 cm (13¾ in)

This viperfish is one of many fearsome predators that prowl the dark depths of the oceans. Its huge teeth ensure that its prey has little hope of escape.

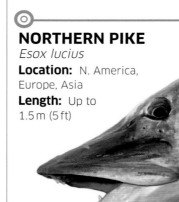

ATLANTIC COD
Gadus morhua
Location: N. Atlantic, Arctic
Length: Up to 2 m (6½ ft)

Familiar as a food fish, this big marine species is a predator that hunts near the sea bed for smaller fish and squid. It has been badly affected by overfishing, with some local populations declining by more than 95 per cent.

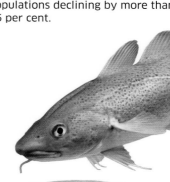

BLACK-BLOTCHED PORCUPINE FISH
Diodon liturosus
Location: Indo-Pacific, S. E. Atlantic
Length: Up to 65 cm (25½ in)

Closely related to the very poisonous pufferfish, this tropical reef fish defends itself from predators by gulping water to inflate itself into a spiny ball. This makes it almost impossible to swallow.

NORTHERN PIKE
Esox lucius
Location: N. America, Europe, Asia
Length: Up to 1.5 m (5 ft)

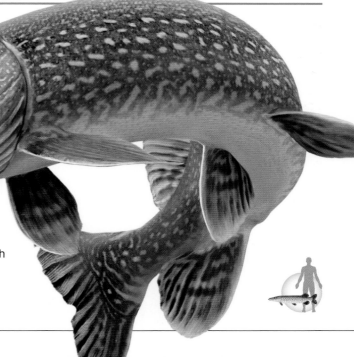

Well known for its ferocity, this freshwater fish is an ambush predator that lurks motionless among water weed and surges out at high speed to seize fish, frogs, and waterbirds. It will even eat smaller pike if prey is scarce.

AMPHIBIANS

Named for the way they live both in the water and on land, amphibians are the most mysterious of the vertebrates. Many are very secretive, emerging only at night and slipping into dark, damp places by day. They have extraordinary lifecycles, and they include some of the most poisonous animals on Earth.

WHAT IS AN AMPHIBIAN?

The first amphibians evolved from fish that were able to breathe air, and crept out of the water on four limb-like fins to find prey on land. But the fish had to lay their eggs in water, and their amphibian descendants still have to breed in pools or damp places. They also have thin skins that lose body moisture easily, so they must take care not to dry out.

TYPES OF AMPHIBIAN

The most familiar amphibians are the frogs and toads, with their big heads and tailless bodies. The long-tailed salamanders and newts lead similar lives, but the worm-like tropical caecilians are secretive burrowers.

Frogs and toads
This is the largest group, with 6,641 species. There is no scientific difference between frogs and toads. They have the same basic form, but typical frogs have smoother skins.

FIRE-BELLIED TOAD

Salamanders and newts
As with frogs and toads, these are basically different names for the same type of animal. There are 683 species; some are wholly aquatic while others spend most of their lives on land.

FIRE SALAMANDER

Caecilians
The 205 species of caecilians have no limbs, and are almost blind. They live underground, using their reinforced heads to burrow in search of worms and insects.

CONGO CAECILIAN

Inside an amphibian

This European common frog has the four-limbed body plan that has been inherited by all land vertebrates, although some amphibians – and reptiles – have lost their legs during the course of evolution.

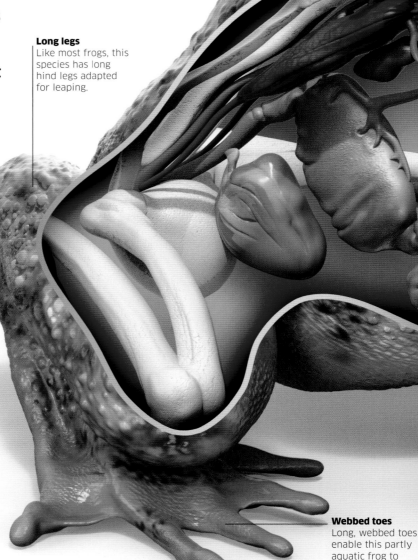

Lungs
A frog breathes by using its throat to pump air into its lungs.

Long legs
Like most frogs, this species has long hind legs adapted for leaping.

Webbed toes
Long, webbed toes enable this partly aquatic frog to swim well.

KEY FEATURES

There are only three types of amphibians, but they include animals with a remarkably wide variety of lifestyles and breeding systems. Despite this, most of them share certain key features. All amphibians are air-breathing, cold-blooded vertebrates, and they have thin skins that are not waterproof. Most lay eggs that must be kept moist, and many spend part of their lives in water.

Vertebrates
Like their bony fish ancestors, all amphibians have internal skeletons made of bone.

Cold-blooded
An amphibian's body temperature is the same as that of the air or water around it.

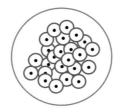

Most lay eggs
Caecilians bear live young, but most amphibians lay eggs with no hard shells.

Aquatic young
Typically the young hatch as aquatic tadpoles that eventually turn into adults.

Moist skin
An amphibian's thin, moist skin loses water easily, but can also absorb oxygen.

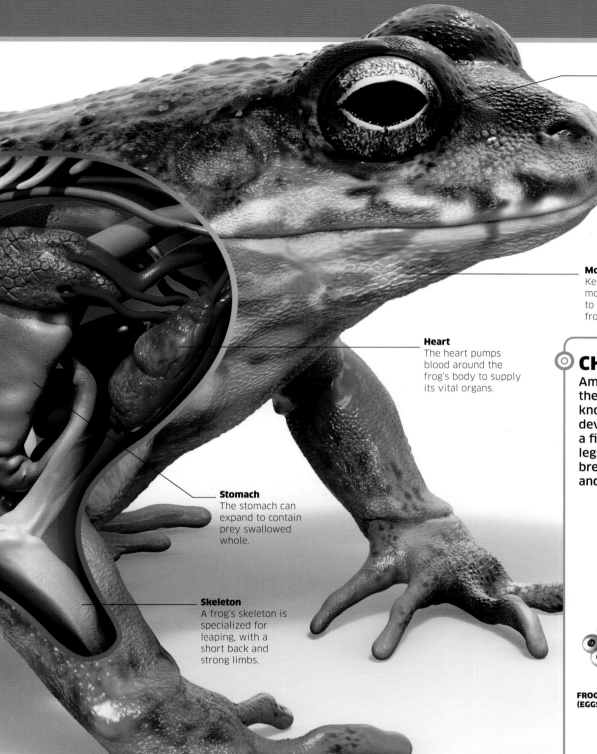

Big eyes
A frog has excellent vision for hunting small animals by sight.

Wide mouth
Frogs have very big mouths for gulping their prey down whole.

Moist skin
Keeping the skin moist allows the frog to absorb oxygen from the air.

Heart
The heart pumps blood around the frog's body to supply its vital organs.

Stomach
The stomach can expand to contain prey swallowed whole.

Skeleton
A frog's skeleton is specialized for leaping, with a short back and strong limbs.

CHANGING SHAPE

Amphibians are the only vertebrates that change their form as they turn to adults – a process known as metamorphosis. A typical frog egg develops into a long-tailed tadpole that lives like a fish for several weeks. Over time it develops legs, and eventually turns into a tiny air-breathing froglet. Finally, its tail shrinks away and it hops onto land to begin its adult life.

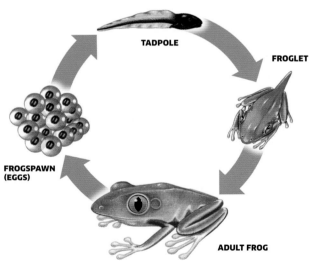

TADPOLE

FROGLET

FROGSPAWN
(EGGS)

ADULT FROG

BREATHING SKIN

Many amphibians start life as aquatic tadpoles, with gills that absorb vital oxygen from the water. When they become adults they develop lungs and can breathe air. But their thin skins can also absorb oxygen from water or air, provided they stay moist, and this allows one group, the lungless salamanders, to survive without either lungs or gills.

LETHAL DEFENCE

The dramatic pattern of this tiny tropical American tree frog warns birds and other enemies that it is extremely dangerous to eat. Its skin oozes poisons made from chemicals in its insect prey, and these are so powerful that these frogs' secretions have been used to make poisoned arrows. Many other amphibians have similar toxic defences.

Warning colours
The bright colours warn predators of the frog's toxicity.

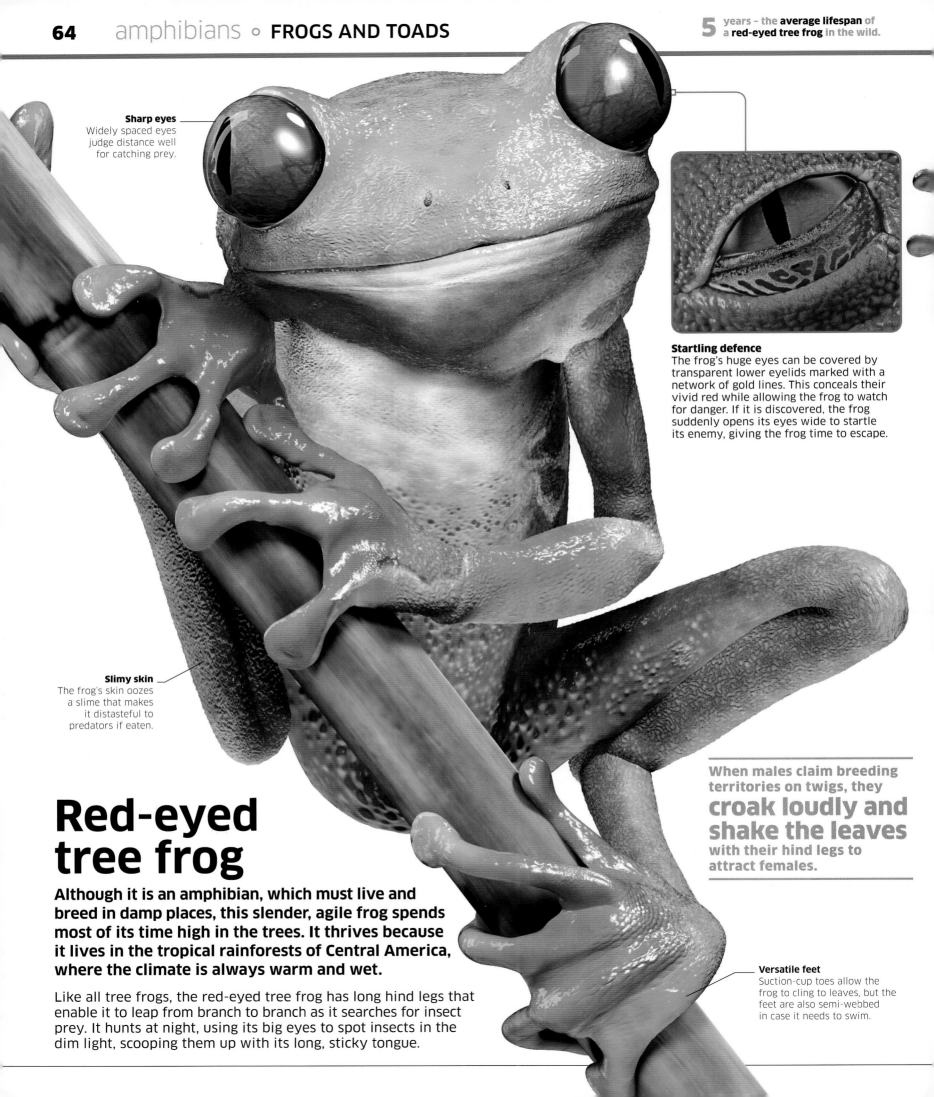

5 years – the **average lifespan** of a **red-eyed tree frog** in the wild.

Sharp eyes
Widely spaced eyes judge distance well for catching prey.

Startling defence
The frog's huge eyes can be covered by transparent lower eyelids marked with a network of gold lines. This conceals their vivid red while allowing the frog to watch for danger. If it is discovered, the frog suddenly opens its eyes wide to startle its enemy, giving the frog time to escape.

Slimy skin
The frog's skin oozes a slime that makes it distasteful to predators if eaten.

When males claim breeding territories on twigs, they **croak loudly and shake the leaves** with their hind legs to attract females.

Red-eyed tree frog

Although it is an amphibian, which must live and breed in damp places, this slender, agile frog spends most of its time high in the trees. It thrives because it lives in the tropical rainforests of Central America, where the climate is always warm and wet.

Like all tree frogs, the red-eyed tree frog has long hind legs that enable it to leap from branch to branch as it searches for insect prey. It hunts at night, using its big eyes to spot insects in the dim light, scooping them up with its long, sticky tongue.

Versatile feet
Suction-cup toes allow the frog to cling to leaves, but the feet are also semi-webbed in case it needs to swim.

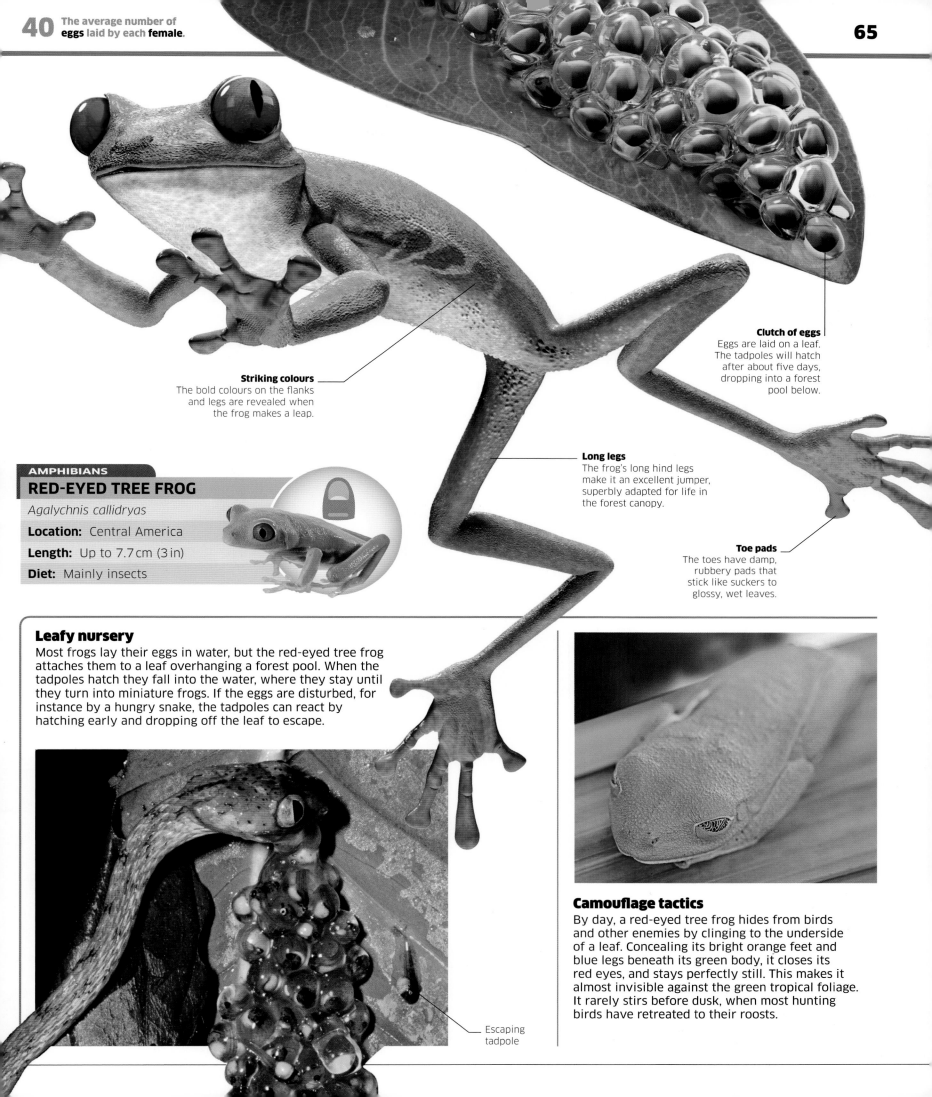

Striking colours
The bold colours on the flanks and legs are revealed when the frog makes a leap.

Clutch of eggs
Eggs are laid on a leaf. The tadpoles will hatch after about five days, dropping into a forest pool below.

Long legs
The frog's long hind legs make it an excellent jumper, superbly adapted for life in the forest canopy.

Toe pads
The toes have damp, rubbery pads that stick like suckers to glossy, wet leaves.

AMPHIBIANS

RED-EYED TREE FROG

Agalychnis callidryas

Location: Central America

Length: Up to 7.7 cm (3 in)

Diet: Mainly insects

Leafy nursery

Most frogs lay their eggs in water, but the red-eyed tree frog attaches them to a leaf overhanging a forest pool. When the tadpoles hatch they fall into the water, where they stay until they turn into miniature frogs. If the eggs are disturbed, for instance by a hungry snake, the tadpoles can react by hatching early and dropping off the leaf to escape.

Escaping tadpole

Camouflage tactics

By day, a red-eyed tree frog hides from birds and other enemies by clinging to the underside of a leaf. Concealing its bright orange feet and blue legs beneath its green body, it closes its red eyes, and stays perfectly still. This makes it almost invisible against the green tropical foliage. It rarely stirs before dusk, when most hunting birds have retreated to their roosts.

Frogs and toads

Instantly recognizable by their big heads and mouths, short tailless bodies, and long hind legs, frogs and toads are the most successful and diverse of the amphibians.

There is no scientific distinction between frogs and toads. The sleeker, more aquatic species are usually called frogs, while the less elegant, land-living types are known as toads. But some toads live in fresh water, and several frogs spend their lives in trees. Many have evolved unusual breeding adaptations.

AFRICAN BULLFROG
Pyxicephalus adspersus
Location: Africa
Length: Up to 24.5 cm (9½ in)

This massively built frog lives in dry places where it spends most of its life buried in the ground to keep moist. During wet seasons it emerges to prey on small mammals, birds, reptiles, other frogs, and indeed anything it can catch. Its huge mouth enables it to swallow its prey whole.

A notorious cannibal, the African bullfrog will even **sometimes eat its own young.**

Teeth
The lower jaw has three big toothlike structures that help the frog grip struggling prey.

Heavyweight
Males are much bigger than females, and may weigh up to 1.4 kg (3 lb).

Stout, blunt toes

RETICULATED GLASS FROG
Hyalinobatrachium valerioi
Location: Central and South America
Length: Up to 2.6 cm (1 in)

The red, beating heart of this small, tropical tree frog can be seen through the transparent skin on its underside. The male attracts several females to lay eggs beneath a leaf, which he then guards until they hatch.

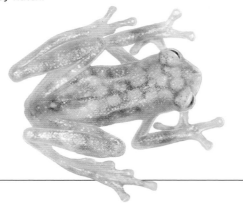

EUROPEAN COMMON FROG
Rana temporaria
Location: Europe, Asia
Length: Up to 9 cm (3½ in)

Like most amphibians, the common frog spends much of its life hunting insects, slugs, and other small animals on land, at night in damp places. It returns to ponds to breed, with the males arriving first and competing to attract females with croaking choruses.

WALLACE'S FLYING FROG
Rhacophorus nigropalmatus
Location: S. E. Asia
Length: Up to 10 cm (4 in)

The big, broad, webbed feet of this Malaysian tree frog act as parachutes when it leaps from tree to tree. They enable it to glide 15 m (50 ft) or more to land on another branch without coming down to ground level. Sticky pads on each toe help it cling to glossy leaves.

50–70 days – the length of time the **Darwin's frog** broods its young in its **vocal pouch**.

7.7 mm (¼ in) – the **length** of the **smallest adult frog** (*Paedophryne amauensis* from New Guinea).

67

ORIENTAL FIRE-BELLIED TOAD
Bombina orientalis
Location: East and S. E. Asia
Length: Up to 8 cm (3¼ in)

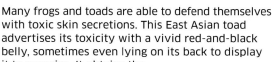

Many frogs and toads are able to defend themselves with toxic skin secretions. This East Asian toad advertises its toxicity with a vivid red-and-black belly, sometimes even lying on its back to display it to enemies. It obtains the red coloration from pigments in the prey it consumes.

LONG-NOSED HORNED FROG
Megophrys nasuta
Location: S. E. Asia
Length: Up to 12 cm (4¾ in)

This frog is spectacularly well camouflaged. Its spiky, angled shape and coloration mimic the litter of dead leaves so well that the frog is almost invisible on the tropical forest floor. It uses this camouflage to ambush small animal prey.

GREAT PLAINS TOAD
Anaxyrus cognatus
Location: North and Central America
Length: Up to 11 cm (4¼ in)

During the breeding season, rival males compete for females with loud calls. This North American toad inflates a big vocal sac to amplify a metallic trill that can last for several minutes.

DYEING POISON-DART FROG
Dendrobates tincturius
Location: South America
Length: Up to 4.5 cm (1¾ in)

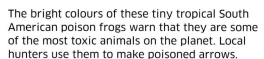

The bright colours of these tiny tropical South American poison frogs warn that they are some of the most toxic animals on the planet. Local hunters use them to make poisoned arrows.

DARWIN'S FROG
Rhinoderma darwinii
Location: South America
Length: Up to 3 cm (1¼ in)

Some frogs and toads have found novel ways of avoiding having to breed in water. The male Darwin's frog gathers up the hatching eggs in his mouth, and keeps the tadpoles in his vocal sac until they turn into tiny frogs.

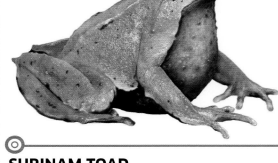

STRIPED BURROWING FROG
Cyclorana alboguttata
Location: Australia
Length: Up to 7 cm (2¾ in)

This Australian frog is one of many that cope with droughts by burrowing underground, storing water in its body and sealing itself inside a cocoon of waterproof mucus. It may stay buried for years before rain enables it to emerge.

TOMATO FROG
Dyscophus antongilii
Location: Madagascar
Length: Up to 10.5 cm (4¼ in)

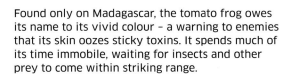

Found only on Madagascar, the tomato frog owes its name to its vivid colour – a warning to enemies that its skin oozes sticky toxins. It spends much of its time immobile, waiting for insects and other prey to come within striking range.

SURINAM TOAD
Pipa pipa
Location: South America
Length: Up to 18 cm (7 in)

Low profile
The toad's body is almost flat, like a leaf.

Precious cargo
Eggs sink into the soft skin of the female's back.

The female Surinam toad has a unique way of rearing her young. The fertilized eggs become embedded in pockets in the skin of her back, and the young develop there. Once the tadpoles turn into tiny toadlets, they emerge to start their independent lives.

AMPHIBIANS
GREAT CRESTED NEWT
Triturus cristatus

Location: Northern Europe

Size: Up to 16 cm (6¼ in)

Diet: Small animals

Jagged crest
In the breeding season the crest on the male's back grows tall.

Elegant tail
The male's tail has a silver streak, and both an upper and lower crest.

Great crested newt

At night in spring the male great crested newt performs an elaborate courtship before a female. He dances in the water, using his tail to fan enticing scents towards her.

Like most amphibians, great crested newts spend much of their lives hunting small animals on land. But in spring they return to ponds to breed, and each night the flamboyantly crested males perform their displays. They prefer large ponds with plenty of water weed where they can hide and where the females can lay their eggs.

Blotchy belly
Both sexes have yellow or orange bellies with black blotches.

Long toes
The five long toes of each hind foot are not webbed like those of a frog.

Precious package
During mating, the female picks up a packet of sperm that the male has placed on the bed of the pond. This fertilizes her eggs, which she can then start laying. She carefully places one egg, or a chain of two or three, on a leaf, and uses her hind feet to wrap the leaf around it. A sticky substance covering the egg holds the folded leaf together.

Aquatic young
Tadpole-like larvae hatch from the eggs after about a month. They have yellow skin and feathery gills that gather oxygen from the water. The front legs grow first, then the back legs. Eventually their skin darkens, their gills disappear, and they climb out of the pond as air-breathing "efts".

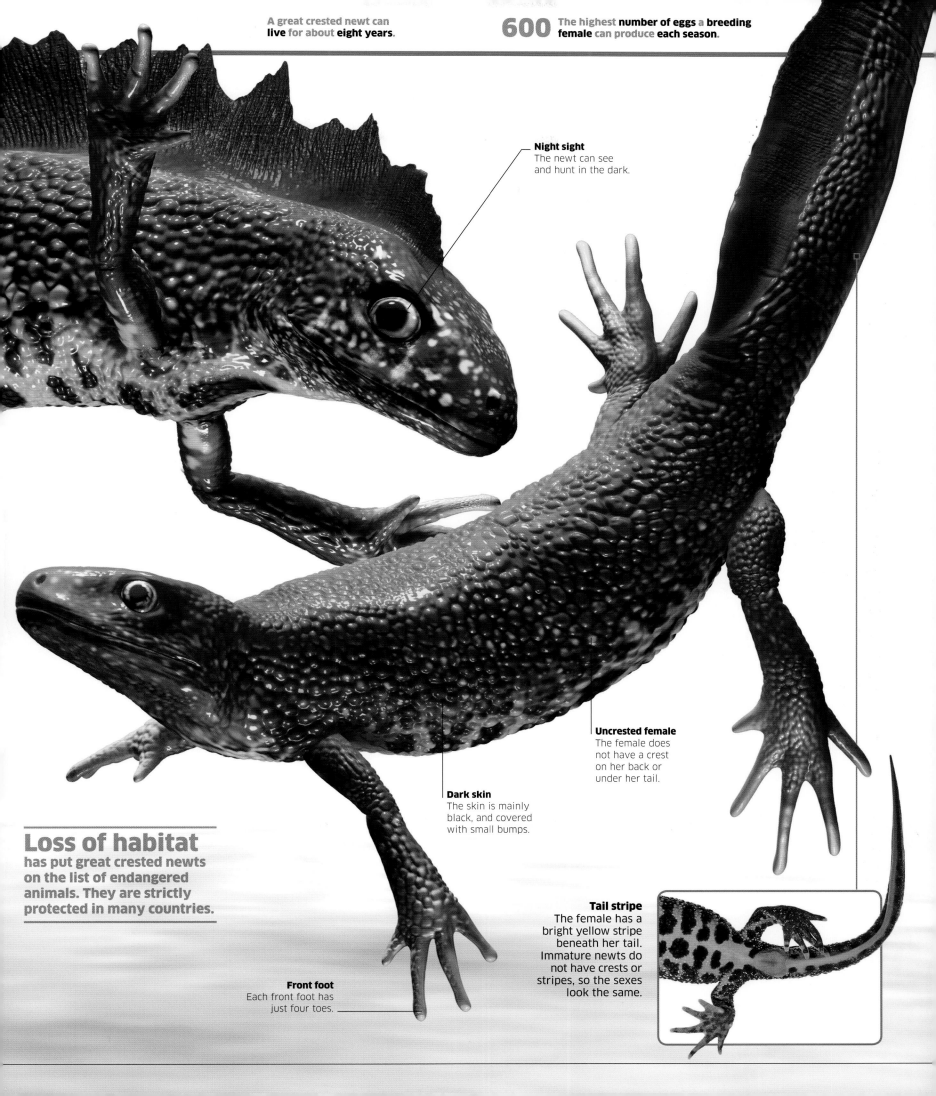

A great crested newt can **live** for about **eight years**.

600 The highest **number of eggs** a breeding **female** can produce **each season**.

Night sight
The newt can see and hunt in the dark.

Uncrested female
The female does not have a crest on her back or under her tail.

Dark skin
The skin is mainly black, and covered with small bumps.

Loss of habitat
has put great crested newts on the list of endangered animals. They are strictly protected in many countries.

Tail stripe
The female has a bright yellow stripe beneath her tail. Immature newts do not have crests or stripes, so the sexes look the same.

Front foot
Each front foot has just four toes.

JAPANESE GIANT SALAMANDER
Andrias japonicus
Location: Japan
Length: Up to 1.4 m (4½ ft)

This super-sized salamander lives in cool mountain streams and never emerges onto land. Like most salamanders, it absorbs vital oxygen from the water through its thin, wrinkled, grey skin.

Tail power
The salamander uses its flattened tail to drive itself through the water.

Poor vision
Tiny eyes cannot see in detail.

Salamanders and newts

Although they look like lizards, with their long tails and short legs, these animals are amphibians related to frogs and toads. They lose body moisture easily, so they cannot survive in dry places. Despite this, many spend their entire lives on land.

Newts are part of the same group of amphibians as salamanders, but tend to be more aquatic, returning to ponds each spring to breed. Most true salamanders lay their eggs in damp places on land. But some salamanders are even more aquatic than newts, and never leave the water.

SIBERIAN NEWT
Salamandrella keyserlingii
Location: Northeast Asia
Length: Up to 15 cm (6 in)

Astonishingly this cold-blooded animal can live in regions where the temperature drops as low as −35°C (−31°F). It can survive being frozen solid for years, returning to its normal lifestyle when it thaws out.

GREATER SIREN
Siren lacertina
Location: Southeastern USA
Length: Up to 90 cm (35½ in)

Many salamanders have very short legs, but the sirens are a group that have lost their hind legs altogether. The greater siren is the biggest of these, and like the others it is aquatic, with feathery gills on each side of its neck for breathing underwater. It hunts at night for insects and other small animals.

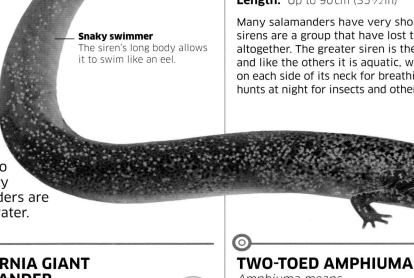

Snaky swimmer
The siren's long body allows it to swim like an eel.

FIRE SALAMANDER
Salamandra salamandra
Location: Central and southern Europe
Length: Up to 28 cm (11 in)

The vivid colour scheme of the fire salamander warns predators that its skin glands ooze dangerous poisons. The salamander can squirt this milky fluid from these openings on its back.

CALIFORNIA GIANT SALAMANDER
Dicamptodon ensatus
Location: Western North America
Length: Up to 30 cm (11¾ in)

Although not nearly as big as the Japanese giant salamander, this is a lot larger than most species. It spends its early life in the water, breathing through feathery gills, and typically lives on land as an adult. But some individuals remain aquatic and keep their gills as adults.

TWO-TOED AMPHIUMA
Amphiuma means
Location: Southeastern USA
Length: Up to 1.1 m (3½ ft)

This is the biggest of three species of amphiumas, a group of aquatic salamanders. It favours the still waters of swamps and ditches. Like many salamanders, its four legs are only vestigial, no longer having any function.

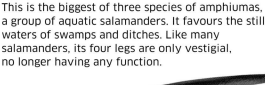

Vestigial limbs

585 The **approximate number of species** of salamanders and newts. **More than half** of these are **lungless salamanders**.

1.7 cm (¾ in) – the length of *Thorius arboreus*, the **smallest salamander**.

71

OLM
Proteus anguinus
Location: Southern Europe
Length: Up to 30 cm (11¾ in)

The strictly aquatic olm is a type of salamander that spends its entire life in the dark, in the waters that flow through limestone caves. It cannot see, hunting by scent, touch, and sound, and its body has lost all colour apart from the red blood that flows visibly through its feathery gills.

Blood-red gills
Thin-walled gills absorb oxygen from the water.

ANDERSON'S NEWT
Echinotriton andersoni
Location: Japan
Length: Up to 16 cm (6¼ in)

Elusive, endangered, and restricted to just a few Japanese islands, this newt has a unique way of defending itself. If it is seized by a predator, its sharp-tipped ribs protrude through wart-like poison glands in its skin, stabbing its enemy in the mouth and causing enough pain to make it release its grip.

Bare bones
Thorn-like rib tips are laced with painful toxins.

MEXICAN AXOLOTL
Ambystoma mexicanum
Location: Mexico
Length: Up to 30 cm (11¾ in)

Juvenile body
Adult axolotls retain tadpole-like gills and tail.

Most amphibians start life in water and breathe through external gills, which are lost as they mature. But the axolotl breeds while in its larval form and normally keeps its gills as an adult. It is now rare, as its habitats have been destroyed.

SALVIN'S MUSHROOMTONGUE
Bolitoglossa salvinii
Location: Central America
Length: Up to 12.5 cm (5 in)

Typical salamanders live on the ground or underwater. But this tropical forest species is adapted for climbing, with a prehensile tail it uses to cling to branches. It has a very long tongue with a sticky tip that it shoots out to catch insects.

SOUTHERN TORRENT SALAMANDER
Rhyacotriton variegatus
Location: Western USA
Length: Up to 11.5 cm (4½ in)

This is one of four species of torrent salamanders that live near rocky, fast-flowing streams in coastal conifer forests. It dries out easily, so although it hunts insects on the forest floor during heavy rain, it retreats to a stream as soon as the rain stops.

RED SALAMANDER
Pseudotriton ruber
Location: Eastern USA
Length: Up to 18 cm (7 in)

All amphibians can absorb oxygen through their thin, moist skin, but most have gills or lungs as well, except for lungless salamanders. This lungless salamander lives on land in summer, but is aquatic in winter.

Breathable skin
The moist skin surface assists in respiration.

REPTILES

Scaly, cold-blooded, and even venomous, reptiles probably inspire more fear than admiration. But they are fascinating creatures, with many special adaptations that enable them to survive. From lumbering tortoises to unusual flying snakes, they include some of the world's most extraordinary animals.

WHAT IS A REPTILE?

Reptiles were the first vertebrates able to live entirely on land. They evolved scaly, waterproof skins that prevent them losing vital body moisture in hot, dry climates. Most reptiles lay eggs that have a tough outer covering for the same reason. As a result, reptiles flourish in all land habitats apart from the very coldest parts of the world.

Protective shell
A tortoise's body is protected by its very strong shell.

Digestion
A big digestive system processes the tortoise's leafy diet.

TYPES OF REPTILE

There are four main orders of reptiles, but one of these contains just one surviving species – the tuatara. The others are the aquatic turtles and land-living tortoises, the crocodiles and alligators, and a single order that consists of the lizards, snakes, and the burrowing, worm-like amphisbaenians.

Turtles and tortoises
These are the most recognizable reptiles, with their domed shells that are fused to the spine and ribs. Tortoises live on land, while turtles live in oceans and fresh waters. There are 340 species.

DIAMONDBACK TERRAPIN

Tuatara
The tuatara is the sole survivor of a group of reptiles that flourished during the age of giant dinosaurs, but mostly died out 100 million years ago. It lives in New Zealand.

TUATARA

Lizards and snakes
Snakes and lizards belong to the largest reptile order, with 9,905 species. The burrowing, limbless amphisbaenians, or worm-lizards, also belong to this group, although there are only a few species.

CORAL SNAKE

Crocodilians
Crocodiles, alligators, and their relatives number only 25 species, but they include the biggest and most formidable of the reptiles. All crocodilians are primarily aquatic, although a few may sometimes hunt on land.

NILE CROCODILE

KEY FEATURES

Reptiles include an amazing diversity of animals adapted for a wide variety of habitats, ranging from oceans to deserts, but they share a number of key features. All living reptiles are cold-blooded vertebrates with tough, waterproof skins that allow them to survive in some of the driest places on Earth. Most reptiles lay eggs with leathery, waterproof shells, but a few give birth to live young.

Vertebrate
A reptile's body is supported by a bony skeleton.

Cold-blooded
Body temperature depends on the environment.

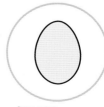

Lay eggs
Reptile eggs are enclosed by waterproof shells.

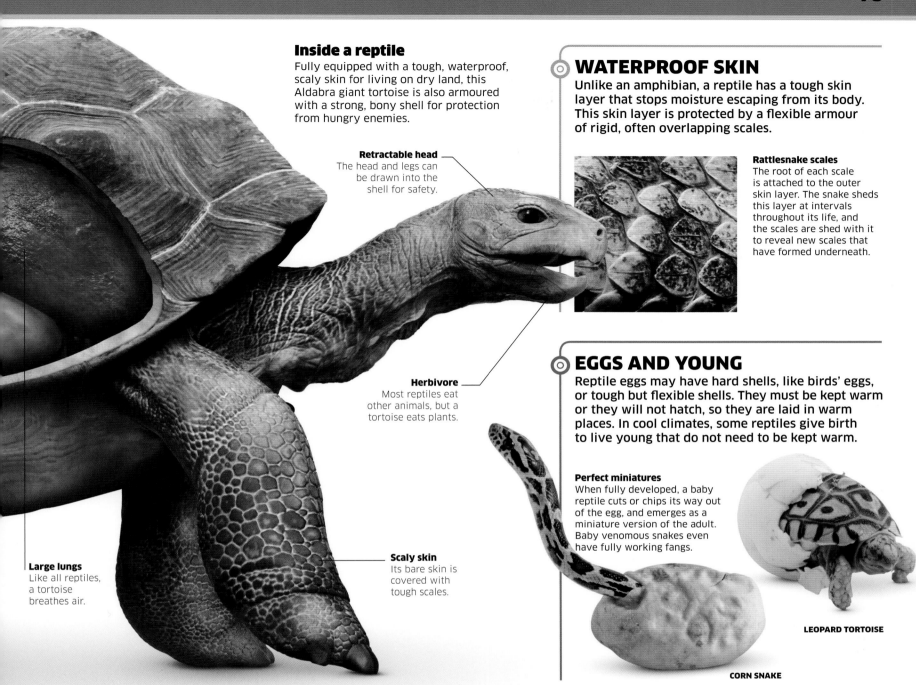

Inside a reptile

Fully equipped with a tough, waterproof, scaly skin for living on dry land, this Aldabra giant tortoise is also armoured with a strong, bony shell for protection from hungry enemies.

Retractable head
The head and legs can be drawn into the shell for safety.

Herbivore
Most reptiles eat other animals, but a tortoise eats plants.

Large lungs
Like all reptiles, a tortoise breathes air.

Scaly skin
Its bare skin is covered with tough scales.

WATERPROOF SKIN

Unlike an amphibian, a reptile has a tough skin layer that stops moisture escaping from its body. This skin layer is protected by a flexible armour of rigid, often overlapping scales.

Rattlesnake scales
The root of each scale is attached to the outer skin layer. The snake sheds this layer at intervals throughout its life, and the scales are shed with it to reveal new scales that have formed underneath.

EGGS AND YOUNG

Reptile eggs may have hard shells, like birds' eggs, or tough but flexible shells. They must be kept warm or they will not hatch, so they are laid in warm places. In cool climates, some reptiles give birth to live young that do not need to be kept warm.

Perfect miniatures
When fully developed, a baby reptile cuts or chips its way out of the egg, and emerges as a miniature version of the adult. Baby venomous snakes even have fully working fangs.

LEOPARD TORTOISE

CORN SNAKE

IN THE DISTANT PAST, THE REPTILES **ALSO INCLUDED THE GIANT DINOSAURS –** THE BIGGEST LAND ANIMALS THAT **HAVE EVER LIVED.**

Scaly skins
The scales protect the skin and resist water loss.

Live young
Some snakes and lizards bear fully formed young.

ENERGY SAVERS

Although reptiles are described as cold-blooded, their bodies need to be warm to function properly. They rely on their environment to provide this warmth, so few reptiles live in regions with cold winters, and those that do are active only in summer. In tropical regions this is not a problem, and a reptile saves so much energy by not generating its own body heat that it can survive on far less food than a warm-blooded animal of similar size.

Basking
This lizard has to bask in the sun before it can become active.

GREEN IGUANA

Temperature control
A reptile such as this green iguana controls its body temperature by its behaviour. When it needs to warm up it basks in the warm sunshine, and if it gets too hot and needs to cool off it slips into the shade.

76 reptiles ○ **TURTLES AND TORTOISES**

150 cm (59 in) – the **length** that the **shell** of a **Galápagos tortoise** can reach.

Galápagos tortoise

Galápagos tortoises are the largest tortoises on Earth, capable of growing to a colossal size and an immense age. They once lived in their thousands on at least seven of the volcanic Galápagos islands off Ecuador, and owed their success to the remoteness of their island homes, where they had no predators or competitors for food.

Isolation of different tortoise populations on the islands led to the evolution of 15 local subspecies, each with its own distinctive features. Today, the Galápagos tortoise is at risk from various introduced species, including rats that prey on young tortoises and goats that compete for food. The number of subspecies has dwindled to 10, with several classified as endangered.

One Galápagos tortoise in captivity is thought to have lived to the **amazing age of 170.**

Growth rings
When a baby Galápagos tortoise hatches from its egg it is no bigger than a mouse, but its shell already has the pattern of scutes (tough scales) that it will keep for life. As the tortoise grows, each scute grows too, adding a ring each year. But the oldest parts wear away over time, so counting the rings does not reveal the tortoise's true age.

Scaly legs
The skin of each leg is covered with strong, protective scales.

400 kg (882 lbs) – the **weight** of the **biggest** Galápagos tortoises on record.

Female Galápagos tortoises **lay 2 to 16 eggs.** The **hatchlings** emerge **4.5 months later.**

77

Defence tactic
The tortoise can pull its legs and head into its shell for protection.

Sensitive nostrils

Horny beak
The tortoise has no teeth. Instead, it gathers food with a sharp-edged horny beak. It eats a variety of plant food in the grassland and forest where it lives, including grass and the succulent stems of the prickly pear cactus. Some of the subspecies have specially shaped shells that allow them to reach high into bushes to gather leaves. The shell above the neck is raised in an arch to allow them to stretch up higher.

Bony carapace
Like all tortoises and turtles, the Galápagos tortoise has a domed, bony upper shell or carapace that is fused to its ribs, and a similar bony plastron (flat shell) beneath its body. The bone is covered with tough scutes (scales) made of horny keratin – the material that our hair and fingernails are made of.

Bony carapace

Shell scutes

Ribs

Skull

Plastron

Armour plate
The underside is protected by a lower shell, or plastron.

Rival males
When mature males come face to face in the mating season, they compete with each other in a ritual dominance display. Standing as tall as they can, they stretch their necks up and open their mouths wide. They may fight, but the shorter-necked tortoise usually backs off first.

GALÁPAGOS TORTOISE

Chelonoidis nigra

Location: Galápagos Islands

Length: Up to 1.2 m (4 ft)

Diet: Leaves, cacti, berries, and lichens

Stout claws
Each front foot has five broad claws. The hind feet have just four.

78 reptiles ∘ **TURTLES AND TORTOISES**

188 The number of **years** one **radiated tortoise** is thought to have **lived** for – longer than any other land animal.

ALLIGATOR SNAPPING TURTLE
Macrochelys temminckii

Location: North America
Length: Up to 80 cm (2½ ft)

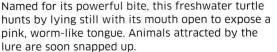

Named for its powerful bite, this freshwater turtle hunts by lying still with its mouth open to expose a pink, worm-like tongue. Animals attracted by the lure are soon snapped up.

PIG-NOSED TURTLE
Carettochelys insculpta

Location: New Guinea, Australia
Length: Up to 75 cm (29½ in)

Unlike other freshwater turtles, the pig-nosed turtle has flippers like those of a sea turtle instead of clawed feet. It owes its name to its fleshy snout, which has pig-like, forward-facing nostrils.

ASIAN NARROW-HEADED SOFTSHELL TURTLE
Chitra chitra

Location: South Asia, Indonesia
Length: Up to 1.6 m (5¼ ft)

Softshell turtles have hard shells or carapaces like other turtles, but with a covering of leathery skin instead of tough scutes. This species is one of the biggest, with males having longer, thicker tails than females.

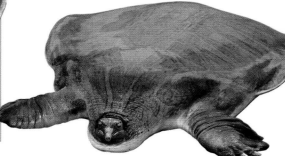

Tempting bait
Few fish can resist the temptation of the turtle's wriggling, worm-like tongue.

Turtles and tortoises

Instantly recognizable by their domed shells, turtles and tortoises come in many shapes and sizes and occupy a variety of habitats. Most of the 341 species are aquatic turtles. The land-dwelling tortoises number only 58 species and all belong to a single family.

These reptiles have a long history, dating back more than 220 million years to a time when the first dinosaurs were evolving. Their bony armour has served them well ever since, especially in the water where its weight is no problem. On land, it is one reason why tortoises are so famously slow.

Carapace
Streamlined, leathery carapace has seven ridges.

Horny beak
The sharp-edged beak is ideal for cropping seagrasses.

GREEN SEA TURTLE
Chelonia mydas

Location: Worldwide
Length: Up to 1.5 m (5 ft)

An elegant, graceful swimmer, the green sea turtle is found in tropical oceans all over the world. Like other sea turtles it makes long migrations to favoured breeding beaches to lay its eggs, often returning to the same beach year after year. Most turtles are carnivorous but this one is a herbivore, feeding mainly on seagrasses and marine algae.

LEATHERBACK SEA TURTLE
Dermochelys coriacea

Location: Worldwide
Length: Up to 2.7 m (8¾ ft)

The biggest turtle by far, this oceanic giant has a carapace covered with leathery, oily skin. It eats jellyfish and other drifting, soft-bodied creatures.

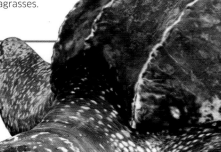

Jellyfish prey

2,600 km (1,615 miles) – the estimated **distance green sea turtles may swim** to reach their **nesting grounds**.

650 kg (1,433 lb) – the **largest** recorded **weight** of a **leatherback sea turtle**.

79

DIAMONDBACK TERRAPIN
Malaclemys terrapin
Location: North America
Length: Up to 23 cm (9 in)

Widespread along the Atlantic coast of North America, this small turtle is adapted for life in tidal saltmarshes and mangrove swamps. It preys mainly on snails, clams, and other molluscs.

Patterned scutes

Shell crushers
Strong jaws are adapted for crushing shells.

Scaly tail
The very long tail is covered with large scales.

STINKPOT TURTLE
Sternotherus odoratus
Location: North America
Length: Up to 14 cm (5½ in)

When alarmed, this small, long-necked turtle releases a foul-smelling liquid from glands beneath its carapace. It eats a wide variety of foods, finding them by walking on the stream bed instead of swimming.

BIG-HEADED TURTLE
Platysternon megacephalum
Location: East Asia
Length: Up to 40 cm (15¾ in)

This freshwater turtle's head is so big that it cannot be pulled back into the animal's shell. The head has its own bony protective shield instead, and the turtle also has a powerful bite.

RADIATED TORTOISE
Astrochelys radiata
Location: Southern Madagascar
Length: Up to 40 cm (15¾ in)

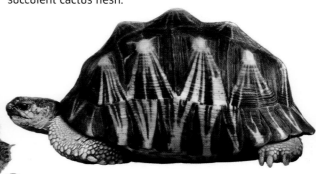

Tortoises are essentially turtles adapted for life on land. This Madagascan species has an unusually ornate carapace. It resides in dry woodland and mainly eats grass, but will also eat fruit and succulent cactus flesh.

PANCAKE TORTOISE
Malacochersus tornieri
Location: East Africa
Length: Up to 20 cm (8 in)

Inhabiting rocky hills, the well-named pancake tortoise has a very flat, flexible shell that enables it to slip into narrow crevices. For a tortoise, it can move very fast, diving into the nearest refuge whenever it senses danger.

COMMON SNAKE-NECKED TURTLE
Chelodina longicollis
Location: Australia
Length: Up to 28 cm (11 in)

Unlike typical turtles, snake-necked turtles hide their heads in their shells by bending their long necks sideways. This species preys on small aquatic animals.

MATAMATA
Chelus fimbriatus
Habitat: South America
Length: Up to 70 cm (27½ in)

Relying on its superb camouflage to conceal it, the matamata lurks in ambush on the bottom of shallow streams and pools. When prey comes within range, the turtle suddenly gapes its mouth wide open so the water rushes in, sucking its victim in with it.

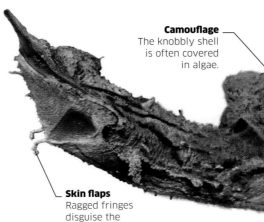

Camouflage
The knobbly shell is often covered in algae.

Skin flaps
Ragged fringes disguise the turtle's outline.

80 reptiles ○ **LIZARDS**

200 The minimum number of **known species of chameleon.** There are probably **many more** that have **not yet been discovered.**

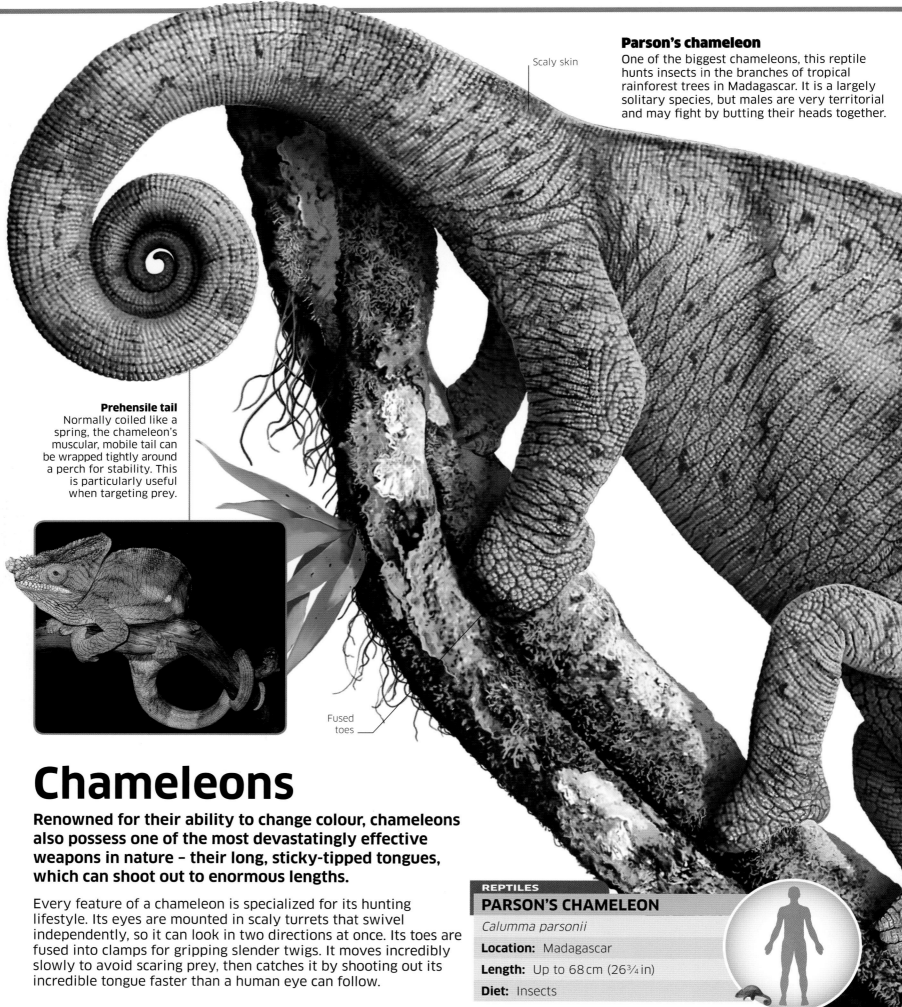

Scaly skin

Parson's chameleon
One of the biggest chameleons, this reptile hunts insects in the branches of tropical rainforest trees in Madagascar. It is a largely solitary species, but males are very territorial and may fight by butting their heads together.

Prehensile tail
Normally coiled like a spring, the chameleon's muscular, mobile tail can be wrapped tightly around a perch for stability. This is particularly useful when targeting prey.

Fused toes

Chameleons

Renowned for their ability to change colour, chameleons also possess one of the most devastatingly effective weapons in nature – their long, sticky-tipped tongues, which can shoot out to enormous lengths.

Every feature of a chameleon is specialized for its hunting lifestyle. Its eyes are mounted in scaly turrets that swivel independently, so it can look in two directions at once. Its toes are fused into clamps for gripping slender twigs. It moves incredibly slowly to avoid scaring prey, then catches it by shooting out its incredible tongue faster than a human eye can follow.

REPTILES
PARSON'S CHAMELEON
Calumma parsonii
Location: Madagascar
Length: Up to 68 cm (26¾ in)
Diet: Insects

A chameleon's **tongue** strikes prey within **one tenth of a second.**

The **tongues** of some chameleons can be **extended to twice their body length** to seize prey.

81

MADAGASCAN DWARF CHAMELEON

Brookesia micra

Location: Madagascar
Length: Up to 2.8 cm (1¼ in)

Discovered in 2012, this is the smallest chameleon and one of the smallest of all vertebrate animals. It sleeps in trees at night but hunts insects by day, foraging on the ground. Unlike most chameleons it is not able to change its colour, and is always brown.

Changing colour
As with many chameleons, this species can undergo dramatic colour changes. Its pattern usually depends on its mood, but may provide camouflage. This one is displaying to a rival.

Neck frill

Warty nose horn

NAMAQUA CHAMELEON

Chamaeleo namaquensis

Location: Southwest Africa
Length: Up to 25 cm (10 in)

Unlike most chameleons this desert species lives on the ground. It often turns black on cool mornings to absorb heat efficiently.

FISCHER'S CHAMELEON

Kinyongia fischeri

Location: East Africa
Length: Up to 30 cm (11¾ in)

Many chameleons live in remote regions, where they forage up in the trees. This species lives only in the forests of Tanzania, where it is rarely seen by humans, and little is known about its behaviour.

MEDITERRANEAN CHAMELEON

Chamaeleo chamaeleon

Location: S. Spain, N. Africa, Middle East, Mediterranean islands
Length: Up to 40 cm (15¾ in)

This chameleon is regularly seen on the Mediterranean islands of Crete and Cyprus. It is a solitary, stealthy hunter that creeps up on insects and captures them with a rapid flick of its telescopic tongue.

PANTHER CHAMELEON

Furcifer pardalis

Location: Madagascar
Length: Up to 50 cm (19¾ in)

Similar to Parson's chameleon, this species lives in dry forests where the males compete vigorously over territory. Rivals glow with vivid colour when they meet, but the loser rapidly fades to drab brown.

JACKSON'S CHAMELEON

Trioceros jacksonii

Location: East Africa
Length: Up to 38 cm (15 in)

As with many chameleons, the male of this species is more ornamented than the female, with three long horns on his snout, which are displayed in clashes over territory.

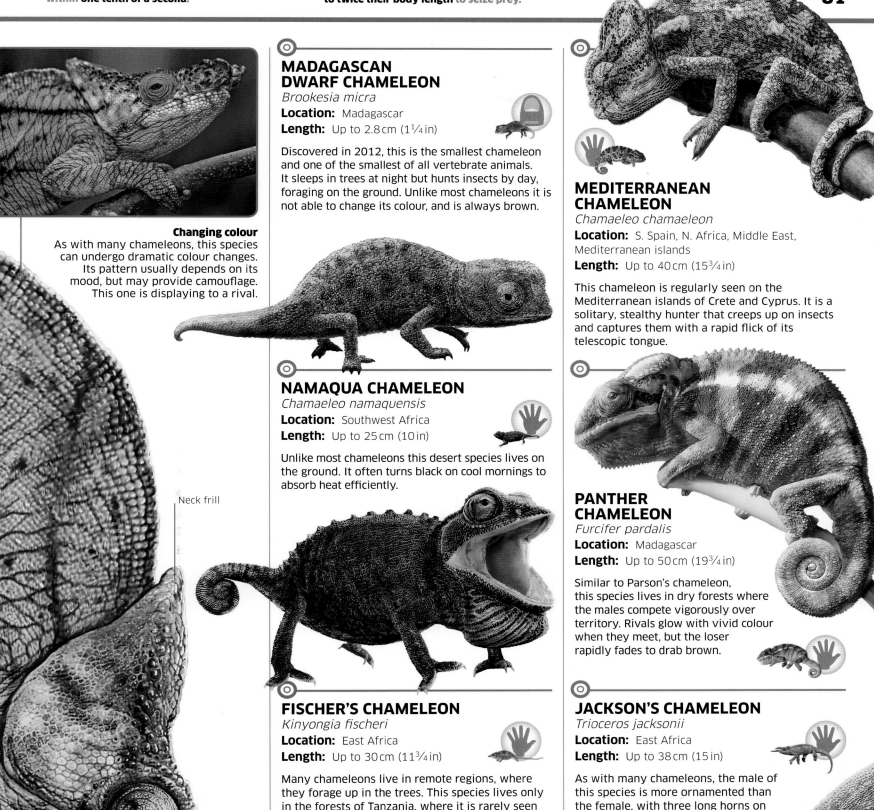

82 reptiles ○ **LIZARDS**

A Komodo dragon can **detect the smell of a dead animal** from 10 km (6 miles) away.

30 The approximate **number of years** a Komodo dragon **can live**.

Komodo dragon

The biggest of the lizards, the mighty Komodo dragon is a fearsome predator, powerful enough to ambush, kill, and devour a fully-grown water buffalo. It will even kill and eat its own kind.

The Komodo dragon lives on the island of Komodo and nearby islands and coasts near Java in southern Indonesia, where it preys on any animals it can catch. An adult Komodo dragon can knock a deer down with one blow of its tail, then hold its victim with its long claws while using its saw-edged teeth to kill the deer and then tear it apart. Rival males also use their strength to fight each other when competing for females or territory, rearing up on their hind legs to wrestle until one manages to force the other to the ground.

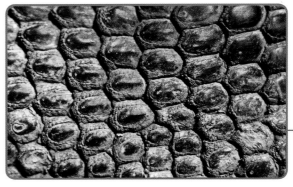

Armoured skin
The skin of a Komodo dragon is covered with scales that contain tiny bones called osteoderms. These form a tough but flexible armour, like the chain mail of linked steel rings worn by medieval soldiers. Similar armour defends other lizards against bigger predators, but in the case of Komodo dragons it protects them from each other.

Safe refuge

The only animals a Komodo dragon has to fear are bigger Komodo dragons, which are likely to kill and eat it if they get the chance. Young dragons take to the trees directly after hatching and do not begin to live on the ground until they have grown to around 1.2 m (4 ft) long. Even then, a smaller dragon has to give way to bigger dragons when feeding. It may even make itself smell disgusting by rolling in the gut contents of its prey, to put off any hungry cannibals.

Big body
The bulky body can hold enough food to last the dragon for a month.

An adult Komodo dragon may eat up to **80 per cent** of its own body weight in a single meal.

Muscular tail
The long, heavy tail acts as a prop when a male rears up to grapple with a rival.

Scaly legs
Strong legs project sideways from the body, giving the dragon the sprawling gait typical of a lizard.

Forked tongue
The long tongue is forked like a snake's, and is flicked out to detect the scent of carcasses and follow scent trails.

Vision
The dragon can see in colour, but has poor night sight and relies on its sense of smell.

Slicing teeth
Up to 60 curved teeth, serrated like steak knives, allow the dragon to slice through the tough hide and flesh of prey.

Venomous bite
The drooling saliva of a Komodo dragon is laced with venom produced by glands in the lower jaw. The venom mixes with the lizard's saliva so it flows into the wounds inflicted by the blade-like teeth. It stops the victim's blood from clotting, and may also trigger internal bleeding. So even if an animal manages to escape the initial attack, it soon collapses from blood loss and shock, making easy prey for the dragon following its trail.

REPTILES

KOMODO DRAGON

Varanus komodoensis

Location: Indonesia

Length: Up to 3.1 m (10¼ ft)

Diet: Carrion and live animals

Long claws
Each foot has five massively powerful claws for seizing prey. Young dragons also use them for climbing.

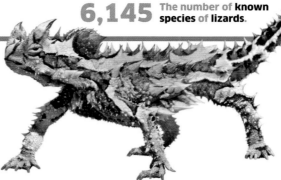

COMMON GREEN IGUANA
Iguana iguana
Location: Central and South America
Length: Up to 1.5 m (5 ft)

Unusually for a lizard, this large tropical species is a herbivore, which climbs trees and uses its sharp, blade-like teeth to feed on leaves and fruit. Its spiky crest helps protect it from hungry hawks and eagles. Despite its name, its skin can be orange, black, or blue.

THORNY DEVIL
Moloch horridus
Location: Australia
Length: Up to 20 cm (8 in)

Native to hot deserts, the thorny devil bristles with conical spines for defence against predators. Channels between the spines collect moisture from the air, which the lizard can drink. It preys almost exclusively on ants.

GREEN BASILISK
Basiliscus plumifrons
Location: Central America
Length: Up to 61 cm (24 in)

This flamboyantly crested lizard is famous for the way it can dash across the surface of deep water supported by the long, flattened toes of its hind feet. It usually does this to escape from enemies.

ARMADILLO GIRDLED LIZARD
Ouroborus cataphractus
Location: Southern Africa
Length: Up to 10 cm (4 in)

Armoured on its back with stout, spiny scales, this lizard defends itself by rolling up and gripping its tail in its mouth. The resulting ball makes a prickly mouthful for any predator. When unrolled, it feeds on insects, spiders, and other small animals, hunting them by day in rocky desert terrain.

BLUE-TONGUED SKINK
Tiliqua scincoides
Location: East Australia
Length: Up to 61 cm (24 in)

One of the biggest skinks – a large family of stumpy, short-legged lizards – this reptile has a bright blue tongue, which it flips out when faced by a predator. The sudden flash of vivid electric blue startles its enemy, giving the skink a chance to make its escape.

Defence display

SANDFISH SKINK
Scincus scincus
Location: North Africa
Length: Up to 20 cm (8 in)

This skink is adapted for moving swiftly through soft, dry sand by making swimming movements like a fish. Its body is superbly streamlined for slipping through the sand, with a wedge-shaped head and smooth, shiny scales. It catches insects by sensing their movements in the sand.

DWARF-PLATED LIZARD
Cordylosaurus subtessellatus
Location: Southern Africa
Length: Up to 15 cm (6 in)

Found in rocky landscapes, this sleek lizard is notable for its very long, blue tail. Like many lizards, when threatened it can snap this off, leaving the tail wiggling to distract an enemy and give the lizard time to escape. Its tail gradually regrows, but is shorter.

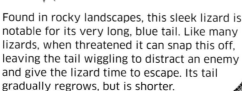

VIVIPAROUS LIZARD
Zootoca vivipara
Location: Europe, Asia
Length: Up to 15 cm (6 in)

Most lizards lay eggs, relying on warm weather to incubate them. But a few, such as this widespread Eurasian species, give birth to live young. This allows it to live in cooler regions than other lizards, as far north as the Arctic. It is mainly an insect-eater.

SLOW WORM
Anguis fragilis

Location: Eurasia, N. W. Africa
Length: Up to 48 cm (19 in)

Neither a worm nor particularly slow, this is one of several species of legless lizard. It resembles a small snake, but unlike a snake, it can blink its eyes, and it cannot swallow large prey whole. It feeds on insects, slugs, and worms.

COMMON FLAT-TAILED GECKO
Uroplatus fimbriatus

Location: Madagascar
Length: Up to 33 cm (13 in)

Geckos are a distinctive group of lizards that are superbly adapted for climbing, with sticky structures under the tips of their toes that can cling to any surface. This species is exquisitely camouflaged, and invisible when crouched on tree bark. It has super-sensitive night vision for hunting insects.

Lizards

With more than 6,000 species worldwide, lizards are the largest and most diverse group of reptiles. They come in all shapes and sizes, ranging from tiny chameleons (see pp.102–103) to giant monitor lizards the size of crocodiles.

A typical lizard has a scaly skin, four legs, and a long tail. Its legs extend sideways from its body, giving it a sprawling stance with its belly close to the ground. Some lizards have very short legs or even none at all. A few species even have a venomous bite.

GILA MONSTER
Heloderma suspectum

Location: North America
Length: Up to 60 cm (23½ in)

Despite being closely related to snakes, very few lizards are venomous. This bulky hunter is one of the exceptions. The venom glands are in its lower jaw, and it uses its venom for defence – a tactic backed up by its bright warning coloration.

Strong forelegs for digging

Frill spread wide

FRILL-NECKED LIZARD
Chlamydosaurus kingii

Location: New Guinea, Australia
Length: Up to 90 cm (35½ in)

The dramatic neck-frill of this Australasian lizard is usually kept folded against its body. But if the lizard is cornered by a predator, it spreads the frill and opens its mouth wide to reveal a brightly coloured lining. It uses the same display for courtship.

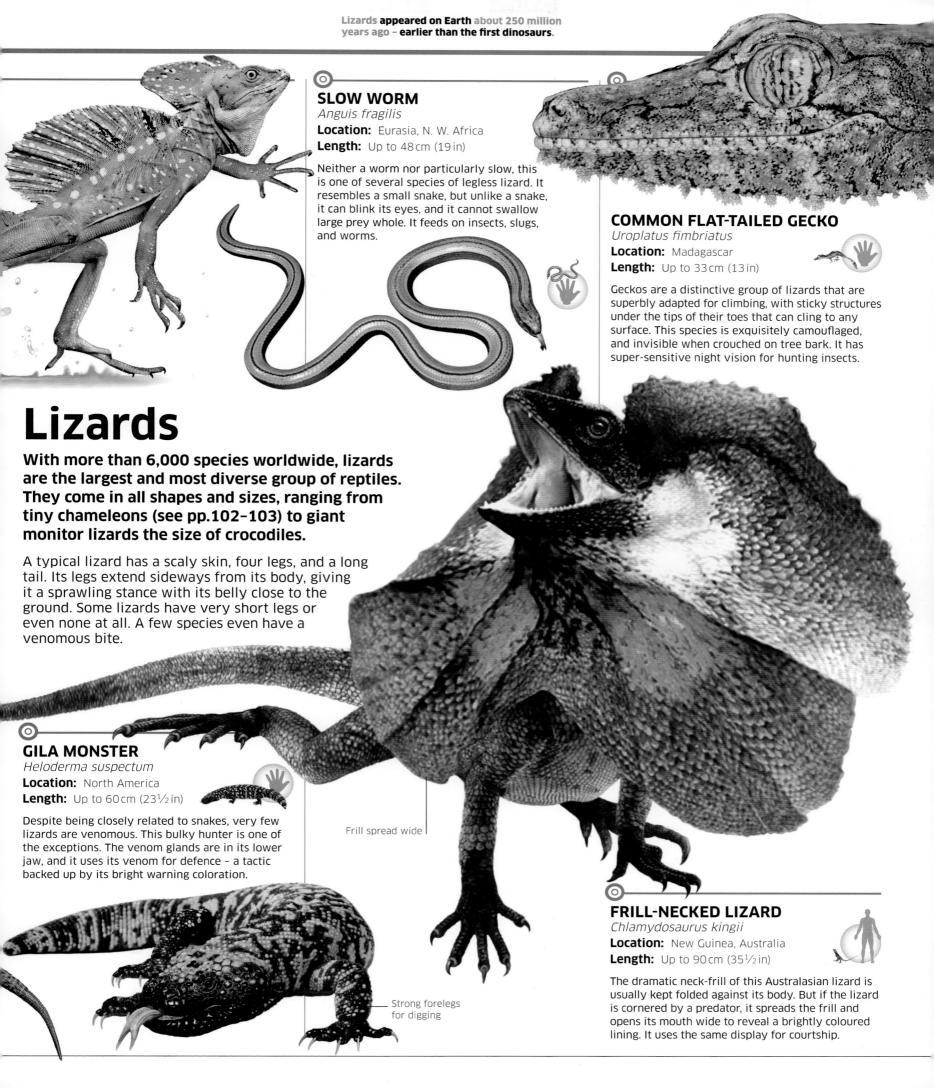

Emerald tree boa

Camouflaged among the tropical forest foliage by its green skin, the emerald tree boa drapes itself over a low branch watching for a victim to stray within striking range.

Like nearly all snakes the emerald tree boa is a hunter. It is mainly nocturnal and preys on the small mammals and birds that live in the lowland tropical forests of South America, using heat-sensitive organs on its lips to detect their warm bodies even in the dark. Unlike some snakes it is not venomous. Instead it seizes prey in its extra-long teeth and squeezes the animal to death in its powerful coils.

White flashes
Pale markings on its back make the snake's outline less obvious to prey or predators.

REPTILES

EMERALD TREE BOA

Corallus caninus

Location: South America

Length: Up to 1.8 m (6 ft)

Diet: Mainly small mammals

Prehensile tail
The boa can use its tail to cling to a branch when striking at prey.

Although the emerald tree boa feeds mainly on small mammals, it can move **fast enough to snatch birds out of the air with its sharp teeth.**

Vertical pupils
Vertical slit-like eye pupils open wide in the dark, when the snake is most active.

Heat-sensing pits
Sensors in each pit detect the body heat of warm-blooded prey.

Teeth are hidden in the gum

Sharp teeth
The boa's long, needle-sharp teeth curve backwards, so once it has a grip there is little chance for its prey to escape. Like all snakes it swallows its prey whole, moving each side of its jaw alternately to drag its victim down its elastic throat. This can take a long time, but each meal may sustain the boa for several weeks.

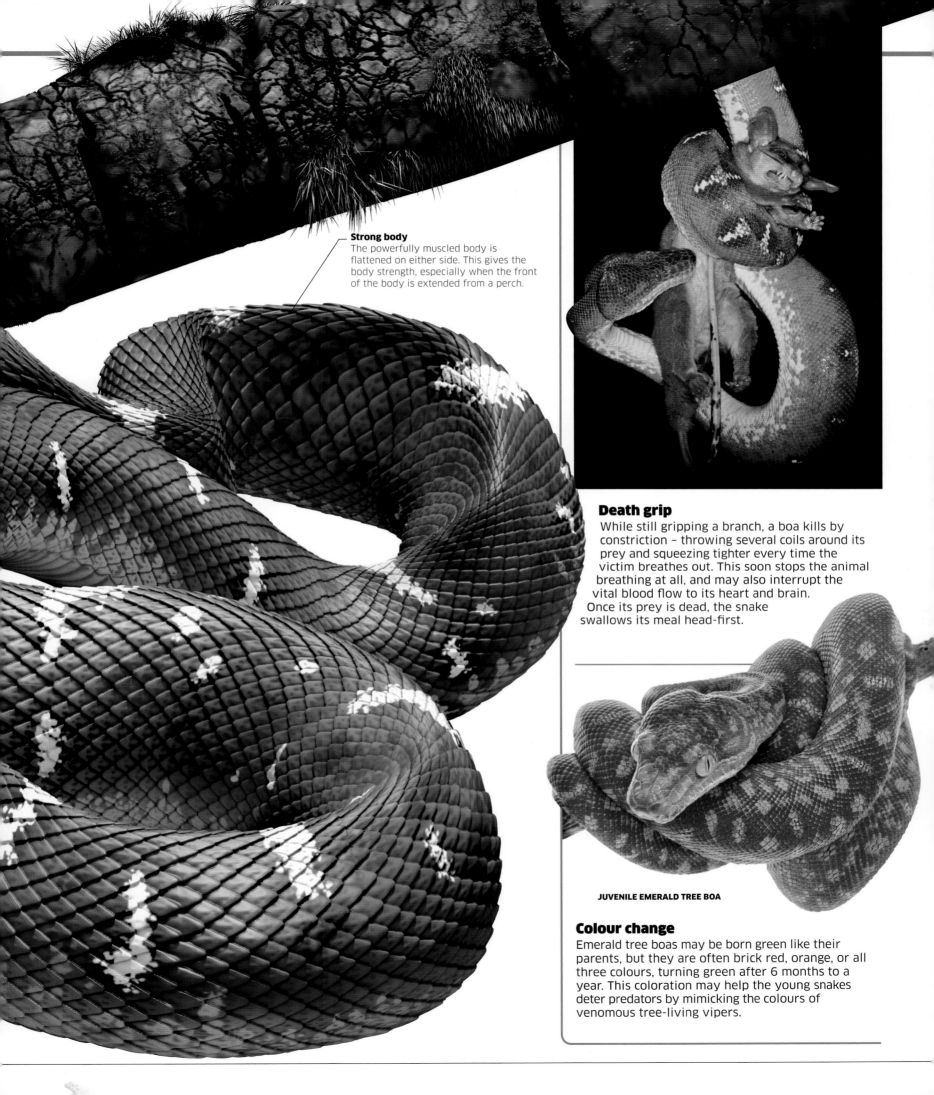

Strong body
The powerfully muscled body is flattened on either side. This gives the body strength, especially when the front of the body is extended from a perch.

Death grip
While still gripping a branch, a boa kills by constriction – throwing several coils around its prey and squeezing tighter every time the victim breathes out. This soon stops the animal breathing at all, and may also interrupt the vital blood flow to its heart and brain. Once its prey is dead, the snake swallows its meal head-first.

JUVENILE EMERALD TREE BOA

Colour change
Emerald tree boas may be born green like their parents, but they are often brick red, orange, or all three colours, turning green after 6 months to a year. This coloration may help the young snakes deter predators by mimicking the colours of venomous tree-living vipers.

5 cm (2 in) – the length a **gaboon viper's fangs** can grow to.

A **golden flying snake** can **glide** for distances of up to **100 m (330 ft)**.

RETICULATED PYTHON
Malayopython reticulatus
Location: S. E. Asia
Length: Up to 10 m (33 ft)

The longest snake, and one of the heaviest, this tropical Asian giant is a constrictor that kills prey by coiling around it and squeezing it to death.

SCHLEGEL'S GIANT BLINDSNAKE
Afrotyphlops schlegelii
Location: Eastern and southern Africa
Length: Up to 1 m (3¼ ft)

Specialized for burrowing, and rarely seen above ground, this African snake does have eyes, but they are very small and covered by stout scales. It has a spade-like snout that it uses to tunnel in search of the termites that are its sole prey.

Snout
The sharp snout is adapted for digging.

Eye
The eyes have vertical pupils like a cat's.

Snakes

Highly specialized for their predatory lifestyle, snakes are among the most efficient of all hunters. Their adaptations also make them some of the most dangerous animals on Earth.

Snakes are dedicated killers. With very few exceptions they hunt live prey, kill it, and swallow it whole. They have specialized senses for detecting their quarry, and they can move surprisingly quickly for animals with no legs. Their jaws and skulls are highly modified for swallowing animals bigger than their own heads, and some snakes are armed with deadly venom.

Forked tongue
The python picks up the scent of prey with its tongue.

BOMBAY EARTH SNAKE
Uropeltis macrolepis
Location: South Asia
Length: Up to 30 cm (11¾ in)

This small, burrowing south Indian forest snake has a curiously wedge-shaped tail, armoured with unusually tough scales. It uses this as a shield to block the end of its burrow when it is tunnelling, and keep out hungry predators.

SIDEWINDER
Crotalus cerastes
Location: North America
Length: Up to 80 cm (31½ in)

Camouflage
Scaly body matches the desert sand.

One of the highly venomous rattlesnakes, the sidewinder is named for the way it crawls over hot, dry, wind-blown desert sand by looping its body sideways. It lives in the deserts of northern Mexico and the southwestern United States.

GABOON VIPER
Bitis gabonica
Location: West and central Africa
Length: 2 m (6½ ft)

The African gaboon viper is a massively built killer that uses its superb camouflage to ambush prey in its tropical forest habitat. It has the longest venomous fangs of any snake.

A large **reticulated python** can **eat a pig** weighing more than 60 kg (132 lb).

25,000 The number of annual **recorded human deaths** from **snake bites**.

89

INDIAN COBRA
Naja naja
Location: South Asia
Length: Up to 2.4 m (7¾ ft)

One of the most dangerous snakes, the highly venomous Indian cobra is famous for its hooded threat display. Compared to a viper it has short fangs, but they deliver a potent venom containing paralyzing nerve toxins.

Hood
The hood is supported by extended ribs.

Scaly skin
Smooth scales protect the body.

EASTERN CORAL SNAKE
Micrurus fulvius
Location: North America
Length: Up to 1.2 m (4 ft)

Bands of vivid colour spell danger for any animal tempted to attack this highly venomous snake. The warning is so effective that harmless species such as the scarlet kingsnake mimic the banded pattern for their own defence.

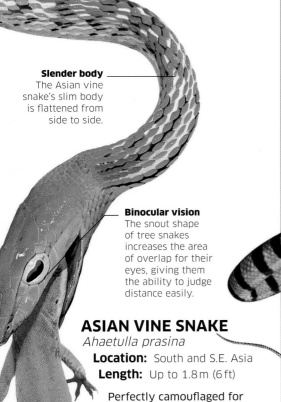

Slender body
The Asian vine snake's slim body is flattened from side to side.

Binocular vision
The snout shape of tree snakes increases the area of overlap for their eyes, giving them the ability to judge distance easily.

ASIAN VINE SNAKE
Ahaetulla prasina
Location: South and S.E. Asia
Length: Up to 1.8 m (6 ft)

Perfectly camouflaged for hunting in trees, the slender vine snake targets lizards, tree frogs, and young birds with its unusually sharp eyesight. Concealed by the foliage, the snake ambushes its prey, killing its victim with a venomous bite.

YELLOW-LIPPED SEA KRAIT
Laticauda colubrina
Location: Indo-Pacific region
Length: Up to 1.5 m (5 ft)

Flattened tail
Paddle-shaped tail helps in swimming.

This snake spends most of its time in shallow coastal waters, but lays eggs on land. It has short fangs, but potent venom for killing fish quickly before they can swim away.

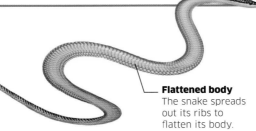

Flattened body
The snake spreads out its ribs to flatten its body.

GOLDEN FLYING SNAKE
Chrysopelea ornata
Location: South and S. E. Asia
Length: Up to 1.3 m (4¼ ft)

This extraordinary south Asian snake hunts small animals in trees, and avoids coming down to ground level by hurling itself into the air and gliding from tree to tree. Once airborne it flattens its body into a big S-shape that floats on the air like a frisbee.

COMMON EGG-EATER
Dasypeltis scabra
Location: Africa, West Asia
Length: Up to 1.2 m (4 ft)

All snakes can eat huge meals, but the African egg-eater can take a whole egg in its mouth. The snake breaks it up with spiny projections of its neck vertebrae, then coughs up the crushed shell.

RING-NECKED SNAKE
Diadophis punctatus
Location: North America
Length: Up to 46 cm (18 in)

If threatened this small American snake coils its tail and flips it over to expose the vividly coloured underside. This may warn enemies that the snake can bite, although its venom is not very strong.

A Nile crocodile can **kill** a full-grown **African buffalo**.

100 years or more – the possible lifespan of a crocodilian.

Crocodilians

The biggest, most powerful reptiles, crocodilians are superbly equipped for their aquatic way of life, and are notorious for their fearsome jaws and their ability to kill and eat almost anything.

The crocodilians consist of three families – the gharials, the alligators and caimans, and the crocodiles. They are all dedicated meat-eaters with the same basic body shape, but their jaws vary in form depending on their diet. They propel themselves through the water with their long, muscular tails, and are able to stay concealed underwater without breathing for long periods as they wait to ambush prey.

REPTILES

NILE CROCODILE

Crocodylus niloticus

Location: Tropical Africa

Length: Up to 6.1 m (20 ft)

Diet: Fish, mammals, birds

Armoured scutes
A crocodile's back is armoured with big, bony plates embedded in thick, oversized scales known as scutes. These protect it from bigger crocodiles, as well as the sharp hooves and horns of struggling prey.

Splayed legs
Short legs are used for steering underwater.

Flattened tail

Food processor
Highly acidic juices in the stomach digest everything, including hair, bones, hooves, and horns.

Renewable teeth
The crocodile has up to 68 teeth. Some are much bigger than others and, as in all true crocodiles, many of the teeth are visible when the jaws are closed. Each tooth is replaced by a new one as it wears out, so a crocodile always has a full set.

Strong, pointed teeth

Death grip
Powerful jaws can exert a colossal biting force for gripping and dismembering prey.

The **closest living relatives** of crocodilians are **birds**.

After a big meal, a crocodilian can go without food for **six months** or more.

91

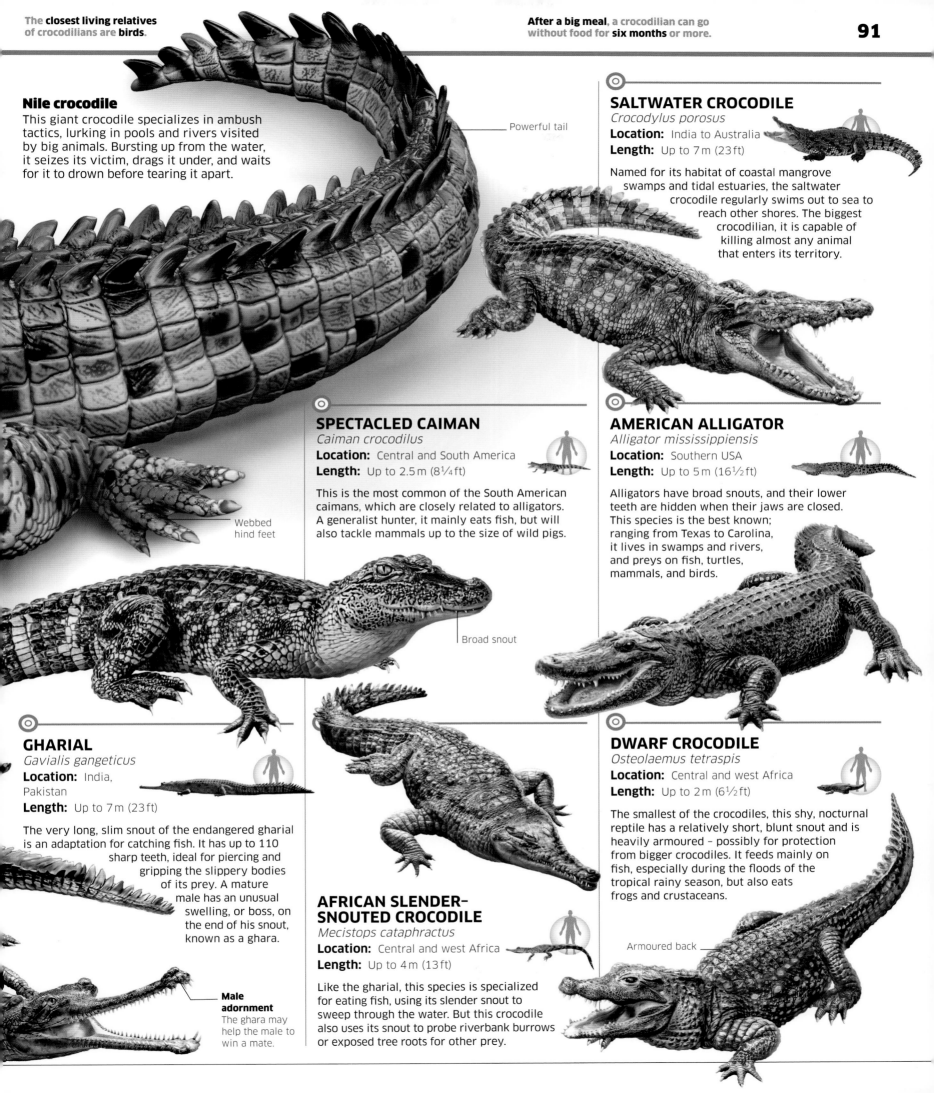

Nile crocodile

This giant crocodile specializes in ambush tactics, lurking in pools and rivers visited by big animals. Bursting up from the water, it seizes its victim, drags it under, and waits for it to drown before tearing it apart.

Powerful tail

Webbed hind feet

SALTWATER CROCODILE
Crocodylus porosus

Location: India to Australia
Length: Up to 7 m (23 ft)

Named for its habitat of coastal mangrove swamps and tidal estuaries, the saltwater crocodile regularly swims out to sea to reach other shores. The biggest crocodilian, it is capable of killing almost any animal that enters its territory.

SPECTACLED CAIMAN
Caiman crocodilus

Location: Central and South America
Length: Up to 2.5 m (8¼ ft)

This is the most common of the South American caimans, which are closely related to alligators. A generalist hunter, it mainly eats fish, but will also tackle mammals up to the size of wild pigs.

Broad snout

AMERICAN ALLIGATOR
Alligator mississippiensis

Location: Southern USA
Length: Up to 5 m (16½ ft)

Alligators have broad snouts, and their lower teeth are hidden when their jaws are closed. This species is the best known; ranging from Texas to Carolina, it lives in swamps and rivers, and preys on fish, turtles, mammals, and birds.

GHARIAL
Gavialis gangeticus

Location: India, Pakistan
Length: Up to 7 m (23 ft)

The very long, slim snout of the endangered gharial is an adaptation for catching fish. It has up to 110 sharp teeth, ideal for piercing and gripping the slippery bodies of its prey. A mature male has an unusual swelling, or boss, on the end of his snout, known as a ghara.

Male adornment
The ghara may help the male to win a mate.

AFRICAN SLENDER-SNOUTED CROCODILE
Mecistops cataphractus

Location: Central and west Africa
Length: Up to 4 m (13 ft)

Like the gharial, this species is specialized for eating fish, using its slender snout to sweep through the water. But this crocodile also uses its snout to probe riverbank burrows or exposed tree roots for other prey.

DWARF CROCODILE
Osteolaemus tetraspis

Location: Central and west Africa
Length: Up to 2 m (6½ ft)

The smallest of the crocodiles, this shy, nocturnal reptile has a relatively short, blunt snout and is heavily armoured – possibly for protection from bigger crocodiles. It feeds mainly on fish, especially during the floods of the tropical rainy season, but also eats frogs and crustaceans.

Armoured back

BIRDS

With their often dazzling plumage and mastery of the air, birds are the most instantly attractive animals. Many also sing, filling the air with music during the spring breeding season. Highly adapted for flight, they are among the most specialized vertebrates, but also some of the most successful.

WHAT IS A BIRD?

Since the 1990s, the discovery of many miraculously preserved fossils has proved beyond doubt that birds are feathered dinosaurs – relatives of two-legged hunters such as *Velociraptor*. Birds inherited their feathers from such animals, along with their warm blood and super-efficient lungs. These enabled the first primitive birds to take to the air more than 140 million years ago, and by 66 million years ago they had evolved into birds very like the ones that fly around us today.

Vivid colour
Feathers can be brightly pigmented, but may also reflect light in ways that create iridescent colours.

Wing anatomy
Each wing is a modified arm, with extended hand bones but reduced fingers.

Flight control
The most highly developed part of the brain is the section controlling flight.

Sharp eyes
All birds depend heavily on their eyes for finding food, and when flying.

BIRD VARIETY

There are well over 10,000 species of birds, belonging to 28 major groups, or orders. One order, the perching birds, accounts for more than half of the species; other orders include distinctive birds such as owls, parrots, and birds of prey.

BEE HUMMINGBIRD

OSTRICH

Biggest and smallest
The biggest bird is the flightless ostrich, which can weigh more than eight times as much as the heaviest flying bird. The smallest bird, the bee hummingbird, is little bigger than the ostrich's eye.

Flight muscles
Big flight muscles anchored to a deep-keeled breastbone power the down-stroke of the wings.

Toothless bill

BILL SHAPES

Bird bills have evolved in different ways to deal with many types of food and ways of feeding, from sipping sweet flower nectar to tearing prey apart.

Nectar-gatherer
A hummingbird's bill is a precision tool, adapted for slipping into narrow, tubular flowers to extract sugary nectar.

Nut-cracker
Seed-eaters have extra-strong bills. The powerful bill of the hawfinch can crack a cherry stone.

Butchery tool
The hooked bill of this white-tailed eagle is used for stripping meat from the bones of fish, birds, and mammals.

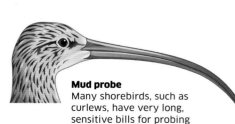

Mud probe
Many shorebirds, such as curlews, have very long, sensitive bills for probing deep into soft mud in search of prey.

Water-sifter
The spoonbill sweeps its highly specialized bill from side to side through shallow water to sift out small animals.

AMAZING LUNGS

A bird's lungs are relatively rigid structures with air tubes passing right through them. The tubes lead to many balloon-like air sacs that pump air through the lung tissue. The system is far more efficient than mammal lungs, absorbing the extra oxygen essential for powering the flight muscles.

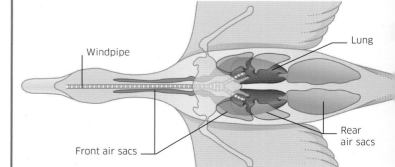

Windpipe

Lung

Front air sacs

Rear air sacs

Inside a bird
The strong yet light skeleton, very powerful muscles, and lightweight feathers of this river kingfisher are all specialized for flight – the feature that has made birds masters of the air.

Flight feathers
Most of the wing area consists of long, overlapping flight feathers.

Scaly legs
The legs have scaly skin, and sharp-clawed feet for gripping and perching.

Tail
Like the wings, the tail is mostly made up of feathers. It is used for steering, and as an air brake.

NESTS AND EGGS
Most birds build nests where they can lay their eggs, keep them warm until they hatch, and then care for their young. Nests range from scrapes on the ground to elaborate constructions woven from a variety of materials. Some are hidden in holes, while others are built in trees or on ledges.

REED BUNTING NEST

FEATHER TYPES
Bird feathers have a number of different functions. Fluffy down feathers, and the downy parts of small body feathers provide insulation from the cold. But the larger wing and tail feathers are stiff and lightweight, ideal for the demands of flight.

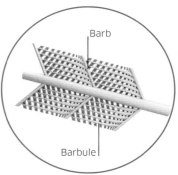

Barb

Barbule

Feather structure
Each branching barb of a flight feather is fringed with hooked barbules that zip together to form a flat surface known as a vane.

DOWN FEATHER

BODY (CONTOUR) FEATHER

FLIGHT FEATHER

KEY FEATURES
All birds share a number of key features. Like mammals, they are warm-blooded vertebrates, but their bodies are covered with feathers instead of fur. They lay eggs, and most can fly, or had flying ancestors. This combination of features defines them as birds.

WE OFTEN THINK OF BIRDS AS **FEATHER-BRAINED,** BUT IN FACT SOME CROWS AND PARROTS **ARE AS INTELLIGENT AS APES AND DOLPHINS.**

Vertebrates
A bird's body is supported by an internal skeleton.

Warm-blooded
Birds generate their own body heat in all environments.

Lay eggs
All birds breed by laying eggs with hard shells.

Most fly
Some birds spend most of their lives in the air.

Feathered
Feathers retain heat and enable birds to fly.

Deadly enemy
The cheetah is one of the few hunters that can overtake an ostrich.

BIRDS
OSTRICH
Struthio camelus

Location: Africa

Height: Up to 2.8 m (9 ft)

Diet: Small plants and animals

Sun shades
An ostrich uses its wings for dancing displays, and to shade its young.

Ratites

The huge, spectacular ostrich is the biggest of the ratites – a group of flightless birds that rely on their running speed to escape predators. Some are also notorious for their ferocity when cornered.

Although ratites do have wings, they cannot fly because their wings have soft, fluffy, or hair-like feathers instead of stiff flight feathers. Their relatively weak wing muscles are attached to a flat breastbone instead of the deep-keeled breastbone found in other birds. They are thought to share a common ancestor with the tinamous – a group of ground-dwelling birds that are able to fly, although only over short distances.

Fluffy feathers
Ostrich feathers are fluffy and soft, and resemble the insulating down feathers of other birds. They lack the rows of hooked barbules that zip together to form stiff vanes on flight feathers.

Powerful legs
Very long legs allow the ostrich to outrun most of its enemies.

Two toes
Each foot has two toes, with a big hoof-like nail on the large inner toe.

Ostrich

The largest of all birds, the ostrich is specialized for roaming the open grassland and deserts of tropical Africa in search of scarce food. The black-and-white males mate with up to seven browner females, which all lay their eggs in one communal nest. The male helps to incubate the eggs.

Ostriches are the world's **heaviest birds** – they can weigh up to **150 kg (330 lbs)**.

At full stretch, an **ostrich can run** at 70 km/h (43 mph) – **as fast as a racehorse**.

97

Huge eye
The eyes of an ostrich are enormous – each eyeball is up to 5 cm (2 in) wide. Like nearly all birds it relies on its acute sense of sight to locate food, detect danger, and find breeding partners.

GREATER RHEA
Rhea americana
Location: South America
Height: Up to 1.5 m (5 ft)

Long neck
The ostrich has a good view of approaching danger thanks to the length of its neck.

An ostrich cannot chew, so it **swallows stones** to help its muscular gizzard grind up its food.

Fine feathers
Males display their wings in courtship.

This is the South American counterpart of the ostrich, with a similar way of life. It lives in flocks on open grassland and feeds on a variety of plant and animal foods.

SOUTHERN CASSOWARY
Casuarius casuarius
Location: Indonesia, New Guinea, Northern Australia
Height: Up to 1.8 m (25½ ft)

Living in tropical rainforest, the big, powerful cassowary has sharp, spear-like claws that can be dangerous to anyone who comes near them. The female is more colourful than the male, with a taller casque (helmet-like crest) on her bill.

Camouflaged chick
A young cassowary's striped plumage breaks up the bird's outline making it more difficult to spot.

EMU
Dromaius novaehollandiae
Location: Australia
Height: Up to 1.9 m (6¼ ft)

The Australian equivalent of the ostrich, the emu wanders nomadically over most of the continent. It prefers wooded country with plentiful food, but can survive for long periods without eating.

SOUTHERN BROWN KIWI
Apteryx australis
Location: South Island, New Zealand
Height: Up to 65 cm (25½ in)

Much smaller than other ratites, the kiwis of New Zealand have fur-like plumage. At night they use their long bills to probe the ground for invertebrates.

Sensitive whiskers

ELEGANT CRESTED TINAMOU
Eudromia elegans
Location: Southern Chile to Argentina
Height: Up to 41 cm (16 in)

The tinamous of South and Central America are now thought to be part of the ratite group of birds, even though they are able to fly. This species lives in flocks in the cold, dry scrublands of Patagonia.

Speckled plumage

50 The **number of years** an emperor penguin **can live**.

A **breeding emperor penguin** often has to **walk 100 km** (62 miles) or more across the ice **to feed in open water**.

Emperor penguin

The emperor is a sleek hunter that dives under the Antarctic ice to catch fish and squid. Emperors breed on sea ice, the female laying a single egg then returning to open waters to feed. The male incubates the egg, waiting patiently for his mate to return before making the long journey across the ice to feed.

Emperors lay their eggs earlier than other penguins so that the chicks can develop all through spring and summer, before winter sets in again. Smaller penguins develop more quickly, so they can wait until after the spring thaw to breed and lay their eggs on rocky shores.

An emperor penguin may dive to
500 m (1,640 ft)
or more to reach the sea bed.

Barbed tongue
An emperor penguin preys on a variety of small fish, squid, and shrimp-like krill, using its swimming speed to pursue and catch each animal individually. Its tongue bristles with rear-facing barbs that stop the prey escaping before the penguin can swallow it.

Sharp barbs

Excellent insulation
The emperor has adapted to withstand extreme cold, with an extra-thick layer of insulating fat, or blubber, beneath the skin. Its feathers are short and stiff, and overlap to form a waterproof covering that keeps out the cold.

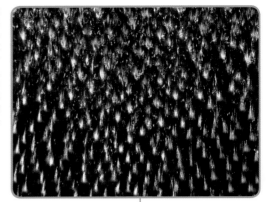

Flightless wings
The penguin's wings are adapted for swimming, acting as stiff flippers to propel the penguin through the water.

Downy chick
When it hatches, the chick is covered with a thick coat of silvery-grey down feathers.

First feathers
The downy feathers will be replaced after about three months by the chick's juvenile plumage.

BIRDS
EMPEROR PENGUIN
Aptenodytes forsteri

Location: Antarctica

Height: 1.2 m (4 ft)

Diet: Fish, squid, and krill

Standing tall
On land, the emperor walks upright with a highly energy-efficient, waddling gait.

Colourful bill
The lower mandible of the bill can be orange, pink, or lilac.

Streamlined body
The emperor's body is long and tapered at each end, forming a streamlined shape for underwater swimming.

Webbed feet
The scaly, webbed feet steer the penguin when it swims underwater.

Winter vigil

All winter, the male guards the egg. It sits on his feet, covered with a fold of skin to prevent it from freezing. While the male incubates the egg, he does not eat, losing up to half his body weight over two months.

In their element

Like all penguins, emperors are superb swimmers. They are fast, with a top speed of 24 km/h (15 mph), and can stay underwater for up to around 20 minutes.

Keeping out the cold

To survive the bitter Antarctic winter, male emperors form tight huddles of up to 5,000 birds. They constantly shuffle around so that each penguin takes a turn on the colder, windy side of the huddle.

The **ancestors of chickens** were first **domesticated** more than **5,000 years ago**.

INDIAN PEAFOWL

Pavo cristatus

Location: India

Length: Up to 2.2 m (7¼ ft)

Diet: Seeds, fruit, insects

Glorious plumes
The "tail" is actually made up of elongated feathers growing from the male's back.

In flight
Their enormous fan of plumes is a slight hindrance, but peacocks can fly well enough to reach a safe perch in a tree to spend the night. In their native forests this is vital to their survival.

Subtle colouring
Female peafowl have far less dramatic plumage, and a shorter train of feathers.

Foraging tools
The bird uses its strong feet to scratch in the soil for insects and seeds.

Indian peafowl
The peafowl is a type of pheasant that has the most dazzling of courtship displays. The vividly coloured male, or peacock, woos the female by spreading a spectacular fan of iridescent feathers, dotted with big glowing "eyes". If the female is sufficiently impressed she may allow him to mate.

25 The number of eggs a **female grey partridge** can lay – the **largest egg clutch** of any bird.

1.8 m (6 ft) – the length a **peacock's feather train** can reach. It makes up over **60 per cent** of the bird's **total body length**.

101

MALLEE FOWL
Leipoa ocellata
Location: Australia
Length: Up to 61 cm (24 in)

This is one of the megapodes – birds that build mounds of warm, decaying vegetation covered with soil to act as incubators for their eggs. The male regularly tests the temperature, and either ventilates the mound, or adds soil to retain heat.

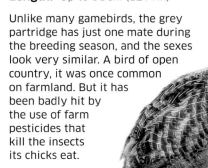

GREAT CURASSOW
Crax rubra
Location: Central America
Length: Up to 92 cm (36¼ in)

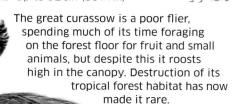

The great curassow is a poor flier, spending much of its time foraging on the forest floor for fruit and small animals, but despite this it roosts high in the canopy. Destruction of its tropical forest habitat has now made it rare.

WILD TURKEY
Meleagris gallopavo
Location: North America
Length: Up to 1.2 m (4 ft)

Like the peacock, the male wild turkey is quite different from the female, and is a huge, highly ornamented bird that performs elaborate strutting displays accompanied by gobbling calls. It eats seeds, fruit, and insects.

GREATER PRAIRIE CHICKEN
Tympanuchus cupido
Location: North America
Length: Up to 47 cm (18½ in)

Gamebirds

Many of these plump, ground-feeding birds have been hunted for food for centuries, which is why they are called gamebirds. But some like the peafowl also have spectacularly beautiful plumage.

Pheasants, partridges, turkeys, grouse, and their relatives are mainly forest or woodland birds that live on the ground and rarely fly. Many have a polygamous breeding system, with each extravagantly ornamented male courting as many females as possible. In most species, females nest and raise their young alone, which is possible because the chicks can feed themselves almost as soon as they hatch.

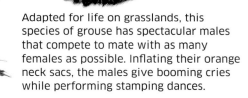

Adapted for life on grasslands, this species of grouse has spectacular males that compete to mate with as many females as possible. Inflating their orange neck sacs, the males give booming cries while performing stamping dances.

GREY PARTRIDGE
Perdix perdix
Location: Europe
Length: Up to 31 cm (12¼ in)

Unlike many gamebirds, the grey partridge has just one mate during the breeding season, and the sexes look very similar. A bird of open country, it was once common on farmland. But it has been badly hit by the use of farm pesticides that kill the insects its chicks eat.

RED JUNGLEFOWL
Gallus gallus
Location: Southeast Asia
Length: Up to 78 cm (30¾ in)

This exotic-looking jungle pheasant is the ancestor of the domestic chicken. In the wild it forages for seeds and insects in bamboo forests, clearings, and nearby scrubland, often in flocks of up to 50. Each male courts and mates with several females.

Lethal weapons
Each of the male's legs is armed with a sharp spur, which is used in fights with rivals.

ANDEAN CONDOR
Vultur gryphus
Location: South America
Length: Up to 1.1 m (3½ ft)

The biggest vulture, and largest bird of prey, the magnificent Andean condor searches for food among the mountains by riding updraughts on huge outspread wings. It may soar for an hour or more without making a single wingbeat.

Naked head
Bare skin on the bird's head allows it to dig deep into flesh without its feathers getting matted with blood.

OSPREY
Pandion haliaetus
Location: Worldwide except Antarctica
Length: Up to 58 cm (22¾ in)

The osprey is a specialized fish hawk that plunges into rivers, lakes, and shallow seas to seize fish in its talons. Its feet have spiny soles that help the bird grip the slippery, struggling fish as it surges up from the water and carry its prey to a perch to eat.

SNAIL KITE
Rostrhamus sociabilis
Location: N., S., and C. America
Length: Up to 43 cm (17 in)

This slow-flying specialist feeds almost exclusively on freshwater snails, which it plucks from marshes and scissors out of their shells with its long-hooked bill. It lives mainly in Central and South American wetlands, but also in the Florida Everglades.

— Snail prey

BALD EAGLE
Haliaeetus leucocephalus
Location: North America
Length: Up to 90 cm (35½ in)

Familiar as the "American eagle", the national symbol of the United States, this powerful hunter feeds mainly on fish but also takes other prey. Although it ranges as far south as Mexico, most bald eagles live in the far north, in Alaska and western Canada.

Not so bald
White head feathers give the eagle its "bald" appearance.

A bald eagle builds the **largest nest** of any bird. It can weigh over 2,700 kg (6,000 lbs) – more than a rhinoceros.

Powerful talons
Huge claws are used to seize fish, birds, rabbits, and squirrels.

Hawks and eagles

Birds of prey are the top predators of the bird world – powerful fliers with sharp claws and hooked bills that attack and eat other animals. Most of them are active hunters, but a few are adapted for scavenging carcasses of dead remains.

Ranging from sparrow-sized falcons to gigantic condors, birds of prey (also known as raptors) are some of the most spectacular and exciting of all birds. They include powerful eagles that can rip monkeys out of trees, fast-flying falcons that pursue and kill other birds in flight, super-agile forest hawks, specialized fish hunters, owl-like harriers, and soaring, scavenging vultures.

A **diving peregrine falcon** can reach a speed of **322 km/h (200 mph)** or more.

The **secretary bird** sometimes kills snakes by leaping on their backs and breaking their necks.

An **Andean condor** may have a wingspan of more than **3 m (9¾ ft)**.

PALM-NUT VULTURE
Gypohierax angolensis
Location: Tropical Africa
Length: Up to 60 cm (23½ in)

Technically a bird of prey and closely related to the scavenging vultures, this big, black-and-white bird feeds mainly on the fruit of oil palm trees. It uses its hooked bill to tear into the husk, which is rich in nutritious oil.

LAMMERGEIER
Gypaetus barbatus
Location: Eurasia, Africa
Length: Up to 1.1 m (3½ ft)

Sometimes called the bearded vulture because of the dark bristles flanking its bill, the lammergeier usually lives in rocky, mountainous habitats. It is well known for seizing large bones and dropping them onto rocks to break them open and expose the bone marrow inside.

NORTHERN HARRIER
Circus cyaneus
Location: Eurasia, N. and C. America
Length: Up to 51 cm (20 in)

Harriers are long-winged, slender birds that specialize in flying low over open ground, looking for small prey. The male northern harrier is a lovely dove-grey colour.

NORTHERN GOSHAWK
Accipiter gentilis
Location: North America, Eurasia
Length: Up to 66 cm (26 in)

This is one of the biggest forest hawks – relatively short-winged, long-tailed hunters adapted for fast, swerving flight through trees. It uses its flying skill to snatch squirrels and birds from their perches, and other prey such as pheasants from the ground.

Short, broad wings

HARPY EAGLE
Harpia harpyja
Location: Tropical America
Length: Up to 1.1 m (3½ ft)

One of the world's most powerful birds of prey, this huge tropical forest eagle uses its formidable talons to rip monkeys and sloths from their perches in the crowns of rainforest trees.

WEDGE-TAILED EAGLE
Aquila audax
Location: Australia, New Guinea
Length: Up to 1 m (3¼ ft)

Identifiable by its pointed tail, this is the biggest bird of prey in Australia. It hunts by soaring over the plains or watching from a perch, and is big enough to seize a small kangaroo.

SECRETARY BIRD
Sagittarius serpentarius
Location: Tropical Africa
Length: Up to 1.5 m (5 ft)

The secretary bird stalks the African savannas on very long legs, using its feet to catch and kill small mammals, insects, and snakes.

PEREGRINE FALCON
Falco peregrinus
Location: Almost worldwide
Length: Up to 48 cm (19 in)

Most falcons specialize in hunting airborne prey, including insects and bats. The peregrine attacks birds, plummeting from a height on half-folded wings to rip into its victims with its talons.

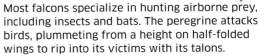

GALAH
Eolophus roseicapilla

Location: Australia
Length: Up to 36 cm (14 in)

Widespread in grassland and woodland across Australia, this is one of the crested parrots known as cockatoos. It feeds on small seeds and grain, including wheat. It forages in flocks, but forms lifelong breeding pairs that nest in holes in trees.

KAKAPO
Strigops habroptila
Location: New Zealand
Length: Up to 60 cm (23½ in)

The kakapo is a giant, flightless ground parrot that evolved in New Zealand at a time when there were no predators to threaten it. The introduction of stoats, rats, and cats led to its near-extinction, and it now survives in forest and scrubland on just a few remote islands.

RAINBOW LORIKEET
Trichoglossus moluccanus
Location: Australia, New Guinea
Length: Up to 30 cm (11¾ in)

Screeching flocks of rainbow lorikeets forage together for food in the forests of Australia and New Guinea. A lorikeet's tongue has a brush-like tip for gathering nectar, but it will also eat fruit and insects. At dusk the birds gather in huge communal roosts to spend the night.

Parrots

Celebrated for their intelligence and ability to mimic human speech, parrots are colourful birds with powerful, hooked bills for cracking seeds and nuts. Most parrots live in tropical forests and grasslands, often in large flocks, but a few are now very rare.

Ranging from mouse-sized pygmy parrots to magnificent giants like the hyacinth macaw, parrots occur on all warm continents south of the equator, as well as Central America and southern Asia. Most are seed-eaters, but the lories and lorikeets are specialized for gathering nectar. Some parrots eat insects, and a few may even scavenge for carrion.

BUDGERIGAR
Melopsittacus undulatus
Location: Australia
Length: Up to 18 cm (7 in)

Wild budgerigars live in big, nomadic flocks on the dry grasslands of Australia, moving from place to place in search of good crops of seeds. They breed in tree holes, whenever and wherever food is plentiful, and a pair may raise several broods of young in a good year.

80 years – the **age** some parrots **in captivity** have reached.

105

Mobile tongue
The hyacinth macaw feeds mainly on palm nuts, cracking their tough shells with its stout bill and using its mobile tongue to extract the kernels. A parrot's tongue is strong and very sensitive, so the bird can use it to explore its environment in the same way that we use our fingers.

Hyacinth macaw
The spectacular hyacinth macaw is the longest and largest of the parrots, though the flightless kakapo is heavier. It lives in the tropical lowland forests of Brazil and nearby regions, where it forages for food in small flocks, and breeds in tree holes.

Agile foot
The feet are very mobile, with two toes pointing forwards, and two pointing back.

BIRDS
HYACINTH MACAW
Anodorhynchus hyacinthinus

Location: South America

Length: Up to 1 m (3¼ ft)

Diet: Nuts, seeds, fruit

ECLECTUS PARROT
Eclectus roratus
Location: Australasia
Length: Up to 43 cm (17 in)

Male and female eclectus parrots are so different that they were once thought to be separate species. While the male is emerald green with patches of red and blue, the female is crimson with a blue belly. They live in the tropical forests of New Guinea and nearby regions.

CONGO AFRICAN GREY PARROT
Psittacus erithacus
Location: Africa
Length: Up to 33 cm (13 in)

This species is well known for its intelligence and vocal mimicry. In the wild the Congo African grey forages in small groups for food such as fruit and nuts, but roosts in large flocks. Like other parrots, it uses its bill as a climbing aid.

GREAT CRESTED GREBE
Podiceps cristatus
Location: Eurasia, Africa, Australia
Length: Up to 51 cm (20 in)

Grebes are highly adapted for diving after prey but their feet are so far back on their bodies that they struggle to walk on land. This species builds a floating nest for easy access from the water, and is famous for its elaborate, "dancing" courtship displays.

Expandable throat pouch

BROWN PELICAN
Pelecanus occidentalis
Location: Caribbean and the Americas
Length: Up to 1.4 m (4½ ft)

Pelicans have huge, expandable throat pouches, used for scooping up water teeming with small fish. Unlike other pelicans, this species hunts by plunge-diving into the sea from the air.

GREAT CORMORANT
Phalacrocorax carbo
Location: Worldwide except South America and Antarctica
Length: Up to 1 m (3¼ ft)

Widespread on coasts and fresh waters, this underwater hunter pursues fish by propelling itself with its big, webbed feet. Its plumage absorbs water, reducing the bird's buoyancy so that when it dives, it can stay submerged more easily.

MAGNIFICENT FRIGATEBIRD
Fregata magnificens
Location: Tropical American seas
Length: Up to 1.1 m (3½ ft)

The long-winged tropical frigatebird soars over the ocean, searching for prey or even stealing it in mid-air from other birds. Males have red throat pouches that they inflate for courtship displays.

Waterbirds, seabirds, and shorebirds

A huge variety of birds are specialized for feeding in or near water. Some hunt at sea, while many more feed on tidal shores or in freshwater wetlands.

Some of these birds have webbed feet and other adaptations for efficient swimming. Others have long legs, for wading in deep water. Many have bills that are modified for special feeding techniques.

PURPLE HERON
Ardea purpurea
Location: S. Eurasia, Africa
Length: Up to 90 cm (35½ in)

Herons mainly hunt in fresh water, standing motionless in the shallows, waiting for prey to approach. Like all herons, the purple heron has a "kink" in its neck. This acts like a hinge, allowing the bird to dart its head forward to seize prey with a quick stab of its spear-like bill.

Spreading the weight
Extra-long toes help the heron to walk over floating vegetation.

GREATER FLAMINGO
Phoenicopterus roseus
Location: S. Eurasia, Africa, Central America
Length: Up to 1.5 m (5 ft)

Flamingos are extraordinary birds, specialized for filter-feeding on tiny aquatic organisms. Some eat microscopic algae, but the greater flamingo feeds on insects and shrimps. Holding its head upside down in the shallows, it pumps water through its specially adapted bill, which has rows of comb-like bristles to trap prey.

The flamingo's rosy pink plumage is **caused by pigments in its food.**

Super sifter
The shape of the bill is ideal for sifting food from the surface of the water.

The Arctic tern **flies between the poles twice a year** – a **round trip** of more than **32,000 km (20,000 miles)**.

With a **record weight** of 15.5 kg (34 lb), the **whooper swan** is one of the **heaviest of all flying birds**.

107

WHOOPER SWAN
Cygnus cygnus
Location: Eurasia
Length: Up to 1.6 m (5¼ ft)

The pure-white whooper swan breeds in the subarctic in summer and migrates south for the winter, gathering in large flocks on freshwater marshes and estuaries. Its name comes from its loud, whooping call.

WOOD DUCK
Aix sponsa
Location: North America
Length: Up to 51 cm (20 in)

The colourful male wood duck makes a striking contrast with the grey-brown female. The male's dazzling plumage is for courtship display, whereas the female's drab colouring keeps her safe while incubating her eggs. Unlike most ducks, the wood duck nests in tree holes.

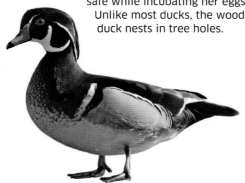

WATER RAIL
Rallus aquaticus
Location: Eurasia, North Africa
Length: Up to 28 cm (11 in)

Rails are short-winged waterbirds that live in freshwater wetlands. The water rail is one of the shyest, with a narrow body ideal for slipping through dense reedbeds. It is more often heard than seen, uttering a variety of pig-like grunts and squeals.

Long toes
The toes spread the bird's weight when walking on soft mud.

EURASIAN CURLEW
Numenius arquata
Location: Eurasia, Africa
Length: Up to 60 cm (23½ in)

Long-legged and long-billed, the Eurasian curlew is one of the largest of the shorebirds or waders – birds adapted for gathering food from tidal shores and wetlands. Its extremely long, curved bill is specialized for probing deep into soft mud for worms, clams, crabs, and other animals.

Out of sight
Mottled plumage provides excellent camouflage.

Probing bill
The highly sensitive bill tip detects hidden prey.

ATLANTIC PUFFIN
Fratercula arctica
Location: North Atlantic, Arctic
Length: Up to 30 cm (11¾ in)

The Atlantic puffin is one of the auks – northern seabirds specialized for hunting underwater using their wings to drive them forwards, like penguins. It has a large, colourful bill, which is adapted for carrying many small fish at once.

ARCTIC TERN
Sterna paradisaea
Location: Arctic and Antarctic regions
Length: Up to 35 cm (13¾ in)

The elegant, slender Arctic tern makes the longest migration of any bird. It breeds in the Arctic in the northern summer, then flies all the way to the Southern Ocean around Antarctica to feed during the northern winter.

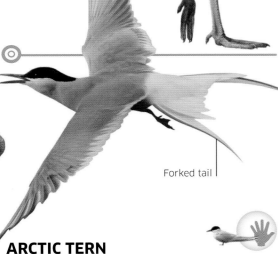

Forked tail

Dual-purpose wings
Short wings act as flippers underwater, but are long enough for flight.

Seasonal colour
Both the bill and the bright orange feet become paler in winter.

Floating flight
The long wings need only beat gently, reducing noise.

Ear tufts
Long, feathery tufts look like ears, but their purpose is not clear.

Eagle owl

This magnificent bird is one of the largest of the owls and a powerful hunter with the strength to kill a young deer. Its huge eyes are highly efficient in dim light, enabling it to fly in near-darkness and even target prey by moonlight.

The eagle owl does most of its hunting at dawn and dusk, when its prey is most active. Like all owls, it has excellent hearing, but it relies on its sharp eyesight more than many other owls. It has a vast range, with more than 12 subspecies found across Europe, Asia, and North Africa.

Eagle of the night
Most owls take prey that they can swallow whole, in one gulp. The eagle owl does hunt like this, but it will also sometimes attack and kill larger animals. It then tears the flesh into bite-sized mouthfuls with its hooked bill, like a true eagle.

Direct view
The owl's eyes are not spherical, like ours, but conical and fixed in place in the skull. An owl cannot simply roll its eyes to look at something, as we can, it has to turn its whole head. Luckily, an owl's flexible neck enables it to swivel its head up to 270°, which is three-quarters of a full turn.

Night sight
Large eyes are up to three times more sensitive in the dark than human eyes.

Feathered feet
The legs and feet are covered with feathers for protection against sharp-toothed prey.

Deadly weapons
Powerful, black-clawed talons grip and kill the owl's prey.

Soft-edged feathers
The owl's flight feathers have special, comb-like leading edges that muffle the noise of air rushing over its wings. This allows the owl to fly silently, so it can listen for prey, then take the animal by surprise.

BIRDS

EAGLE OWL

Bubo bubo

Location: Eurasia, North Africa

Length: Up to 75 cm (29½ in)

Diet: Mainly small mammals

There are up to **50 species of toucans**, and more than **200 species of woodpeckers**.

Compared to its size, the **toco toucan** has the **biggest bill** of any bird.

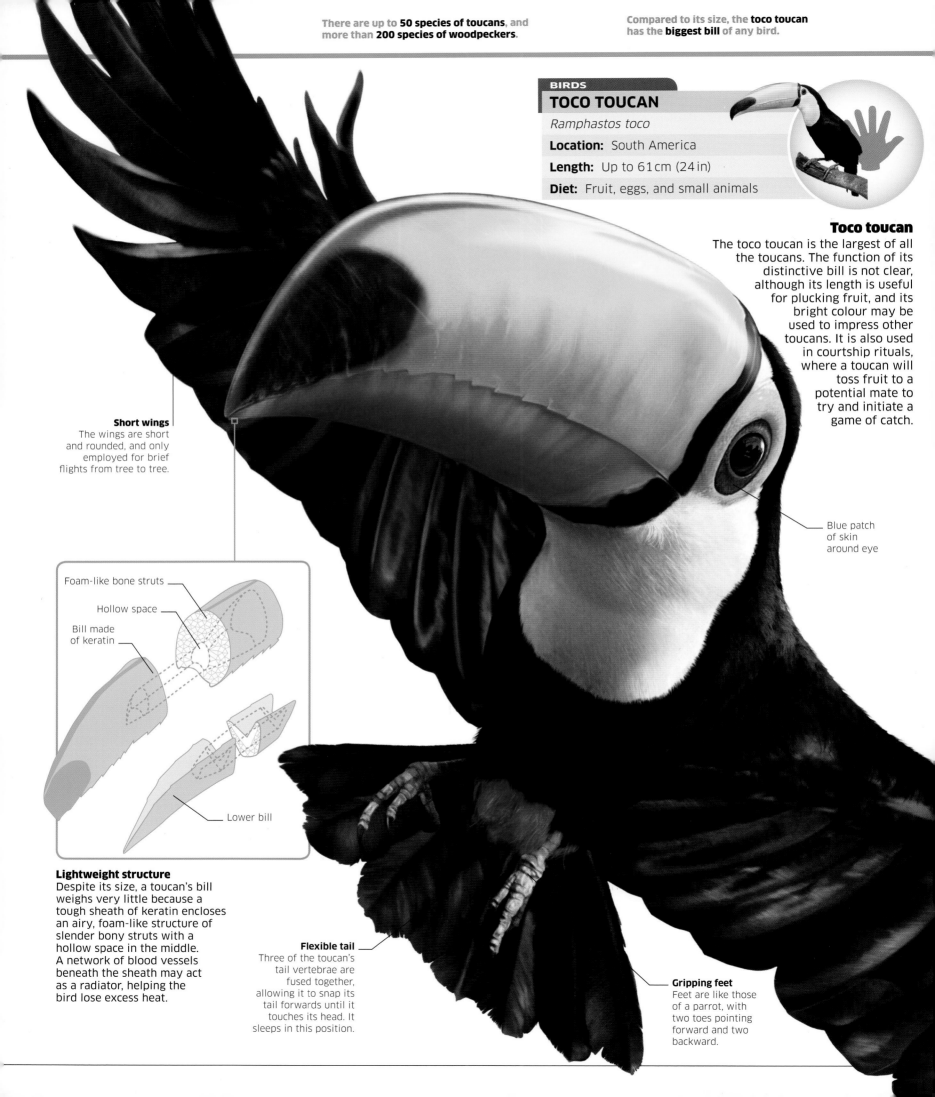

BIRDS

TOCO TOUCAN

Ramphastos toco

Location: South America

Length: Up to 61 cm (24 in)

Diet: Fruit, eggs, and small animals

Toco toucan

The toco toucan is the largest of all the toucans. The function of its distinctive bill is not clear, although its length is useful for plucking fruit, and its bright colour may be used to impress other toucans. It is also used in courtship rituals, where a toucan will toss fruit to a potential mate to try and initiate a game of catch.

Short wings
The wings are short and rounded, and only employed for brief flights from tree to tree.

Blue patch of skin around eye

Foam-like bone struts

Hollow space

Bill made of keratin

Lower bill

Lightweight structure
Despite its size, a toucan's bill weighs very little because a tough sheath of keratin encloses an airy, foam-like structure of slender bony struts with a hollow space in the middle. A network of blood vessels beneath the sheath may act as a radiator, helping the bird lose excess heat.

Flexible tail
Three of the toucan's tail vertebrae are fused together, allowing it to snap its tail forwards until it touches its head. It sleeps in this position.

Gripping feet
Feet are like those of a parrot, with two toes pointing forward and two backward.

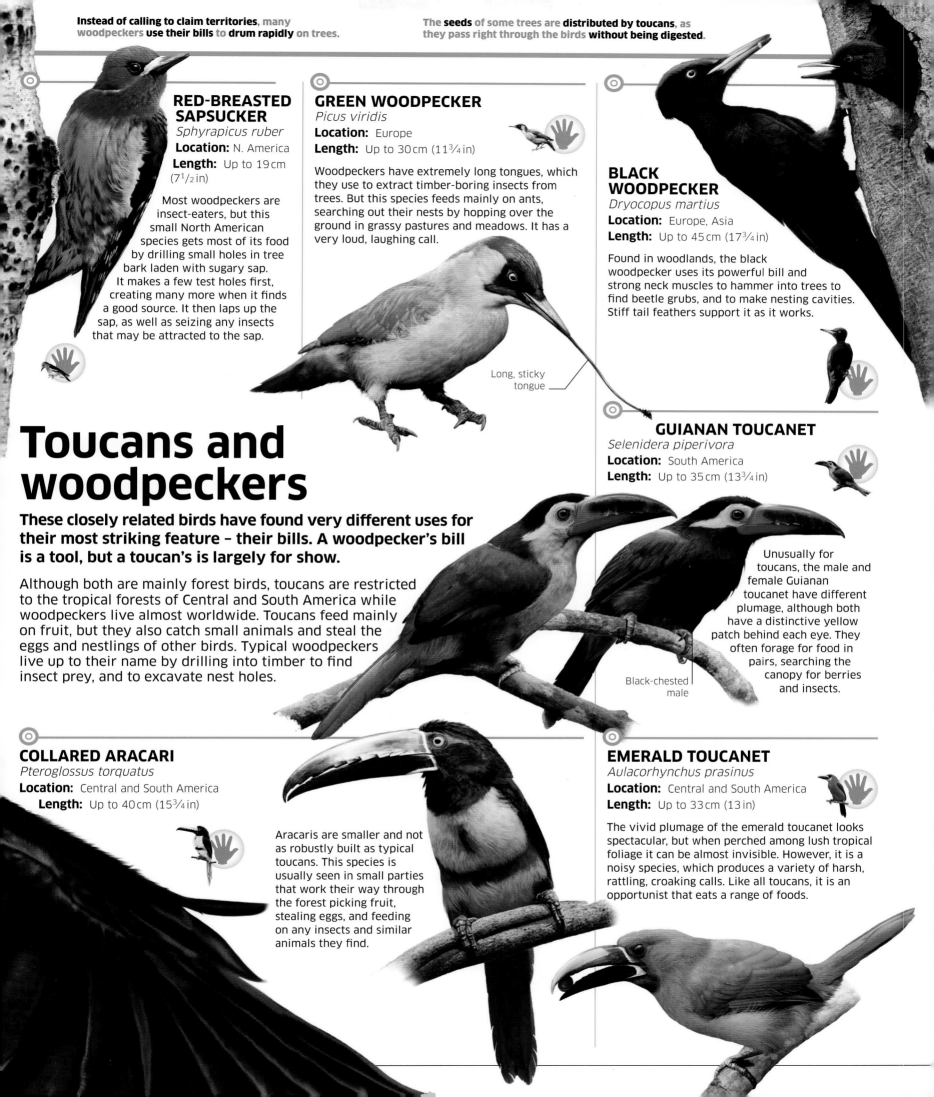

Instead of calling to claim territories, many woodpeckers use their bills to drum rapidly on trees.

The seeds of some trees are distributed by toucans, as they pass right through the birds without being digested.

RED-BREASTED SAPSUCKER
Sphyrapicus ruber
Location: N. America
Length: Up to 19 cm (7½ in)

Most woodpeckers are insect-eaters, but this small North American species gets most of its food by drilling small holes in tree bark laden with sugary sap. It makes a few test holes first, creating many more when it finds a good source. It then laps up the sap, as well as seizing any insects that may be attracted to the sap.

GREEN WOODPECKER
Picus viridis
Location: Europe
Length: Up to 30 cm (11¾ in)

Woodpeckers have extremely long tongues, which they use to extract timber-boring insects from trees. But this species feeds mainly on ants, searching out their nests by hopping over the ground in grassy pastures and meadows. It has a very loud, laughing call.

Long, sticky tongue

BLACK WOODPECKER
Dryocopus martius
Location: Europe, Asia
Length: Up to 45 cm (17¾ in)

Found in woodlands, the black woodpecker uses its powerful bill and strong neck muscles to hammer into trees to find beetle grubs, and to make nesting cavities. Stiff tail feathers support it as it works.

Toucans and woodpeckers

These closely related birds have found very different uses for their most striking feature – their bills. A woodpecker's bill is a tool, but a toucan's is largely for show.

Although both are mainly forest birds, toucans are restricted to the tropical forests of Central and South America while woodpeckers live almost worldwide. Toucans feed mainly on fruit, but they also catch small animals and steal the eggs and nestlings of other birds. Typical woodpeckers live up to their name by drilling into timber to find insect prey, and to excavate nest holes.

GUIANAN TOUCANET
Selenidera piperivora
Location: South America
Length: Up to 35 cm (13¾ in)

Unusually for toucans, the male and female Guianan toucanet have different plumage, although both have a distinctive yellow patch behind each eye. They often forage for food in pairs, searching the canopy for berries and insects.

Black-chested male

COLLARED ARACARI
Pteroglossus torquatus
Location: Central and South America
Length: Up to 40 cm (15¾ in)

Aracaris are smaller and not as robustly built as typical toucans. This species is usually seen in small parties that work their way through the forest picking fruit, stealing eggs, and feeding on any insects and similar animals they find.

EMERALD TOUCANET
Aulacorhynchus prasinus
Location: Central and South America
Length: Up to 33 cm (13 in)

The vivid plumage of the emerald toucanet looks spectacular, but when perched among lush tropical foliage it can be almost invisible. However, it is a noisy species, which produces a variety of harsh, rattling, croaking calls. Like all toucans, it is an opportunist that eats a range of foods.

Eurasian starling

One of the most widespread and adaptable of the perching birds, this noisy, very sociable starling has spread far beyond its native Eurasian range, partly through human introductions.

Some birds are specialized for a particular way of life, but the Eurasian starling is an adaptable opportunist that can use its sharp, strong bill to find food almost anywhere. It feeds mainly on open ground, foraging in groups that probe the earth for small animals, but it may also catch airborne insects in flight. In winter it gathers in vast flocks to roost for the night in trees, or on buildings.

BIRDS

EURASIAN STARLING

Sturnus vulgaris

Location: Europe, western Asia, introduced elsewhere

Length: Up to 22 cm (8¾ in)

Diet: Insects, worms, seeds, berries

Short tail
A short, square tail helps the starling manoeuvre in the air.

Changing plumage
In winter, a starling's dark plumage is peppered with buff spots. These are the pale tips of its feathers, which wear off by spring to reveal a breeding plumage of glossy black with an iridescent green and purple sheen. The birds then moult after the breeding season and return to their winter plumage.

Strong legs
A starling walks on its very sturdy legs, rather than hopping like many perching birds.

Seasonal plumage
The starling's feathers have flecked tips during winter.

An estimated 150 million Eurasian starlings live in North America, all descended from just 60 birds released in New York in 1890.

1.5 million – the **number of starlings** **a winter roost** may contain.

Starlings can sometimes **imitate artificial sounds** such as those of **ringing telephones, lawnmowers, and doorbells**.

113

Triangular wings
The starling's wings are sharply triangular, giving it an arrow shape in flight.

Dark brown wing feathers

Hole nesters
Starlings nest in any holes they can find – in trees, rocky crevices, or in the roofs of buildings. Each pair line their nest hole with dry grass, moss, feathers, and other soft materials to form a cushion for a clutch of pale blue eggs. Both parents incubate the eggs and feed the young when they hatch.

Probing the ground
When a starling is searching for food on soft ground, it uses an unusual foraging technique. As it walks forwards, it thrusts its strong, sharp bill into the ground and then opens it to enlarge the hole. It does this time after time until it locates an insect grub or worm that it can pull out and swallow.

Noisy song
Many perching birds have musical songs, but the starling is not one of them. Its song is a throaty medley of whistles, gurgles, clicks, and creaking noises, which often includes mimicry of other bird calls. Each bird has its own repertoire, and they can even be trained to mimic human sounds.

Winter beak
In winter, both the male and female birds have a dark bill. In summer it becomes yellow.

Sky dance
As the summer breeding season ends, starlings abandon their nests and start spending the night in mass communal roosts. Before settling down for the night these flocks perform spectacular manoeuvres known as murmurations, which involve thousands of birds swooping through the sky in coordinated waves that resemble clouds of black smoke.

TEST PROBE

SUCCESS!

VERMILION FLYCATCHER
Pyrocephalus rubinus

Location: North, Central, and South America

Length: Up to 15 cm (6 in)

Flycatchers feed by flying up from a perch and snatching insects out of the air. The male of this species has a vivid red body and black wings; females are grey and white, for camouflage when incubating eggs.

SUPERB LYREBIRD
Menura novaehollandiae

Location: Southeastern Australia

Length: Up to 96 cm (37¾ in)

Lyrebirds spend their days on the forest floor and roost in trees at night. Males have spectacular tail plumes, which they use in elaborate courtship displays, designed to attract as many females as possible.

Typical passerine toes

BARN SWALLOW
Hirundo rustica

Location: Worldwide except Antarctica

Length: Up to 18 cm (7 in)

Like many passerines, this bird is an excellent flier – a graceful, aerial hunter that catches insects in flight and makes long migrations to and from the tropics each year. It often nests in buildings so, unlike many bird species, it has benefitted from the worldwide growth of the human population.

Forked tail
The outer tail feathers, called tail streamers, are longer in males.

Long, curved, pointed wings

NIGHTINGALE
Luscinia megarhynchos

Location: Europe, western Asia, Africa

Length: Up to 16.5 cm (6½ in)

Many passerines are described as songbirds, with males that sing to claim territory and attract females. The song of the male nightingale is one of the most tuneful and inventive of all. The bird's brown plumage hides it from hungry predators.

SUPERB FAIRY-WREN
Malurus cyaneus

Location: Southeastern Australia

Length: Up to 14 cm (5½ in)

Most perching birds raise their young in pairs, but this species has devised a way of spreading the workload – the vividly coloured breeding male and his mate recruit their relatives to help. These are usually younger, less colourful males, which help gather food for the young.

EURASIAN NUTHATCH
Sitta europea

Location: Europe, Asia

Length: Up to 14 cm (5½ in)

The perching birds' specialized, gripping feet allow many of them to be highly acrobatic when foraging for food. The Eurasian nuthatch is one of the most agile; it can run head-first up and down tree trunks, and even search tree bark for insects while hanging upside down.

Nutcracker
The long bill is often used to break open nut shells.

Perching birds

More than half of the world's bird species are passerines, or perching birds. They share an ability to perch on the most slender twigs, and include all the most musical songbirds.

These birds all have the same foot structure, with three toes pointing forwards and one toe pointing back. This allows them to grip twigs and branches securely. Apart from their feet, they are very diverse, ranging from delicate nectar-feeders to powerful scavengers.

SOUTHERN DOUBLE-COLLARED SUNBIRD
Cinnyris chalybeus
Location: Southern Africa
Length: Up to 12 cm (4¾ in)

Sunbirds are the African equivalents of hummingbirds – nectar-feeders with males that have dazzling, iridescent plumage. The long bill of this species gives easy access to flowers.

RED-BACKED SHRIKE
Lanius collurio
Location: Europe, western Asia, Africa
Length: Up to 18 cm (7 in)

Shrikes are hunters that behave like hawks, seizing lizards, mice, and large insects and tearing them apart with their hooked bills. The red-backed shrike has a habit of impaling its prey on thorns, for eating later.

Impaled prey

RAVEN
Corvus corax
Location: North America, Europe, Asia
Length: Up to 69 cm (27¼ in)

The raven is the biggest of the crows, and the most powerful perching bird. It eats a wide variety of foods, from seeds to meat scavenged from the carcasses of animals. Like most crows, it is very intelligent, possessing excellent problem-solving skills.

BAYA WEAVER
Ploceus philippinus
Location: India to Southeast Asia
Length: Up to 15 cm (6 in)

Many perching birds lay their eggs in carefully made nests. The bottle-shaped nest of the baya weaver is one of the most elaborate, woven by the male from grass blades and strips of palm leaf. Many pairs of birds may nest together, with up to 30 nests hanging from branches of the same tree.

RED CROSSBILL
Loxia curvirostra
Location: North America, Europe, Asia
Length: Up to 16.5 cm (6½ in)

The bills of passerines are adapted for feeding on a variety of different foods. Among the most specialized are the crossed mandibles of the crossbills, used for prizing open pine cones and extracting the seeds. Males of this species are red, but females are green.

SNOW BUNTING
Plectrophenax nivalis
Location: North America, Europe, Asia
Length: Up to 16.5 cm (6½ in)

Although many perching birds are small, they are surprisingly tough. The sparrow-sized snow bunting, for example, breeds further north than any other land bird, even nesting on the northern tip of Greenland. Its mainly black and white plumage provides good camouflage on the icy Arctic tundra.

MAMMALS

Furry mammals are the most familiar animals to us because we are also mammals, with most of the same features and needs. Mammals include an amazing diversity of creatures with very different lifestyles, ranging from delicate bats to giant whales, adapted to thrive in every habitat on Earth.

WHAT IS A MAMMAL?

Mammals first appeared about 220 million years ago, at about the same time as the first big dinosaurs. These early mammals were very small, but when the giant dinosaurs were wiped out at the end of the Mesozoic Era, 66 million years ago, mammals started evolving into bigger forms that took their place. Mammals' warm-blooded, furry bodies have enabled them to live almost anywhere and spread all over the world, from tropical forests to icy polar oceans.

Bony skeleton
The elephant's huge body is supported by very strong bones.

Unborn young
This female elephant has a baby developing in her womb.

Long legs
The elephant is supported by legs beneath its body.

Broad feet

TYPES OF MAMMAL

Mammals occur in various shapes and sizes, with bodies specialized for life in many habitats. Despite this they all share the same basic biology apart from a fundamental difference in the way they reproduce.

Monotremes
Many of the earliest mammals laid eggs, and a few still do. Known as monotremes, they include the platypus and four species of spiny echidnas, which all live in Australia and nearby New Guinea. The babies that hatch from the eggs feed on their mothers' milk, just like other mammals.

PLATYPUS

Marsupials
A female marsupial, such as a kangaroo, gives birth to very small, barely formed young that crawl into a pouch on her belly. There the young drink milk enriched with all the nutrients they need to develop into fully-formed babies. Most marsupials live in Australia, New Guinea, and South America.

RED KANGAROO

Placentals
The vast majority of mammals give birth to well-formed young that have developed for a long time inside the mother's body. The unborn young are nourished by fluids passing through an umbilical cord attached to the mother by an organ called the placenta, so they are known as placental mammals.

Mother's milk
All baby mammals are fed on milk.

BACTRIAN CAMEL

KEY FEATURES

Whether they are monotremes, marsupials, or placentals, all mammals share a number of key features. They are warm-blooded vertebrates, which feed their infant young on milk until their digestive systems can cope with solid food. Most mammals have hair, although some have spines or even scales. Finally, all mammals except monotremes give birth to live young.

Vertebrates
All mammals have internal skeletons made of bone.

Warm-blooded
A mammal turns food energy into heat to keep warm.

Most bear live young
They give birth to young instead of laying eggs.

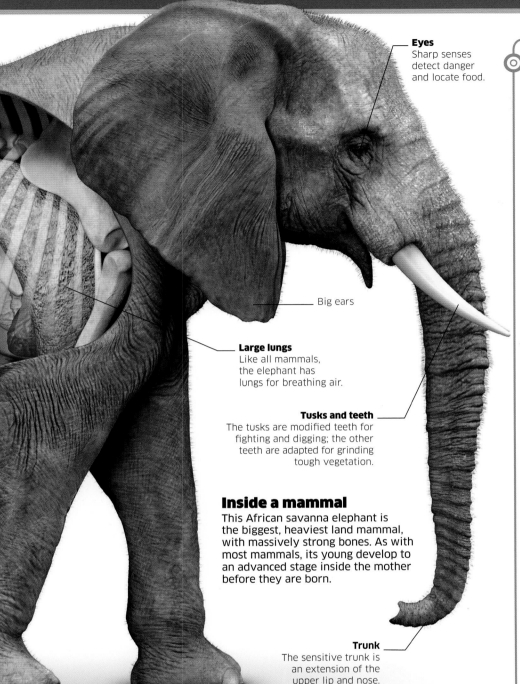

Eyes
Sharp senses detect danger and locate food.

Big ears

Large lungs
Like all mammals, the elephant has lungs for breathing air.

Tusks and teeth
The tusks are modified teeth for fighting and digging; the other teeth are adapted for grinding tough vegetation.

Inside a mammal
This African savanna elephant is the biggest, heaviest land mammal, with massively strong bones. As with most mammals, its young develop to an advanced stage inside the mother before they are born.

Trunk
The sensitive trunk is an extension of the upper lip and nose.

WARM AND SAFE
Most of the energy that a mammal gets from its food is used to generate body heat. This allows mammals to live in cold climates, but also means they need to eat a lot. Good insulation reduces heat loss and saves energy, which is why many mammals have coats of dense, warm fur. The tough keratin that forms hair and fur may also form defensive spines or scales.

Blubber
Nothing saps body heat faster than cold water, so marine mammals need a lot of insulation. Dolphins have thick layers of insulating fat, known as blubber, beneath their skin.

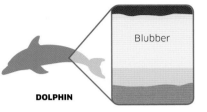

Blubber

DOLPHIN

Fur
A bear has an outer coat of long, tough guard hair that protects an inner coat of dense, woolly underfur. The guard hair sheds water, keeping the underfur dry so it retains an insulating layer of air.

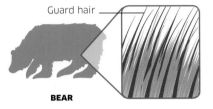

Guard hair

BEAR

Spines
The spines of a porcupine are modified hair, made of the same material but much thicker, stiffer, and very sharp, to protect the animal from its enemies. Hedgehogs and echidnas have the same adaptation.

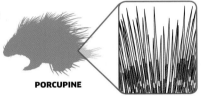

PORCUPINE

Scales
A pangolin's overlapping scales are modified hairs, made of keratin and fused together. An armadillo also has scaly armour, but it is reinforced by large bony plates.

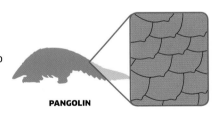

PANGOLIN

TO MAKE ENOUGH
ENERGY TO KEEP WARM, **SOME SMALL MAMMALS** MUST EAT MORE THAN **TWICE THEIR WEIGHT** IN FOOD EVERY DAY.

Young fed on milk
The milk contains nutrients vital to young mammals.

Most have hair or fur
Hair or fur traps air to help retain vital body heat.

MOTHER'S MILK
All young mammals feed on milk during their early lives. The nutrient-rich liquid is produced in the mother's body and secreted through mammary glands. This timber wolf is nursing a litter of several cubs, but many mammals give birth to just one or two infants at a time. A baby orangutan, for example, stays with its mother for up to eight years, and is nourished by her milk for its first two to three years of life.

Monotremes

The monotremes are an extraordinary group of mammals that lay eggs like those of reptiles, instead of giving birth to live young. There are just five living species, all found in Australia and New Guinea.

Monotremes were once more widespread, at least in the southern continents – in 1991 fossil remains were found in South America. But the only surviving monotremes are the spiny echidnas and the platypus. With its rubbery bill and broad tail, the platypus looks very different from the echidnas, and they probably started evolving in different ways more than 20 million years ago.

Sensitive surface
The rubbery, pliable bill is dotted with electroreceptors. These detect the faint electrical nerve activity of animals such as worms and insect larvae hidden in the mud at the bottom of streams. The bill is also highly sensitive to touch.

Small eyes
The eyes are in a groove that is closed when the platypus dives underwater.

Duck-like bill
A platypus's bill is shaped like that of a duck, but it is covered with smooth skin.

Nostrils
The nostrils are located on top of the bill. They close up when the animal is underwater.

Cheek pouch
Any food caught on a dive is stored in the platypus's cheeks until it returns to the surface.

Short legs
The legs extend sideways from the body, more like those of a reptile than a mammal.

Egg-laying mammals

Whereas a platypus usually lays two small, leathery eggs, and incubates them in a nesting burrow, an echidna lays a single egg (shown below). The female echidna retains the egg in a pouch on her body for 10 days until it hatches.

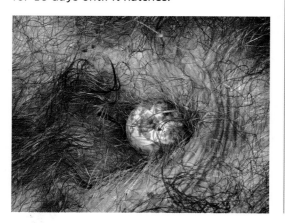

Tiny young

When the tiny young of monotremes hatch they have no fur or spines, and are nourished by their mothers' milk. A young echidna stays in its mother's pouch until its spines begin to grow and then it is placed in a nursery burrow.

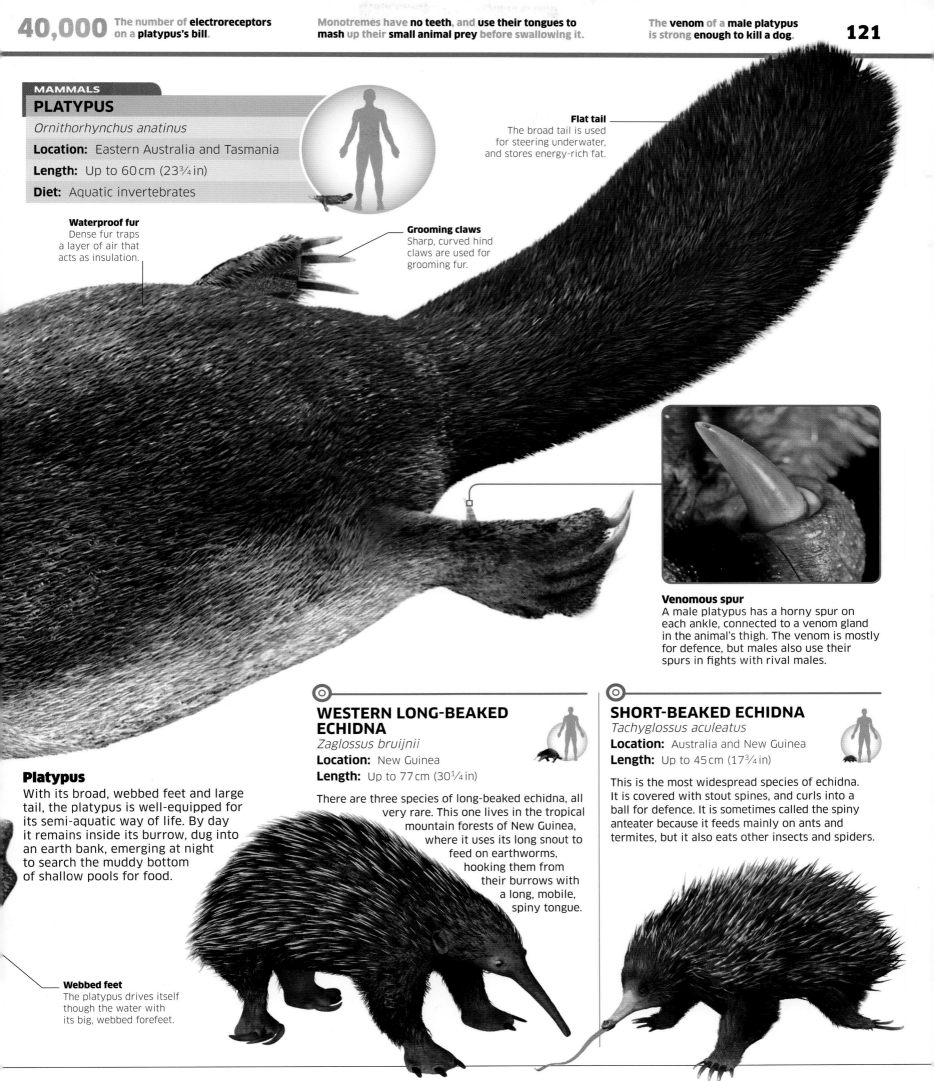

40,000 The number of **electroreceptors** on a **platypus's bill**.

Monotremes have **no teeth**, and **use their tongues to mash** up their **small animal prey** before swallowing it.

The **venom** of a **male platypus** is strong **enough to kill a dog**.

121

MAMMALS
PLATYPUS

Ornithorhynchus anatinus

Location: Eastern Australia and Tasmania

Length: Up to 60 cm (23¾ in)

Diet: Aquatic invertebrates

Flat tail
The broad tail is used for steering underwater, and stores energy-rich fat.

Waterproof fur
Dense fur traps a layer of air that acts as insulation.

Grooming claws
Sharp, curved hind claws are used for grooming fur.

Venomous spur
A male platypus has a horny spur on each ankle, connected to a venom gland in the animal's thigh. The venom is mostly for defence, but males also use their spurs in fights with rival males.

Platypus
With its broad, webbed feet and large tail, the platypus is well-equipped for its semi-aquatic way of life. By day it remains inside its burrow, dug into an earth bank, emerging at night to search the muddy bottom of shallow pools for food.

Webbed feet
The platypus drives itself though the water with its big, webbed forefeet.

WESTERN LONG-BEAKED ECHIDNA
Zaglossus bruijnii

Location: New Guinea

Length: Up to 77 cm (30¼ in)

There are three species of long-beaked echidna, all very rare. This one lives in the tropical mountain forests of New Guinea, where it uses its long snout to feed on earthworms, hooking them from their burrows with a long, mobile, spiny tongue.

SHORT-BEAKED ECHIDNA
Tachyglossus aculeatus

Location: Australia and New Guinea

Length: Up to 45 cm (17¾ in)

This is the most widespread species of echidna. It is covered with stout spines, and curls into a ball for defence. It is sometimes called the spiny anteater because it feeds mainly on ants and termites, but it also eats other insects and spiders.

Red kangaroo

The biggest Australian mammal, and the largest of all marsupials, the red kangaroo is a spectacularly agile creature adapted for life on dry grassland. Its powerful hind legs enable it to bound across the open landscape at speed with minimal effort.

Kangaroos have evolved one of the most efficient ways of moving at speed. Instead of running, they hop, and every time a kangaroo lands, its long hind feet flex at the ankle and stretch the strong elastic tendon at the back of each leg. The tendon then recoils, hurling the animal back into the air. It works so well that a red kangaroo can cover up to 9 m (29¹/₂ft) in a single bound, easily outdistancing any enemy.

Boxing males
Mature males are not territorial, but they do fight over females. These fights usually take the form of ritual boxing matches, as each male jabs at his rival with strong arms, trying to knock him over. If this does not work they may wrestle, or kick with both legs while supporting their weight with their tails.

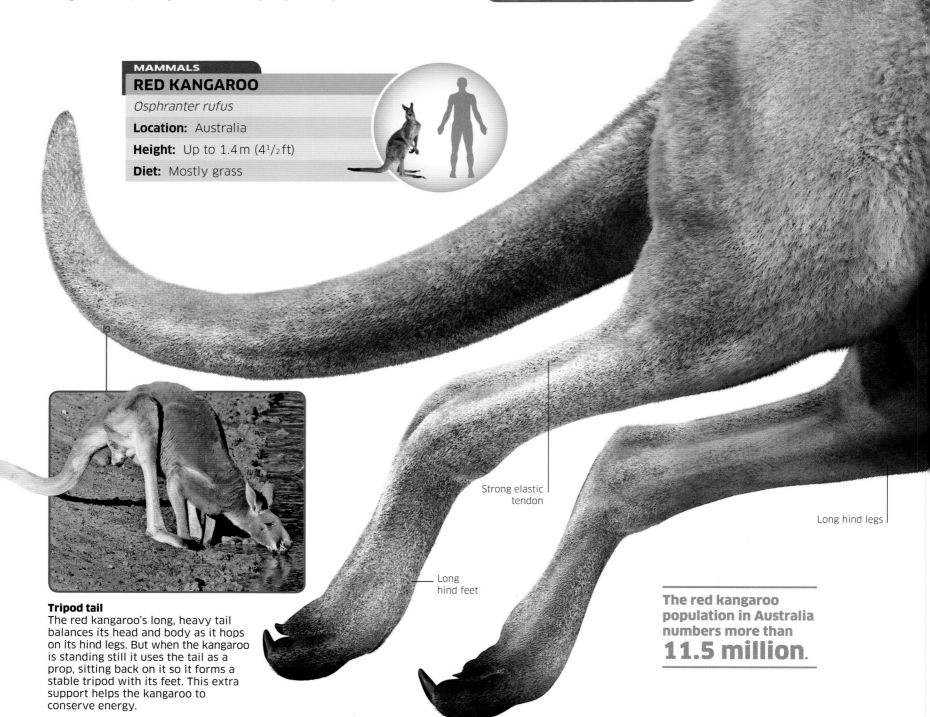

MAMMALS	
RED KANGAROO	
Osphranter rufus	
Location: Australia	
Height: Up to 1.4 m (4¹/₂ft)	
Diet: Mostly grass	

Strong elastic tendon

Long hind legs

Long hind feet

Tripod tail
The red kangaroo's long, heavy tail balances its head and body as it hops on its hind legs. But when the kangaroo is standing still it uses the tail as a prop, sitting back on it so it forms a stable tripod with its feet. This extra support helps the kangaroo to conserve energy.

The red kangaroo population in Australia numbers more than **11.5 million.**

50 km/h (31 mph) – the **speed** a red kangaroo can reach, **bounding across open country**.

If it gets too hot, a red kangaroo licks its arms to cool itself.

123

Red male
A male has short, reddish-brown fur on his back, and paler fur on his belly.

Mobile ears
The large, sensitive ears can swivel to pick up sounds.

Cheek teeth
As the kangaroo's cheek teeth are worn down, they are replaced by unworn teeth which slide forwards in its jaws.

Broad chest
A male has broad shoulders and a muscular chest for fighting with rivals.

Short forelimbs
The forelimbs end in dextrous paws that are used for grooming, self-defence, and feeding.

Clawed paws

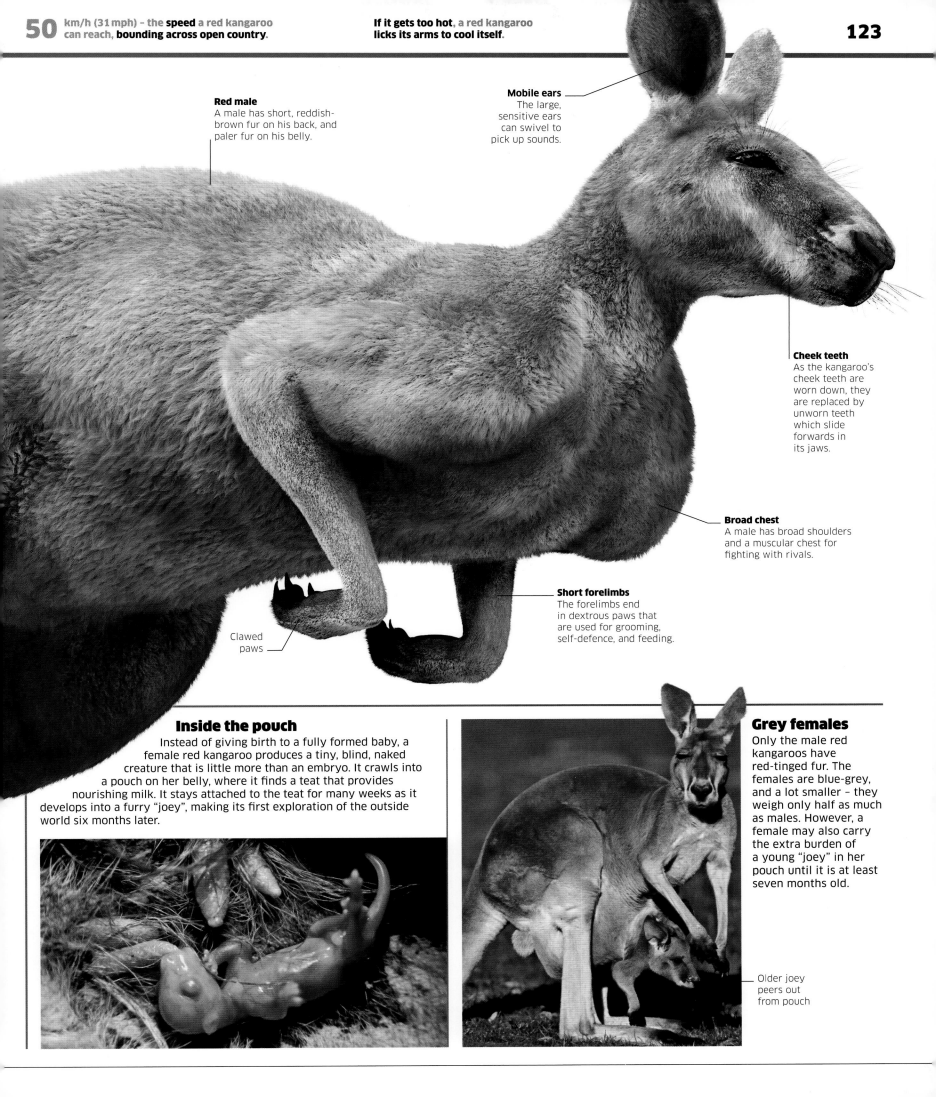

Inside the pouch

Instead of giving birth to a fully formed baby, a female red kangaroo produces a tiny, blind, naked creature that is little more than an embryo. It crawls into a pouch on her belly, where it finds a teat that provides nourishing milk. It stays attached to the teat for many weeks as it develops into a furry "joey", making its first exploration of the outside world six months later.

Grey females

Only the male red kangaroos have red-tinged fur. The females are blue-grey, and a lot smaller – they weigh only half as much as males. However, a female may also carry the extra burden of a young "joey" in her pouch until it is at least seven months old.

Older joey peers out from pouch

VIRGINIA OPOSSUM
Didelphis virginiana

Location: North and
Central America
Length: Up to 50 cm
(19¾ in)

A highly adaptable opportunist eater that can
thrive on a diet of scraps scavenged from bins, the
Virginia opossum is common
in many US cities. It is well
known for its defence
tactic of playing dead,
lying with its
mouth
open and
its tongue
hanging out.

SOUTHERN MARSUPIAL MOLE
Notoryctes typhlops

Location: Australian deserts
Length: Up to 14 cm (5½ in)

This burrower has enormous claws on its front feet
for digging, a cylindrical body with short fur, and a
horny protective shield on its nose. It is quite blind,
relying on scent to locate the insect larvae and
earthworms that it eats.

NUMBAT
Myrmecobius fasciatus

Location: Southwestern
and southern Australia
Length: Up to 29 cm (11½ in)

The stripy numbat is a specialist termite eater,
finding the insects mainly by scent and scooping
them up with its long, sticky tongue. Once
widespread, it is now endangered and
restricted to a few protected areas.

TASMANIAN DEVIL
Sarcophilus harrisii

Location: Tasmania
Length: Up to 65 cm (25½ in)

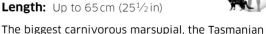

The biggest carnivorous marsupial, the Tasmanian
devil is a hunter and scavenger with massively
powerful jaws for killing prey and
crushing bones. It hunts alone, and
can take prey up to the size of
a small kangaroo.

YELLOW-FOOTED ANTECHINUS
Antechinus flavipes

Location: Eastern and
southwestern Australia
Length: Up to 13 cm (5 in)

With a diet of insects, spiders, worms,
and similar animals, this small marsupial
is remarkable for the way the male has
just one breeding season throughout his
whole life. He has multiple partners but
uses up so many of his body's resources
that he soon dies.

GREATER BILBY
Macrotis lagotis

Location: Australian deserts
Length: Up to 55 cm (21¾ in)

With its long ears
and burrowing
habit, the greater
bilby is like a rabbit,
but has a much broader
diet and is adapted for survival
in the desert. Active only at
night, it gets all the moisture
its body needs from its
food, and never has
to drink.

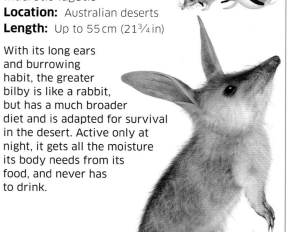

KOALA
Phascolarctos cinereus

Location: Eastern Australia
Length: Up to 82 cm (32¼ in)

One of the most familiar
marsupials, the koala feeds
exclusively on the leaves of
certain eucalyptus trees – a
very poor diet that is hard
to digest and has little food
value. Koalas cope with this
by using very little energy,
spending most of their
lives asleep.

Tree climber
Strong, sharp claws
give a secure
grip on tree bark.

COMMON WOMBAT
Vombatus ursinus

Location: Eastern Australia, Tasmania

Length: Up to 1.15 m (3¾ ft)

A ground-dwelling relative of the koala, with a similar sturdy, bear-like build, the wombat eats grass and can sometimes be seen grazing in fields alongside sheep. It has long claws that it uses to dig an extensive tunnel system. It usually spends the day underground, emerging at night to feed.

COMMON BRUSHTAIL POSSUM
Trichosurus vulpecula

Location: Australia, New Zealand

Length: Up to 55 cm (21½ in)

One of the most widespread Australian marsupials, this nocturnal climber has adapted well to life in cities. Although mainly a leaf-eater, it also preys on small animals and eats kitchen scraps.

SUGAR GLIDER
Petaurus breviceps

Location: Australia, New Guinea

Length: Up to 21 cm (8¼ in)

As its name suggests, this small nocturnal marsupial can glide from tree to tree on a furry membrane of skin stretched between its limbs. The "sugar" part of its name refers to its taste for sugary tree sap and flower nectar, but during the summer it feeds mainly on insects.

Big eyes for night vision

In flight
Stretching from toe to toe, the flight membrane acts as a wing or parachute.

Marsupials

All marsupials give birth to young that are at an early stage of development, and continue to grow inside a protective pouch or under a flap of skin where they feed on their mother's milk.

Most marsupials live in Australia, where they have been isolated from other land mammals for at least 50 million years. They have a wide variety of lifestyles ranging from sleepy leaf-eaters to fierce carnivores. Other marsupials – the opossums – live in North and South America, where most species are omnivores that will eat almost anything. These American marsupials are flourishing, but many Australian species are now rare.

HONEY POSSUM
Tarsipes rostratus

Location: Southwestern Australia

Length: Up to 9 cm (3½ in)

The tiny honey possum feeds almost exclusively on flower nectar and pollen, gathering them with a very long tongue that has a brush-like tip. This means that it can live only in places where flowers open all year round.

GOODFELLOW'S TREE-KANGAROO
Dendrolagus goodfellowi

Location: New Guinea

Length: Up to 84 cm (33 in)

This is one of 10 kangaroo species that are adapted for life in trees. It has shorter back legs than a typical kangaroo, and strong front legs with hooked claws for gripping branches. It feeds at night on leaves and fruit.

A giant anteater's **tongue** is up to **60 cm (2 ft) long**.

GIANT ANTEATER

Myrmecophaga tridactyla

Location: Central and South America

Length: Up to 1.2 m (4 ft)

Diet: Ants, termites

Giant anteater

Highly specialized for its insect-eating way of life, the giant anteater is one of the most distinctive of all mammals. Its huge front claws, elongated snout, and extra-long tongue enable it to rip into the nests of its ant and termite prey, and devour them by the thousand.

Widespread across tropical America, the anteater is a relative of the tree-living sloths, which feed exclusively on leaves. But the anteater is an insectivore, adapted for gathering large numbers of small prey. It occasionally raids the nests of wild bees, but usually targets ants' nests and termite mounds. Unlike other American anteaters, this species hunts and sleeps on the ground, relying on camouflage and powerful claws for defence against predators.

Striped fur
Long, coarse fur has a distinctive pattern that may act as camouflage.

Small eyes

Powerful front legs

Massive claws
Each front foot has huge hook-like claws on the two central toes.

Knuckle walk
A giant anteater keeps its claws sharp by walking on its knuckles with its claws folded into the palms.

Bulk-feeder
A hunting anteater breaks into an ants' nest with its claws, inserts its long snout, and starts feeding. It can flick its long tongue in and out at an astonishing rate – nearly three times a second – and each time the tongue's sticky surface traps numerous ants and drags them into the anteater's mouth.

30,000 The number of **insects** a giant anteater may **devour in one day**.

The giant anteater's **sense of smell** is **40 times more sensitive** than a human's.

127

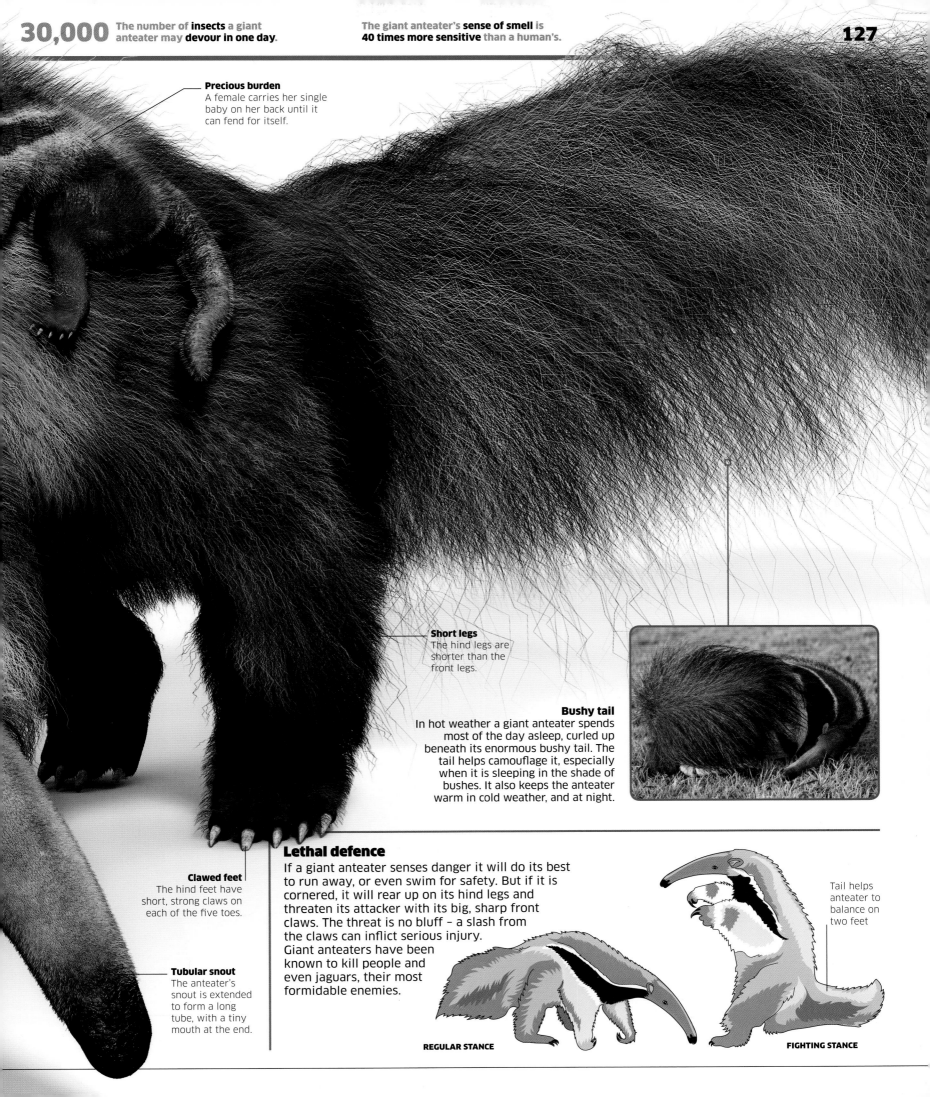

Precious burden
A female carries her single baby on her back until it can fend for itself.

Short legs
The hind legs are shorter than the front legs.

Bushy tail
In hot weather a giant anteater spends most of the day asleep, curled up beneath its enormous bushy tail. The tail helps camouflage it, especially when it is sleeping in the shade of bushes. It also keeps the anteater warm in cold weather, and at night.

Clawed feet
The hind feet have short, strong claws on each of the five toes.

Tubular snout
The anteater's snout is extended to form a long tube, with a tiny mouth at the end.

Lethal defence

If a giant anteater senses danger it will do its best to run away, or even swim for safety. But if it is cornered, it will rear up on its hind legs and threaten its attacker with its big, sharp front claws. The threat is no bluff – a slash from the claws can inflict serious injury. Giant anteaters have been known to kill people and even jaguars, their most formidable enemies.

Tail helps anteater to balance on two feet

REGULAR STANCE

FIGHTING STANCE

100 kg (220 lb) – the **weight** of a **newborn African elephant calf** – as much as a **heavyweight boxer**.

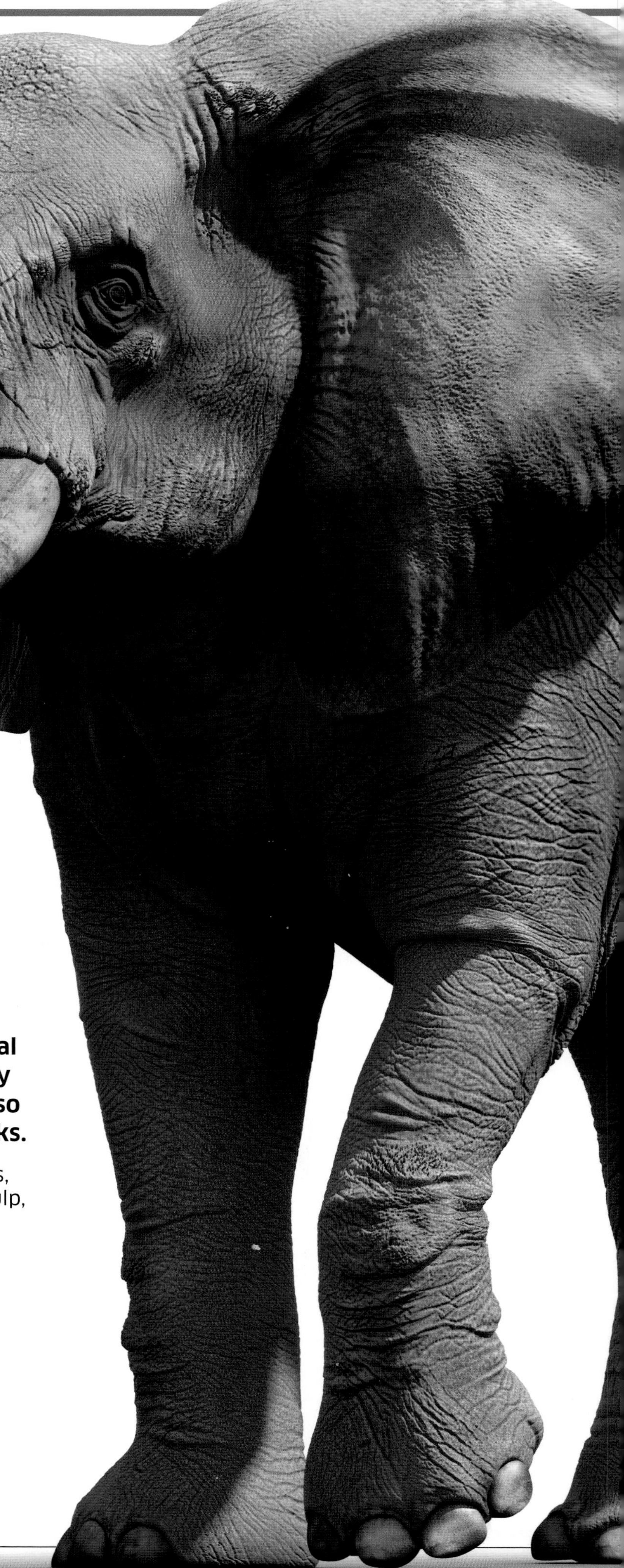

Mobile tip
An African elephant's trunk has two mobile "fingers" at the tip for grasping food.

Air head
The huge skull has a honeycomb-like structure, with many air pockets, to make it lighter.

Curved tusks
The tusks are hugely extended teeth that grow throughout life.

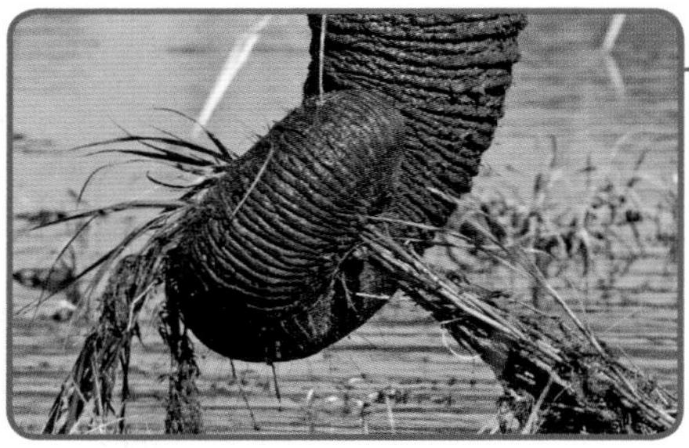

Multi-purpose tool
The elephant's trunk is formed from its nose and upper lip. Highly mobile and strong, yet very sensitive, the trunk makes an ideal tool for investigating and gathering food, drawing in water, signalling to other elephants, and generating loud, trumpeting calls.

Elephants

Instantly recognizable by their long, mobile trunks and colossal size, elephants are the biggest and heaviest land animals. They are renowned for their intelligence and long memories, but also seriously endangered by hunting for their meat and ivory tusks.

Elephants are adapted for eating large quantities of coarse grass, leaves, and bark. They have massive teeth for grinding their tough food to a pulp, and extensive digestive systems for processing it. They spend at least three-quarters of their time feeding or looking for food, travelling in closely bonded social groups led by mature females.

MAMMALS

AFRICAN SAVANNA ELEPHANT

Loxodonta africana

Location: Sub-Saharan Africa

Length: Up to 7.5 m (24½ ft)

Diet: Grass, leaves, bark

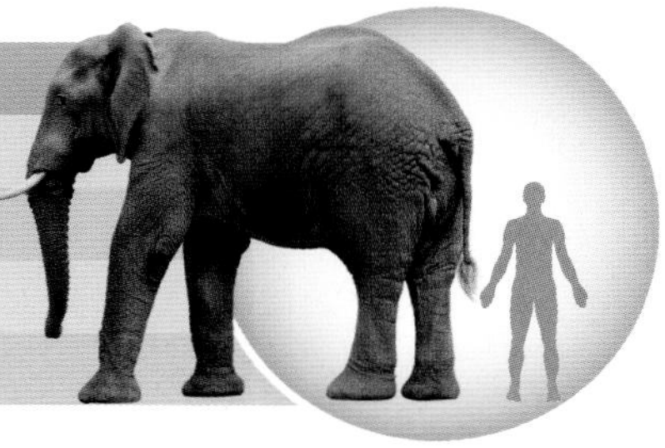

16 hours – the time an elephant spends **eating** every day, consuming up to **250 kg (550 lb) of vegetation**.

An **elephant's trunk** contains **no bones**.

An African elephant **drinks** up to **200 litres (44 gallons) of water** every day.

129

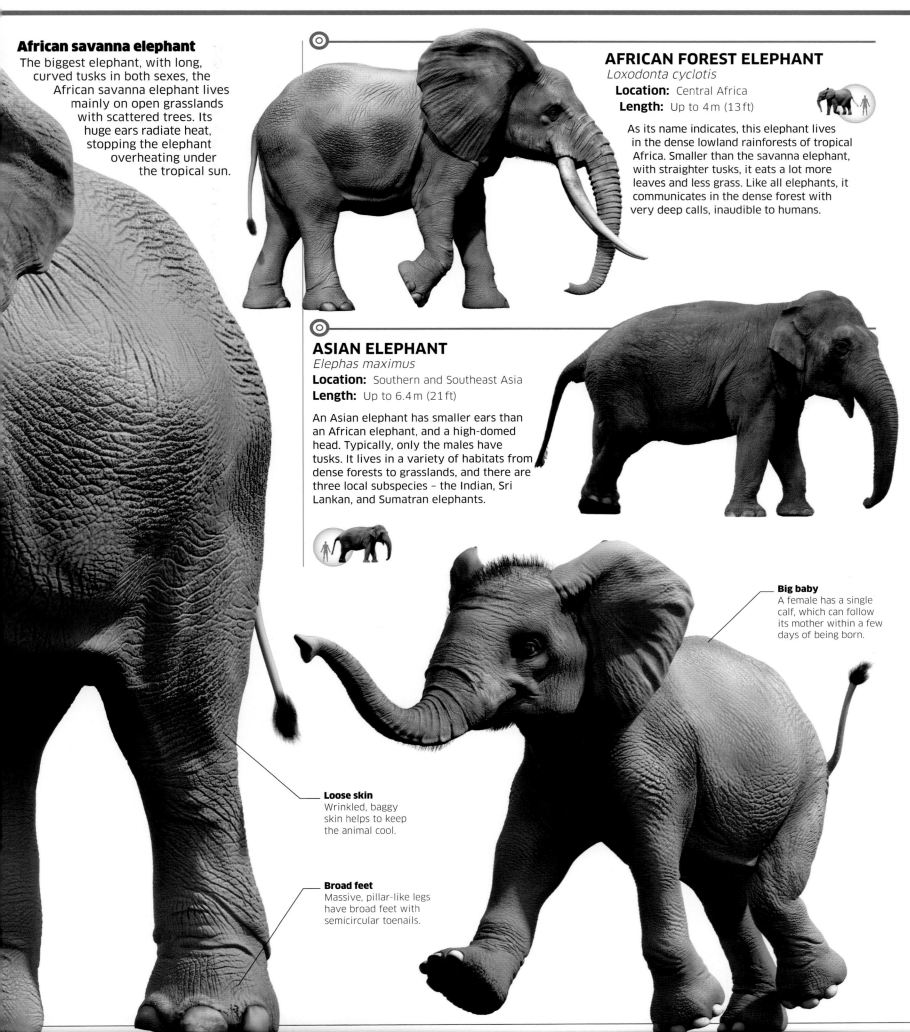

African savanna elephant

The biggest elephant, with long, curved tusks in both sexes, the African savanna elephant lives mainly on open grasslands with scattered trees. Its huge ears radiate heat, stopping the elephant overheating under the tropical sun.

AFRICAN FOREST ELEPHANT
Loxodonta cyclotis

Location: Central Africa
Length: Up to 4 m (13 ft)

As its name indicates, this elephant lives in the dense lowland rainforests of tropical Africa. Smaller than the savanna elephant, with straighter tusks, it eats a lot more leaves and less grass. Like all elephants, it communicates in the dense forest with very deep calls, inaudible to humans.

ASIAN ELEPHANT
Elephas maximus

Location: Southern and Southeast Asia
Length: Up to 6.4 m (21 ft)

An Asian elephant has smaller ears than an African elephant, and a high-domed head. Typically, only the males have tusks. It lives in a variety of habitats from dense forests to grasslands, and there are three local subspecies – the Indian, Sri Lankan, and Sumatran elephants.

Big baby
A female has a single calf, which can follow its mother within a few days of being born.

Loose skin
Wrinkled, baggy skin helps to keep the animal cool.

Broad feet
Massive, pillar-like legs have broad feet with semicircular toenails.

North American beaver

One of nature's busiest architects, the beaver uses its tree-felling skills to transform the landscape of its native forests – creating dams, lakes, and impregnable fortresses where it is safe from its enemies.

A beaver is a giant nocturnal rodent – an aquatic relative of squirrels and mice. Like them, it has big, chisel-bladed front teeth for gnawing its food, but the beaver also uses them to cut down trees. It needs trees to build its lodge, which it surrounds with a defensive moat of deep water by using more timber and mud to dam a forest stream. When the water freezes over in winter the beavers stay active beneath the ice, feeding on the leaves and buds of branches stored underwater.

Webbed feet
When swimming fast, the beaver drives itself through the water with its large webbed rear feet and using its paddle-shaped tail like a rudder. It can swim slowly using its tail alone.

Flat tail
Highly adapted for swimming, the tail is scaly, hairless, and flattened like a paddle. The beaver slaps it on the water to warn other beavers of danger.

MAMMALS
NORTH AMERICAN BEAVER
Castor canadensis

Location: North America, Mexico

Length: Up to 88 cm (34½ in)

Diet: Tree bark, leaves, twigs

The longest-known beaver dam extended **for 850 m (2,790 ft).**

In the **early 19th century**, beavers were almost **hunted to extinction** for their **fur**.

15 minutes – the length of time a **beaver can hold its breath**.

4 m (13 ft) – the **height** of a large **beaver dam**.

131

Waterproof fur
The dense, dark-brown or reddish fur is waterproofed with an oily substance called castoreum, secreted from scent glands.

Chisel teeth
The huge incisor teeth are coated with a hard enamel, which includes iron and turns them orange. They are worn away at the back, where they are softer, by the action of the lower incisors passing behind the upper incisors. This gives them a sharp edge. Like most rodents, beavers' teeth continue to grow throughout their life.

Protective membrane
A transparent eyelid covers each eye when the beaver is underwater.

Gripping paws
The small front paws have unwebbed toes and sharp claws for digging and to grip and manipulate materials.

Living chamber

Mud-covered sticks

Ventilation holes

Underwater entrance

Dam

Pond

Fortified lodge

The beaver's dam can be well over 1.8 m (6 ft) high, and creates a pond that is about 0.9 m (3 ft) deep. The water floods the entrance to the lodge, which is built from a pile of sticks hollowed out to create a living space. Mud plastered over the sticks freezes in winter, so no predator can get in. Occasionally, muskrats will cohabit with beavers.

EURASIAN RED SQUIRREL
Sciurus vulgaris

Location: Eurasia

Length: Up to 22 cm (8³/₄ in)

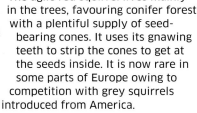

The agile red squirrel lives mainly in the trees, favouring conifer forests with a plentiful supply of seed-bearing cones. It uses its gnawing teeth to strip the cones to get at the seeds inside. It is now rare in some parts of Europe owing to competition with grey squirrels introduced from America.

BLACK-TAILED PRAIRIE DOG
Cynomys ludovicianus

Location: North America

Length: Up to 38 cm (15 in)

This ground squirrel lives on the virtually treeless American prairie grasslands, in burrow systems known as prairie dog towns. In the past some of these were colossal, covering huge areas and occupied by millions of animals.

Fluffy tail
The furry tail wraps around the dormouse when it hibernates.

HAZEL DORMOUSE
Muscardinus avellanarius

Location: Europe

Length: Up to 9 cm (3¹/₂ in)

Resembling a miniature squirrel, this small woodland animal spends more than half its life asleep, hibernating from November to May. When awake it feeds mainly in the trees, gathering berries, nuts, flowers, and sometimes insects.

Rodents

Almost half of all mammal species are rodents. Mostly small, plant-eating animals such as mice and squirrels, they are all equipped with big, self-sharpening front teeth for gnawing tough foods.

Rodents live in virtually every habitat from tropical rainforests to the Arctic tundra and scorchingly hot, dry deserts. Most live on seeds, nuts, fruit, and juicy roots, but a few are hunters of small animals, or omnivores that will devour almost anything.

LONG-EARED JERBOA
Euchoreutes naso

Location: Eastern central Asia

Length: Up to 9 cm (3¹/₂ in)

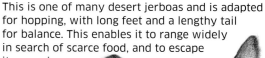

This is one of many desert jerboas and is adapted for hopping, with long feet and a lengthy tail for balance. This enables it to range widely in search of scarce food, and to escape its enemies.

NORWAY LEMMING
Lemmus lemmus

Location: Northern Scandinavia

Length: Up to 13.5 cm (5¹/₄ in)

This Arctic species is a prolific breeder and may produce so many young in a good year that food shortages can occur. This forces the lemming to make mass migrations to find new habitats. It is the staple prey of Arctic foxes and snowy owls.

A **springhare** can cover 2 m (6½ ft) or more in **one bound**.

Lions have been known to **die of wounds inflicted** by the **quills of porcupines** they have attacked.

133

Scorpion prey

NORTHERN GRASSHOPPER MOUSE
Onychomys leucogaster

Location: North America
Length: Up to 13 cm (5 in)

Most rodents are dedicated vegetarians, but this one is a hunter. It mainly preys on insects, but has been known to kill and eat smaller mice and even small snakes and lizards. It is also known for its remarkably loud, shrill calls.

BLACK RAT
Rattus rattus

Location: Eurasia, Africa, Australasia, North America
Length: Up to 22.5 cm (8¾ in)

Along with some other species, the black rat has been accidentally spread around the world by travelling on human ships. It is famous as a carrier of bubonic plague, the disease that killed half the human population of Europe in the 14th century.

SOUTH AFRICAN SPRINGHARE
Pedetes capensis

Location: Southern Africa
Length: Up to 43 cm (17 in)

Despite its name this is not a hare, but a rodent. However, it can certainly spring, leaping like a kangaroo on its long hind legs, balanced by its long, bushy tail. It lives in deserts, hiding in a burrow by day and only feeding at night.

NAKED MOLE RAT
Heterocephalus glaber

Location: Eastern Africa
Length: Up to 9.2 cm (3½ in)

This extraordinary rodent lives in colonies that are each controlled by a single breeding queen, rather like colonies of honeybees. The colonies occupy burrows that the mole-rats dig with their teeth, kicking the loose earth out of the burrow entrance.

Prominent teeth
Large incisor teeth are used for digging and eating.

Hairless skin

LONG-TAILED CHINCHILLA
Chinchilla lanigera

Location: Chile and South America
Length: Up to 23 cm (9 in)

The chinchilla lives in the Andes mountains, where it survives the harsh climate thanks to a dense coat of fur. It emerges at night when temperatures are at their lowest to feed on seeds and grasses, and other small animals.

CRESTED PORCUPINE
Hystrix cristata

Location: Africa, Italy
Length: Up to 1 m (3¼ ft)

If attacked, this porcupine raises up its spectacularly long quills and shakes its tail, which is equipped with special broad, hollow quills that produce a hiss-like rattle. If its enemy takes no notice, the porcupine may charge it tail-first, to embed the sharp quills in its attacker's skin.

CAPYBARA
Hydrochoerus hydrochaeris

Location: Tropical South America
Length: Up to 1.3 m (4¼ ft)

The biggest of all rodents, the pig-sized capybara lives in swamps and flooded grasslands where it has a semi-aquatic way of life, feeding mainly on grasses and aquatic plants. It has a scent gland on top of its snout, which is much bigger in mature males.

Rabbits and hares

With their long ears and bounding gait, rabbits and hares are instantly recognizable. They live almost worldwide, from the tropics to the High Arctic, and some occur in vast numbers.

Together with the rodent-like pikas, they form a group called the lagomorphs, which means "hare-shaped". They are closely related to rodents such as squirrels and mice, but have slightly different teeth and are more strictly vegetarian. Rabbits are typically burrowers that bolt underground for safety when threatened, but most hares are long-legged athletes that live in open country and rely on fast getaways to escape their enemies.

Able to hit 70 km/h (43 mph), the brown hare can run as fast **as a greyhound.**

Wide field of view
Big, bulging eyes high on the sides of the head give virtually all-round vision.

Big ears
Very long ears catch the slightest sound that could betray a predator.

Strong legs
The hare's very long hind legs allow it to run at high speeds.

Brown hare
Renowned for its agility, the brown hare can easily outrun most of its enemies, often changing direction rapidly to evade pursuers. During the spring breeding season, reluctant females drive off over-eager males by sparring with their paws like boxers.

Front incisors

Peg teeth

Peg teeth
A hare has big, rodent-like incisor teeth that grow constantly to compensate for wear, with a big gap behind them that allows it to hold a lot of food in its mouth. However, unlike a rodent, a hare also has a pair of small peg teeth that have almost no function.

Brown fur sometimes turns reddish

MAMMALS
BROWN HARE
Lepus europaeus

Location: Eurasia; introduced elsewhere

Length: Up to 70 cm (27½ in)

Diet: Grass, herbs, bark

24 European rabbits were **introduced to Australia** in 1859. They reproduced rapidly and **there are now billions of them.**

Arctic hares **live in regions** where the average temperature is **below -27°C (-16°F).**

135

BLACK-TAILED JACKRABBIT
Lepus californicus
Location: Mexico, Western USA
Length: Up to 60.5 cm (23¾ in)

The enormous ears of the jackrabbit are vital to its survival in hot, dry deserts and grasslands, since they act as radiators that give off excess heat to the air and help the animal keep cool. Despite its name the jackrabbit is a hare, with long legs that give it the speed to escape a coyote.

Heat radiator
A network of blood vessels in the ears radiates excess body heat.

ARCTIC HARE
Lepus arcticus
Location: Arctic Canada, Greenland
Length: Up to 67 cm (26½ in)

This incredibly hardy hare lives in large groups and is adapted for the freezing climate with a very thick coat of white fur. It has shorter ears than is usual for a hare, reducing heat loss.

AMAMI RABBIT
Pentalagus furnessi
Location: Amami islands, Japan
Length: Up to 51 cm (20 in)

An elusive, nocturnal inhabitant of dense forest, the Japanese Amami rabbit is a survivor of a type of rabbit that was once widespread in Asia, but is now almost extinct. It lives in burrows that it digs with its long claws.

EUROPEAN RABBIT
Oryctolagus cuniculus
Location: Western Europe; introduced elsewhere
Length: Up to 55 cm (21¾ in)

Once restricted to Spain, France, and North Africa, the European rabbit has been spread to many other parts of the world, and in Australia it has become a pest. It digs extensive burrow systems, emerging mainly at night to nibble on grasses and leaves.

Leg power
Powerful hind legs give the rabbit the speed to bolt for cover.

VOLCANO RABBIT
Romerolagus diazi
Location: Mexico
Length: Up to 36 cm (14¾ in)

With a stumpy body and short ears, this is one of the smallest and rarest rabbits. It lives only on the forested slopes of four volcanoes to the south of Mexico City, where its habitat and future are threatened by farming and road building.

Short, thick fur

EASTERN COTTONTAIL
Sylvilagus floridanus
Location: North and Central America
Length: Up to 48.5 cm (19 in)

The most common of many similar species known as cottontails, this is the American equivalent of the European rabbit. But instead of digging its own burrows, it occupies holes dug by other animals such as ground squirrels.

Large hind feet

RING-TAILED LEMUR
Lemur catta
Location: Madagascar
Length: Up to 46 cm (18 in)

Its distinctive tail makes this the most recognizable of the lemurs. It lives in large, noisy groups, searching for fruit, leaves, and small animals in the forest trees, but unusually it also spends a lot of time on the ground.

WHITE-FOOTED SPORTIVE LEMUR
Lepilemur leucopus
Location: Madagascar
Length: Up to 26 cm (10¼ in)

The sportive lemurs were given their name because they look like boxers when they are defending themselves. This species is probably the smallest of the family – a dedicated leaf-eater that, because of the very low food value of its leafy diet, devotes most of its time to either eating or resting.

Dense fur

Firm grip
The feet are padded for clinging to branches.

BLUE-EYED BLACK LEMUR
Eulemur flavifrons
Location: Madagascar
Length: Up to 45 cm (17¾ in)

The males and females of most lemurs look the same, but in this critically endangered species only the males are black. Females are reddish-brown, with paler fur on their underside. Apart from many humans, this is the only primate with blue eyes. It feeds mainly on fruit and flowers.

Lemurs

Found only in Madagascar, the lemurs are a diverse group of primates related to the ancestors of monkeys and apes. Highly adapted for life in the forest trees, many are superbly acrobatic climbers.

Arriving in Madagascar at least 40 million years ago, the lemurs evolved into up to 120 species ranging from tiny mouse lemurs to gorilla-sized giants. Each species was adapted to a particular way of life on an island with a wide variety of habitats – some were adaptable omnivores, while others were specialists. But 17 species (including the giant lemurs) are now extinct, and many more are endangered by destruction of their wild habitats.

Balancing tail
The long tail is held out for balance.

MADAME BERTHE'S MOUSE LEMUR
Microcebus berthae
Location: Madagascar
Length: Up to 9.5 cm (3¾ in)

This huge-eyed, nocturnal animal is the smallest of the tiny mouse lemurs, and the smallest of all primates. It is very agile, climbing through trees and shrubs in search of fruit, flowers, nectar, insects, and small vertebrates such as geckos and chameleons.

During the dry season, the
mouse lemur eats sugary honeydew
produced by sap-sucking flower bugs.

Long tail
The tail is longer than the body.

Lemurs use their **front teeth like combs** for **grooming** their fur.

10 m (33 ft) – the **distance** Verreaux's sifaka can **leap between branches**, propelled by its **strong hind legs**.

137

Verreaux's sifaka

Highly specialized for climbing, this big lemur cannot walk or run in the usual way. Instead, it skips sideways over the ground on its hind legs, with its arms held out for balance, like a dancer.

Thick, soft fur

INDRI
Indri indri
Location: Madagascar
Length: Up to 72 cm (28¼ in)

The biggest lemur, this strikingly patterned near relative of Verreaux's sifaka is unique in having only a very short tail. Like other lemurs it holds its body vertically while leaping through the trees, and clings to branches with its large hands.

Long hands
Verreaux's sifaka spends most of its life in the treetops, foraging for leaves and fruit. Both its hands and feet are adapted for gripping branches with long thumbs and opposable, thumb-like big toes.

AYE-AYE
Daubentonia madagascariensis
Location: Madagascar
Length: Up to 37 cm (14½ in)

This extraordinary animal has a very slender middle finger that it uses to extract timber-boring insect grubs from their burrows – almost like the mammal equivalent of a woodpecker. It also uses its finger to scoop out the pulp of ripe fruit.

Powerful hind legs
This lemur can make impressive leaps from branch to branch.

Bushy tail

MAMMALS
VERREAUX'S SIFAKA
Propithecus verreauxi
Location: Madagascar
Length: Up to 48 cm (19 in)
Diet: Leaves, fruit, bark

A howler monkey **can smell ripe fruit** up to 2 km (1¼ miles) away.

77 per cent of a **howler monkey's day** is **spent resting.**

Tight hold
Baby howlers are born with a golden coat. They cling to the fur on their mother's back to be transported around.

Keeping track
Groups of howlers start and end each day by whooping at each other. This tells them where their competitors are.

Hyoid bone

Lower jaw

Voice box
A howler monkey has an enlarged larynx (voice box) for producing deep, resonant calls. It is supported by a huge, hollow hyoid bone behind the massive lower jaw. The jaw and hyoid of a male howler (shown above) are bigger than those of a female.

Shared mothering
Mother howler monkeys care for and carry each others' babies in a practice called "allomothering".

Long tail
The tail measures up to 65 cm (25½ in) long, matching the length of the body.

Mobile toes
Long toes give the monkey a secure grip on branches high above the ground.

Sensitive underside
The underneath of the tail lacks hair. It is extra sensitive and able to identify things by touch.

Paraguayan howler

The booming calls of tropical American howler monkeys are the loudest noises made by any land animal on Earth. The monkeys howl to defend their feeding territory and their females, with each troop calling in unison to warn neighbouring troops not to trespass on their patch.

The males howl loudest, filling the rainforest with sound at dawn and during the day as each troop responds to its neighbours, but females howl too. Unusually the females are a different colour from the males, being olive-buff while the males are black. Howler monkeys usually live in small troops in the tropical forests of central South America. They spend most of their time high in the tree canopy feeding on fruit and leaves.

The guttural, roaring territorial calls of Paraguayan howlers **can be heard 5 km (3 miles) away.**

22 The **highest number** of howlers in a troop. Usually there are **between 5 and 8**.

A Paraguayan howler monkey can **live for up to 20 years**.

139

Colour vision
These monkeys have excellent colour vision for detecting red and orange, the colours of ripe fruit.

Sniffing the air
A keen sense of smell enables howlers to track down food by its scent.

Grasping tail
Wrapped around a branch, the tail is strong enough to support the monkey's weight.

MAMMALS

PARAGUAYAN HOWLER

Alouatta caraya

Location: Central South America

Length: Up to 65 cm (25½ in)

Diet: Leaves, fruit

Leafy diet

Unusually for a monkey, the Paraguayan howler eats a lot of leaves as well as fruit. Leaves are easier to find, but are far less nutritious. The monkeys select the youngest leaves, but they have to eat a lot of them. They save energy by spending much of the day asleep and not moving far.

Monkeys

From big, powerful, dog-faced baboons to miniature, silky-coated marmosets, monkeys are the most varied of all primates, famous for their agility, sociable natures, and intelligence.

Most monkeys are tropical tree-dwellers that feed mainly on fruit. In tropical forests, trees are in fruit all year round, but fruiting trees can be scattered and hard to find. So typical monkeys have become very skilled at moving through trees, and have good colour vision for spotting ripe fruit among the leaves. Their excellent memories also help them remember where to find good food sources. Monkeys are divided into two categories: Old World monkeys from Africa and Asia, and New World monkeys from tropical America.

JAPANESE MACAQUE
Macaca fuscata
Location: Japan
Length: Up to 65 cm (25½ in)

Sometimes called the snow monkey because of its chilly mountain habitat, this monkey is unusual because it does not live in the tropics. It eats fruit, plus green plants, juicy roots, and seeds when fruit is scarce. It is most famous for bathing in hot volcanic springs to keep warm in winter.

Warm coat
Thick fur keeps out the winter chill.

DE BRAZZA'S MONKEY
Cercopithecus neglectus
Location: Central Africa
Length: Up to 54 cm (21¼ in)

This is one of the most colourful and widespread species of guenon, a type of long-tailed African monkey, mainly found in tropical forests. It prefers swampy forests, where small groups forage for food.

ANGOLAN COLOBUS
Colobus angolensis
Location: Central and East Africa
Length: Up to 66 cm (26 in)

Also called the black-and-white colobus, this slender rainforest monkey is one of the most striking Old World species, with a white ruff around its face and a silky, white mantle over its shoulders. An agile climber, it lives high in the trees in large troops, feeding mainly on leaves.

MANDRILL
Mandrillus sphinx
Location: Central Africa
Length: Up to 1.1 m (43¼ in)

The mandrill is the largest monkey and closely related to the baboon. Males have bright red-and-blue faces, with the colouring most vivid in dominant males. Mandrills spend most of their time on the ground and eat a wide variety of foods, from fruit, eggs, and leaves to small mammals.

Long snout

Sturdy limbs

An **Angola colobus** can **eat** up to 3 kg (6½ lb) of **leaves** a day – **a third of its body weight**.

A male **proboscis monkey's nose** can grow **so long** that he has to **push it out of the way** to feed.

141

GEOFFROY'S TUFTED-EAR MARMOSET
Callithrix geoffroyi
Location: Eastern tropical Brazil
Length: Up to 23 cm (9 in)

Squirrel-sized marmosets are the smallest monkeys. Like other species, this marmoset gouges holes in tree bark with its teeth so it can eat the sugary gum that oozes out.

PROBOSCIS MONKEY
Nasalis larvatus
Location: Borneo
Length: Up to 76 cm (30 in)

Named for its large, fleshy nose, this Old World monkey lives in tall forest trees where it eats fruit and leaves. Always found close to water, it is an excellent swimmer.

Fleshy nose
The nose is much longer in adult males.

BALD UAKARI
Cacajao calvus
Location: Western Amazonia
Length: Up to 57 cm (22½ in)

The vivid red face of this monkey is a sign of its good health – weaker individuals have paler faces, and are not as successful at finding mates. It lives mainly in the seasonally flooded forests of the upper Amazon, foraging in the treetops for seeds and fruit.

GOLDEN LION TAMARIN
Leontopithecus rosalia
Location: Eastern tropical Brazil
Length: Up to 33 cm (13 in)

Once widespread, this small, sleek tamarin is now very rare. An agile climber, it uses its long, clawed fingers to search among dense foliage for fruit and insects.

BLACK-HEADED NIGHT MONKEY
Aotus nigriceps
Location: Western Amazonia
Length: Up to 42 cm (16½ in)

The huge eyes of this tropical American monkey allow it to forage by night for fruit and insects, and even leap through the treetops in the dark. Its nocturnal lifestyle keeps it safe from monkey-hunting eagles.

Long, thin digits with straight nails

WHITE-FACED SAKI
Pithecia pithecia
Location: Northern South America
Length: Up to 41.5 cm (16½ in)

Only the male of this species has the distinctive white face, which contrasts with his black fur; females are browner. Pairs often remain together for life.

GUIANAN BROWN CAPUCHIN
Sapajus apella
Location: South America
Length: Up to 46 cm (18¼ in)

Widespread in South America, the capuchins include a wide variety of sociable, mainly tree-living species. The Guianan brown capuchin is one of the most common – an adaptable omnivore that can thrive in many different types of forest.

CENTRAL AMERICAN SPIDER MONKEY
Ateles geoffroyi
Location: Central America
Length: Up to 63 cm (24¾ in)

This spider monkey gets its name from its extremely long, spidery limbs, and even longer, prehensile (grasping) tail. These equip the monkey perfectly for its acrobatic way of life, searching for fruit high in the rainforest canopy. It uses its almost thumbless hands as hooks to swing from tree branches.

Fifth limb
The prehensile tail is strong enough to support the monkey's weight.

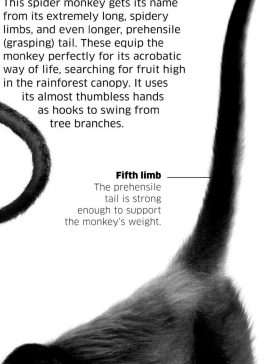

The birth rate for orangutans is very low. On average a female orangutan has **one baby every 9.3 years.**

Baby is carried by its mother

Close ties
An orangutan mother will spend eight or nine years raising her young.

Four hands
The orangutan's feet are just like its hands, capable of gripping branches.

Flexible legs
An orangutan's legs are shorter than its arms.

Red ape
The fur ranges from orange or chestnut to chocolate brown.

The word **orangutan** is Malay for "forest person".

58 The **number of years** wild **orangutans can live for**.

Flanged male orangutans are **twice the size of** mature females.

143

FLANGED MALE

UNFLANGED MALE

Late developers

A dominant male has broad, fleshy flanges on his cheeks, a big throat pouch for amplifying his calls, and a cape of long hair. He uses these features to impress females and rivals, including unflanged males. Unflanged males exhibit a kind of arrested development and may never develop flanges, though they can still reproduce.

Nesting in the trees

Every day an orangutan builds two types of nests high in the trees – a day nest and a night nest. These are woven from branches and foliage. Orangutans learn how to make these from each other, so the first nest this baby builds will be an attempt to copy the one she is sharing with her mother.

Sumatran orangutan

Superbly adapted for swinging through the canopy of their native forests, orangutans move slowly, always testing first that branches can hold their weight. They spend their lives high in the branches, rarely visiting the ground.

Orangutans live on the South East Asian islands of Borneo and Sumatra. Although they look similar, the two populations are now considered separate species. They feed mainly on fruit gathered from high in the rainforest trees, as well as tree-living termites and birds' eggs. Orangutans are highly intelligent but less sociable than other apes, often preferring to forage and sleep alone. Sumatran orangutans are longer and slimmer than Bornean orangutans, and more endangered due to rainforest destruction.

MAMMALS

SUMATRAN ORANGUTAN

Pongo abelii

Location: Sumatra

Height: Up to 99 cm (39 in)

Diet: Fruit, leaves, and insects

Using tools
Orangutans use sticks as tools to dig for termites or collect honey from beehives.

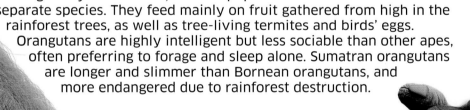

Thumb and fingers
Four long fingers and an opposable thumb, like on a human hand, give a strong grip.

Quick learners
Each local group of orangutans has its own ways of finding food, building nests, and even communicating with its neighbours. Baby orangutans learn skills from their mother, such as how to use tools to dig insects out of their timber burrows. A baby lives with its mother until it is at least 7 years old.

Long arms
An orangutan's armspan can measure up to 2.25 m (7½ ft) from fingertip to fingertip.

Mountain gorilla

The mighty gorilla is the biggest of the apes – a forest giant that is one of our closest living relatives. Highly intelligent, it lives in family groups defended by a single mature "silverback" male, who uses his prodigious strength to keep rival males at bay.

There are two species of gorilla, western and eastern. Mountain gorillas are a subspecies of the eastern. They live in the upland forests of eastern central Africa, where most of their food consists of leaves and stems gathered near the ground. Since these items have poor nutritional value, the gorillas must spend most of their time eating, chewing each mouthful thoroughly with their massive cheek teeth to extract as much nutrition as possible.

Silverback
The short, silver-grey hair on a mature male's back begins to grow when he reaches 14 years old.

Shaggy coat
Mountain gorillas have longer coats than other gorillas.

Fighting stance
Gorillas get around by "knuckle walking" on all fours; they only stand to fight or to beat their chests.

Rival males may fight to the death, but first they try to scare each other away by roaring and beating their chests.

Family structure
A typical mountain gorilla family group is made up of three or four adult females, with four or five young of different ages, fathered by one mature male. The male defends the family from predators and any rival males who might try to drive him out and kill his young. As long as this does not happen, the family group will stay together.

A wild gorilla **may live for 40 years** or more.

The mountain gorilla is the **rarest gorilla species**, with **fewer than 1,000** left in the wild.

Skull crest
A ridge of bone anchors massive jaw muscles.

Unique prints
Each gorilla has its own individual fingerprints.

Sharp weapons
Males have long, sharp canine teeth for fighting.

Big build
The arms are longer and the chest is broader than those of chimps.

Hairy hands
A gorilla's hands are very like human hands but stronger and a lot hairier.

Toe grip
All apes have very mobile toes. Their big toes are opposable, like their thumbs, so they can grip branches with their feet. Mountain gorillas spend most of their time on the ground because they eat pith, stems, leaves, bark, and occasionally ants and don't need to climb to find food. Despite their weight, adult west African gorillas regularly climb trees to gather fruit.

Seeing in colour

Gorillas and other apes have excellent colour vision. In particular, and unlike many mammals, they are sensitive to red and orange. This enables them to pick out ripe fruit, which is a valuable part of their diet.

On the defence
The defending silverback first barks and stares at his attacker, then he starts hooting and stands upright, throwing vegetation at him. If the attacker still doesn't back down, he will charge.

MAMMALS
MOUNTAIN GORILLA
Gorilla beringei beringei

Location: Eastern Central Africa

Height: Up to 1.96 m (6½ ft)

Diet: Leaves, pith, bark, stems, fruit

WESTERN HOOLOCK GIBBON

Hoolock hoolock

Location: South Asia

Length: Up to 81 cm (32 in)

Like all gibbons, the hoolock has very long arms and powerful shoulders adapted for swinging from branch to branch. The male has white eyebrows that contrast dramatically with his black fur; the female is a grey-brown colour.

White-browed male

Brown female
Females have brownish fur and white-ringed faces.

Whitish hands and feet

Long reach
Extra-long arms give the reach needed to swing between branches.

Stabilizing legs
Like all apes, the hoolock can walk upright for short periods of time.

LAR GIBBON

Hylobates lar

Location: S. E. Asia

Length: Up to 42 cm (16½ in)

The lar gibbon varies from black to sandy brown, but always has a ring of white hair surrounding its black face. It lives in family groups high in the trees of tropical rainforests, where it feeds mainly on fruit. It rarely, if ever, comes down to the forest floor.

Legs are shorter than arms

Apes

There are two main groups of apes. The first consists of the long-armed gibbons, adapted for life high in the trees. The other is the great apes, which includes the chimpanzee and its two close relatives, bonobos and humans. Orangutans and gorillas (see pp.182–185) also belong to this group.

The apes include the most spectacularly agile primates. The 19 species of gibbons use their long arms to swing gracefully through the treetops. The great apes are the largest of the apes and are considered the most intelligent primates.

NORTHERN WHITE-CHEEKED CRESTED GIBBON

Nomascus leucogenys

Location: S. E. Asia

Length: Up to 53 cm (20¾ in)

Only the black-furred male of this species has white cheeks; the female is pale brown with a dark face. Like other gibbons, they form long-lasting pairs. They mainly eat fruit, supplemented by young, tender leaves and small animals.

Social grooming
For all apes, grooming is important both for cleaning fur and for social bonding.

Black-furred male

The **calls of the siamang** can be **heard through the forest** up to 2 km (1¼ miles) away.

Chimpanzees live in **societies** of up to **150 members**, but **split up into smaller groups** to find food.

147

SIAMANG
Symphalangus syndactylus
Location: S. E. Asia
Length: Up to 90 cm (35½ in)

All gibbons defend their territories with loud calls, but the siamang has the loudest – a resonant hooting amplified by an inflatable throat sac. Pairs often call in duet for 15 minutes or more, especially in the early morning, and are answered by neighbouring siamangs.

Hooting sac
The throat sac can inflate to the size of the head.

Strong hands
The long hands are ideal for grasping branches.

BONOBO
Pan paniscus
Location: Central Africa
Length: Up to 83 cm (32¾ in)

This is the rarer of the two species of chimpanzee, with longer legs and a lighter build. It lives both in the trees and on the ground in tropical rainforests, travelling over the forest floor by "knuckle walking" on all fours. It eats mainly fruit supplemented by leaves, eggs, insects, and small vertebrates.

Distinctive hair
A bonobo has long black hair on its head, with a central parting.

Pink lips

Coarse, black fur

COMMON CHIMPANZEE
Pan troglodytes
Location: Central and west Africa
Length: Up to 96 cm (37¾ in)

With a stockier build than the bonobo, the common chimpanzee lives in male-dominated territorial groups in a variety of habitats. It eats a lot of fruit, but uses tools to forage for insects and also kills larger animals, including monkeys.

Chimpanzees have been known to sharpen sticks to spear bushbabies hiding in tree holes.

Long legs

Feet can grip branches

Tough knuckles

Using echolocation, a bat can **detect a flying moth** from up to 6 m (19½ ft) away.

INDIAN FLYING FOX
Pteropus giganteus
Location: India, S.E. Asia
Length: Up to 25 cm (10 in)

This big, tropical fruit bat is one of many that range through the forest at night looking for fruit to eat. During the day it roosts in trees, hanging upside down from branches by its feet. Several hundred flying foxes can live in the same tree.

GREATER HORSESHOE BAT
Rhinolophus ferrumequinum
Location: Europe, Asia
Length: Up to 7 cm (2¾ in)

Like most small bats, this species catches insects whilst flying. It detects airborne moths and beetles by echolocation – emitting a stream of high-pitched clicks and listening for echoes. A horseshoe-shaped structure on its nose focuses the clicks.

GHOST BAT
Macroderma gigas
Location: N. Australia
Length: Up to 14 cm (5½ in)

This big, tropical bat owes its name to its very thin, almost transparent wings and its ghostly pale grey fur. It is a powerful hunter with very large teeth, able to seize, kill, and eat lizards, mice, small birds, and even other bats.

LESSER LONG-NOSED BAT
Leptonycteris yerbabuenae
Location: North and Central America
Length: Up to 9 cm (3½ in)

This unusual bat is a nectar-feeder, which targets the flowers of cacti and agaves in the deserts. The plants bloom at night to attract the bat, which has an extra-long, brush-tipped tongue for lapping up nectar. It can also can hover to drink from the flowers.

GREATER BULLDOG BAT
Noctilio leporinus
Location: Central and South America
Length: Up to 13.2 cm (5¼ in)

Big bats can hunt large prey, and the greater bulldog bat specializes in catching fish. Able to detect ripples in the water made by fish as they surface, it scoops them up with its tail membrane and claws. Many males have bright orange fur.

Bats

A quarter of all mammal species are bats – the only living vertebrates apart from birds that are capable of powered flight. Other mammals, reptiles, and even frogs can glide, but bats can fly, with such agility and precision that most of them live by catching insect prey in mid-air.

A bat's wings consist of sheets of stretchy skin supported by hugely elongated finger bones. The skin membranes extend to the bat's legs, and often to its tail. Some bats have long, narrow wings for speed; others have shorter, broader wings for agility. Unlike typical birds they fly at night, and most use echolocation to navigate in the dark.

MAMMALS
BROWN LONG-EARED BAT
Plecotus auritus
Location: Europe and Central Asia
Length: Up to 5.5 cm (2¼ in)
Diet: Insects, spiders

1,240 The **number of species** of **bat** worldwide.

A brown long-eared bat **may live** for up to **22 years.**

COMMON VAMPIRE BAT
Desmodus rotundus

Location: Central and South America
Length: Up to 9.5 cm (3¾ in)

The vampire bats of tropical America feed on blood. They use their razor-sharp front teeth to make small slits in the skin of large animals, then lap up the blood with their long tongues. Vampire bats can also run and jump over the ground, using their folded wings as legs.

Folding ears
The bat tucks its enormous ears away under its wings when it is roosting by day.

Wing fingers
Elongated finger bones stretch the wing membrane and support it in flight.

Echolocation
All insect-eating bats are equipped with a sophisticated echolocation system. As a bat flies, it produces a stream of high-frequency clicks. These are reflected from obstacles and prey as echoes, which the bat's ears pick up and translate into a "sound picture" of its surroundings. This allows it to navigate and hunt in total darkness.

Bat

Brown long-eared bat
The enormous ears of this European bat enable it to hear the faintest sounds made by insects or spiders in the dark. They also allow the bat to use unusually quiet echolocation calls for finding its way through the trees, and targeting insect prey in flight.

A long-eared bat has excellent eyesight, and often uses it **to hunt prey on moonlit nights.**

——— CLICKS
········· ECHOES

Insect

Meat-slicing teeth
Like nearly all the carnivores (mammals of the order Carnivora), a wolf has special cheek teeth known as carnassials. They are modified chewing teeth that work together like scissor blades to slice meat from bone. Wolves also have long, pointed canine teeth for seizing prey.

Upper canine

Upper carnassial

Lower carnassial

Lower canine

Mobile ears
The wolf uses its mobile ears to locate prey and to express its mood.

Sensitive whiskers detect air movements

Howling
Wolf packs howl to warn neighbouring packs off their territory.

Grey wolf

The ancestor of all domestic dogs, the grey wolf was once familiar across all northern continents. Now, its eerie howl is rarely heard outside the remote regions of the far north and a few mountain refuges.

The wolf is a member of the order Carnivora – a group of mammals that take their name from the fact that many are specialized carnivores, or meat-eaters. Wolves prey mainly on other mammals, ranging from mice to full-grown bison, but are rarely strong enough to tackle large prey alone. Instead an extended family works together as a hunting pack. Using their intelligence and communication skills, the wolves mount a joint attack, then share the spoils between them.

Fur layers
A dense layer of fur lies underneath the outer coat, keeping the wolf insulated against the cold.

MAMMALS
GREY WOLF
Canis lupus
Location: Europe, Central Asia
Length: Up to 1.6 m (5¼ ft)
Diet: Mainly large mammals

Apart from human hunters, the grey wolf's **main enemies are Siberian tigers.**

A **pack may chase its prey** for more than 5 km (3 miles) before **bringing it down**.

Most wolf packs consist of between **5 and 12 wolves**, but some may have **as many as 36**.

151

Long snout
The wolf's long snout contains extended nasal passages that help give it an acute sense of smell. Wolves rely heavily on detecting scents for both tracking their prey and communicating with each other. They can also assess the health of an individual from its smell.

Night sight
A wolf has poor colour vision but can see well at night, when it is often active.

Variable colour
The coat ranges from very dark to almost white, depending on local race.

Long legs
Slender, long legs allow the wolf to sustain a prolonged chase without tiring.

Running spikes
Stout claws grip the ground as the wolf pursues its quarry.

Body language
Wolves are highly social animals that use gestures and body language to communicate. Each pack is led by a breeding pair. Here a female shows submission to the "alpha male" by crouching with her ears lowered while he raises his tail in a gesture of dominance.

Early learning
Although only the alpha female breeds, the whole pack helps to raise and feed her pups. By degrees they learn to fend for themselves, playfighting and competing for food around the den, then eventually accompanying the adults on hunting expeditions.

The raccoon dog is the **only canid** that **hibernates in winter**.

The **hairy soles** of the **fennec fox's feet** offer **protection** from **hot desert sand**.

ETHIOPIAN WOLF
Canis simensis

Location: E. Africa
Length: Up to 1 m (3¼ ft)

This elegant, tawny red relative of the grey wolf lives in the high, cold mountains of central Ethiopia, where it hunts grass rats and other small mammals. Habitat destruction and human activity have made it the rarest, most threatened canid.

Canids

Wolves, wild dogs, and foxes all belong to the Canidae family – the canids. They are among the most successful carnivores, although most of them also eat other foods.

With their long legs and lithe bodies, many canids are built for running after prey in open country. However, it is because they are so adaptable and eat a variety of foods that they are successful. Most foxes hunt in wooded terrain where there is plenty of cover for stalking prey, while the bat-eared fox is a specialized insect-eater. Many canids hunt alone, but nearly all of them live in groups based on close family ties and social interaction.

CRAB-EATING FOX
Cerdocyon thous

Location: South America
Length: Up to 77.5 cm (30½ in)

Like most canids, this South American fox is an opportunist that will eat all kinds of foods, from fruit to small mammals. But it gets its name from its habit of hunting crabs on muddy riverbanks.

MANED WOLF
Chrysocyon brachyurus

Location: South America
Length: Up to 1.15 m (3 ft)

Big ears enable exceptional hearing

DHOLE
Cuon alpinus

Location: Asia
Length: Up to 1.35 m (4½ ft)

The south Asian equivalent of the African wild dog, the almost wholly meat-eating dhole hunts in packs for large prey such as deer and young water buffalo. It has a complex social life, living in large clans that may include several breeding females.

Fox on stilts
Very long legs help the maned wolf to see over tall grass, and allow it to cover long distances in its nightly search for prey.

Although it looks like a big, very long-legged red fox, the South American maned wolf is neither a wolf nor a fox but belongs to a group of its own. It hunts alone on the grassland for small prey, using its big ears to locate victims in the long grass. This canid also eats a lot of fruit, especially a type of wild tomato known as the wolf-apple.

The red fox is **one of the most widely distributed mammals** on Earth.

The bush dog's **partially webbed feet** make it an **efficient swimmer**.

An arctic fox **does not shiver** until the temperature drops to **-70°C (-94°F)**.

153

CULPEO
Lycalopex culpaeus
Location: South America
Length: Up to 92 cm (36¼ in)

One of several closely related South American foxes known locally as "zorros", this adaptable hunter ranges high into the Andes mountains in search of prey.

RACCOON DOG
Nyctereutes procyonoides
Location: Europe, Asia
Length: Up to 70 cm (27½ in)

Well described by its name, this east Asian canid has a dark raccoon-like mask and very long, thick winter fur. Unusually, it is well able to climb trees to reach fruit – part of a broad diet that includes insects, mice, toads, and even fish.

BAT-EARED FOX
Otocyon megalotis
Location: E. and southern Africa
Length: Up to 60 cm (23½ in)

Uniquely for a canid, this fox is a specialist. It uses its huge ears to locate termites and beetles on the African grasslands, crunching them up with its many small chewing teeth.

BUSH DOG
Speothos venaticus
Location: Central and South America
Length: Up to 75 cm (29½ in)

Typical dogs and foxes are lean, long-legged animals, but the South American bush dog is the exception. Built like a terrier, with short legs and a compact head, it is a dedicated predator, hunting in packs for large rodents and pig-like peccaries.

Short ears

NORTHERN GREY FOX
Urocyon cinereoargenteus
Location: S. Canada to South America
Length: Up to 66 cm (26 in)

Found throughout much of the United States and Central America, this fox is closely related to the ancestors of all other canids. It has several primitive features, including an ability to climb trees and jump from branch to branch to find food.

FENNEC FOX
Vulpes zerda
Location: N. Africa
Length: Up to 41 cm (16 in)

The smallest of the canids, this North African desert fox has huge ears that it uses to locate mice, lizards, and other prey in the dark. Its ears also radiate heat, helping the fox to keep cool.

Sandy coat
The fox's fur provides perfect camouflage in its desert habitat.

RED FOX
Vulpes vulpes
Location: Arctic, North America, Europe, Asia, N. Africa, Australia
Length: Up to 90 cm (35½ in)

Widespread in all the northern continents, and introduced to Australia, the red fox can live almost anywhere, from Arctic tundra to big cities. It hunts small mammals, but also eats insects, worms, fruit, and carrion.

Thick coat
The dense fur is usually red with a white chest and tail tip, and black paws.

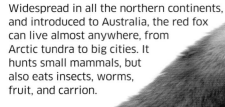

ARCTIC FOX
Vulpes lagopus
Location: N. Canada, Alaska, Greenland, N. Europe, N. Asia
Length: Up to 39.5 cm (15½ in)

Specialized for life in the bitter chill of the far north, the Arctic fox has an amazing resistance to cold thanks to its extremely thick fur. This is typically pure white in winter, but far darker in summer.

Grizzly bear

**Bulky and powerful, the grizzly bear and its close
relatives are the biggest American carnivores
living south of the Arctic.**

The grizzly bear is a North American subspecies of the
brown bear, which also lives in Europe and Asia. The grizzly
is named for its "grizzled" or silvered fur, not its grisly habits,
although it is certainly capable of killing and eating large
animals. Usually it feeds on smaller animals, plants, berries,
and nuts in late summer, and Alaskan bears eat salmon
caught during their annual spawning migration.

MAMMALS	
GRIZZLY BEAR	
Ursus arctos horribilis	
Location:	North America
Length:	Up to 2.8 m (9 ft)
Diet:	Fruit, plants, meat, fish

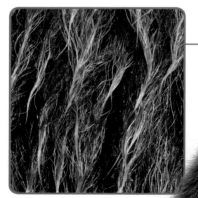

Winter sleep
In winter, food is scarce. The bears cope by fattening
up in late summer, then spending the winter asleep
in a snug den. Their body temperature drops by just
a few degrees while they sleep so that they can
become active again relatively quickly.

Grizzled fur
The fur of a grizzly bear
has pale silvery or golden
tips, giving it a pale-flecked
or "grizzled" appearance. The
fur of other subspecies such
as the Alaskan Kodiak bear
is a deeper, richer brown.

A grizzly bear can
**sleep for more
than six months**
without eating or drinking.

Flat-footed
A bear walks on the soles
of its feet and not on its
toes like most other carnivores.

An adult male grizzly bear can **weigh up to 360 kg (793 lb)**.

A bear **preparing for its winter sleep eats so much** that **it doubles its weight**.

Scavenging grizzly bears are **powerful enough** to **drive wolves away** from their kills.

155

Small eyes
Grizzlies have reasonable eyesight, though their sense of smell is better.

All-purpose teeth
Although the bear has long canines, its other teeth are not specialized for eating meat because it is an omnivore (eats many foods).

Massive claws
The bear has long, strong but blunt claws that it uses for digging and hooking fish. Young bears may use them to climb trees, but the adults weigh too much.

Salmon fishing

In coastal Alaska, grizzly bears satisfy more than half of their annual food needs by catching salmon that swim upriver from the sea in summer to spawn. The bears gather in large numbers at some sites, with the biggest males claiming the best fishing spots.

Watching and waiting
A bear wades into the water and waits. The fish will have to leap this waterfall to swim upstream.

Leaping prey
Intent on making its way upriver to its spawning site, the salmon does not notice the bear waiting in ambush.

Success!
With a snap of its jaws, the bear seizes the salmon in mid-leap. It will carry its prize on shore to eat it.

A giant panda must eat up to 14 kg (31 lb) of bamboo a day to get the nutrients it needs.

1,600 The estimated number of giant pandas in the wild.

MAMMALS
GIANT PANDA
Ailuropoda melanoleuca

Location: East Asia

Length: Up to 1.8 m (6 ft)

Diet: Bamboo

Thumb pad
A thumb-like growth of one of the panda's wrist bones can clamp against its "fingers" to grip bamboo stalks.

Rearing young
Females usually give birth only once every two years. Although twins are common, the mother rarely raises more than one cub. A newborn panda is tiny, blind, and helpless. For its first few months, the cub is cared for by its mother in a special den, only beginning to walk at around three months old. It remains dependent on its mother until it is two years old.

Giant panda

A familiar symbol of the world's endangered wildlife, the giant panda is under threat of extinction. It is a type of bear that feeds almost exclusively on bamboo – a giant grass that grows abundantly in the upland forests of the panda's native central China.

All bears, except the polar bear, eat a lot of plant material. But the giant panda is a specialist that eats meat only very rarely. It is equipped for its bamboo diet with big chewing teeth and a unique adaptation of its forepaws, which allows it to grip its food. However, bamboo is so low in nutrition that the panda has to spend most of its day picking and eating the juiciest shoots it can find.

Bulky body
Its big, muscular stomach allows the panda to digest large amounts of bamboo.

Black and white
Bold-patterned fur may help conceal the panda in snowy, shady forests.

A giant panda spends
16 hours
eating every day.

Foot pads
Like other bears, the giant panda walks on the soles of its feet.

Bamboo shoot

Broad,
crushing,
cheek teeth

Lower jaw

Sharp canine
teeth

Grinding teeth

Compared to other bears, the panda has massive cheek teeth
to crush and grind its food and release the juices inside the
fibrous plant cells. Its large, muscular stomach helps reduce
the bamboo to a pulp. However, its digestive system is more
like that of a carnivore than a typical grazing animal, and it
cannot digest much of the tough plant fibre it eats.

Surrounded by food

The giant panda is a bamboo-eating specialist
because bamboo is so plentiful in its native forests.
But much of the bamboo it eats passes through its
body without being digested, so the panda must eat
a huge amount. When it is not feeding, it saves
energy by sleeping.

Conservation

For thousands of years the giant panda flourished.
But much of its forest habitat has been cleared for
farming, and the panda is now threatened with
extinction. It survives in the wild thanks to special
panda reserves, and it is also being bred in captivity.

SUN BEAR
Helarctos malayanus
Location: Southeast Asia
Length: Up to 1.5 m (5 ft)

The smallest bear, with short fur well suited to its tropical habitat, the sun bear is a good climber and spends much of its life in the trees. It feeds mainly on fruit, but also breaks into bee nests so it can use its very long tongue to lap up honey.

Long tongue
The tongue can protrude up to 25 cm (9³/₄ in) to reach for honey.

SPECTACLED BEAR
Tremarctos ornatus
Location: South America
Length: Up to 1.9 m (6¹/₄ ft)

Also known as the Andean bear, this is the only South American bear. Restricted to the northern Andes mountains, it can be found in scrubby desert and grassland, but favours mountain forests where it climbs trees in search of nuts, fruit, and bark. It consumes very little meat, but does eat insects, snails, and small mammals.

Long, narrow snout

Sharp teeth
The teeth of a polar bear are sharper than those of other bears, and are used for killing prey and tearing it apart. But its teeth are not as well adapted for meat-slicing as those of other predators, since it evolved from omnivorous brown bears that started hunting seals in the far north.

Bears

The bears are the biggest of the carnivores – the order of mammals that includes hunters such as wild dogs and tigers. But while at least one bear can rival the tiger in ferocity, most are omnivores that feed mainly on fruit, nuts, and even insects.

The ancestors of bears were dog-like hunters, but over time most bears became adapted for eating a variety of nutritious foods. Their teeth became less specialized than those of typical carnivores, and the sharp meat-slicing blades gave way to broader cheek teeth for crushing and grinding vegetable foods. But many bears still kill and eat animals, and the polar bear is a full-time meat-eater.

MAMMALS	
POLAR BEAR	
Ursus maritimus	
Location: Arctic seas and coasts	
Length: Up to 2.8 m (9 ft)	
Diet: Seals, small whales, seabirds	

SLOTH BEAR
Melursus ursinus

Location: India

Length: Up to 1.9m (6¼ft)

The sloth bear is a specialized insect-eater that preys largely on ants and termites. Its upper and lower lips can be protruded to form a tube for sucking up swarming insects, and it has large, powerful claws for breaking into termite nests.

Long, tubular snout

Waterproof coat
Its thick, white coat provides the bear with warmth and excellent camouflage.

Polar bear

As well as being the largest bear, and the only one that is a dedicated predator, the polar bear is the largest land predator. It preys mainly on seals – especially ringed seals, which it kills as they surface at breathing holes among the floating pack ice. Its dense, white fur and thick layer of fat allow this bear to hunt on the sea ice throughout the polar winter, and in fact its true habitat is the frozen ocean.

Gripping feet
Huge paws spread the bear's weight on thin ice, and have dimpled pads for extra grip.

V-shape on chest

ASIATIC BLACK BEAR
Ursus thibetanus

Location: Himalayas and eastern Asia

Length: Up to 1.9m (6¼ft)

This forest bear spends up to half its time in the trees, searching for a wide variety of foods including insects, honey, fruit, nuts, and fungi. But it also attacks and eats larger animals such as mountain goats and even water buffalo.

AMERICAN BLACK BEAR
Ursus americanus

Location: North America

Length: Up to 1.9m (6¼ft)

One of the best-known bears, and the most common, this is an adaptable opportunist that can thrive in a wide variety of habitats and eat almost anything, from tender leaves to fish and young deer. Despite this, it sleeps through the winter, for up to eight months in the far north.

A polar bear can smell a seal on the ice from
more than 1km (½ mile) away.

California sea lion

California sea lions are sociable and live in noisy, crowded groups called colonies, near rocky ocean shores. They are also intelligent, highly efficient hunters of fast-swimming fish and squid. They can dive to depths of 30 m (100 ft) or more, holding their breath for up to ten minutes.

Sea lions and fur seals are known as "eared seals" because they have visible ear flaps, unlike true seals such as the harp seal. They also have much longer front flippers, which they use both for moving on land and driving themselves through the water. While the females are sleek and graceful, the males are burly, aggressive heavyweights.

Temperature control
To raise or lower its body temperature, the sea lion raises one flipper out of the water as it swims. This exposes blood vessels, which either absorb warmth from the sun or release excess heat into the atmosphere.

Ear flaps
The sea lion's ears look small, but it has good hearing, especially underwater.

Taking the air
When a sea lion wants to take a breath, it has to contract its cheek muscles to open its nostrils. When it relaxes, its nostrils automatically close to keep the water out as it dives. Unlike a human, the sea lion breathes out before diving, reducing its buoyancy.

Touch sensitive
Sea lions have up to 60 super-sensitive whiskers to help them detect prey in dark or murky waters.

Streamlined shape
A sea lion's neck and body are long and flexible, making it a fast, powerful swimmer.

Powerful forelimbs
The front flippers are used like wings to drive the sea lion through the water.

390 kg (860 lb) – the **maximum weight** of a **male California sea lion**.

A sea lion can **slow its heart rate** from 95 to **20 beats per minute** whilst it is underwater, **to conserve oxygen.**

A sea lion **lives for up to 24** years in the wild.

161

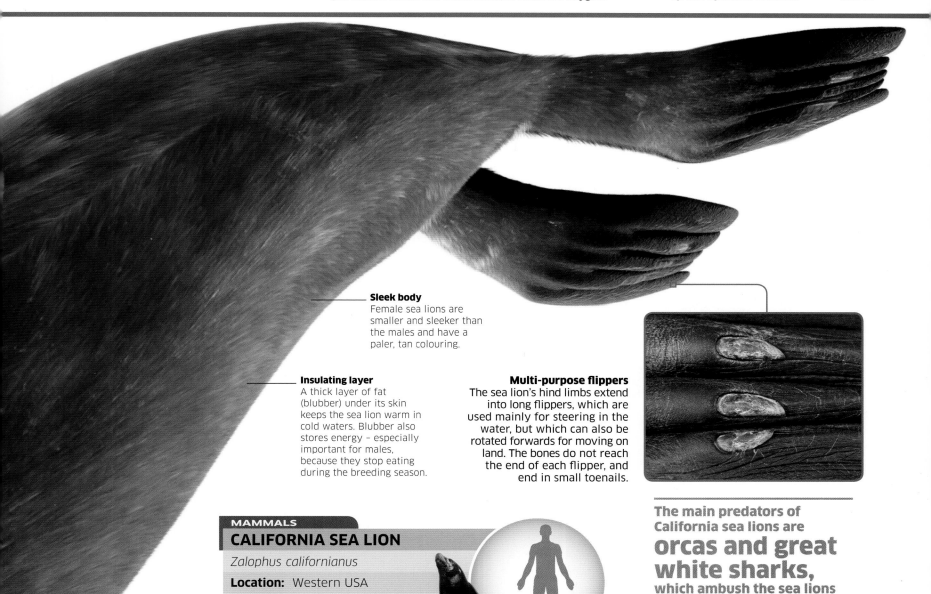

Sleek body
Female sea lions are smaller and sleeker than the males and have a paler, tan colouring.

Insulating layer
A thick layer of fat (blubber) under its skin keeps the sea lion warm in cold waters. Blubber also stores energy – especially important for males, because they stop eating during the breeding season.

Multi-purpose flippers
The sea lion's hind limbs extend into long flippers, which are used mainly for steering in the water, but which can also be rotated forwards for moving on land. The bones do not reach the end of each flipper, and end in small toenails.

The main predators of California sea lions are

orcas and great white sharks,

which ambush the sea lions while they are swimming at the surface.

MAMMALS

CALIFORNIA SEA LION

Zalophus californianus

Location: Western USA

Length: Up to 2.4 m (8 ft)

Diet: Fish, squid

On all fours

To move on land, a sea lion supports most of its weight on its front flippers, turning its hind flippers forwards so it stands on all fours. Then, by arching its back, it moves both its hind limbs forwards, and raises its front end to do the same with its front flippers. It can move surprisingly fast in this manner.

Heavyweight males

In the breeding season, male sea lions fight each other fiercely for females, which they gather together in harems. The winners defend their harems, barking aggressively to discourage rivals. The largest males are the most successful in these conflicts, so they get to breed with the most females and pass on their genes to the next generation. An adult male sea lion can be three times as heavy as a female.

NORTHERN FUR SEAL
Callorhinus ursinus
Location: North Pacific
Length: Up to 2.1 m (6¾ ft)

Similar to sea lions, the fur seals are eared seals with extra-thick fur that helps them survive colder waters. This species is the biggest, with massively built males that compete to mate with the sleeker, lighter females.

WALRUS
Odobenus rosmarus
Location: Arctic waters
Length: Up to 3.5 m (11½ ft)

Instantly recognizable by its long tusks, the walrus uses its sensitive whiskers to locate clams buried in soft, shallow sea beds. Both sexes have tusks, but a male's are bigger. The walrus's thick, wrinkled skin turns pink as it warms up after emerging from the sea.

HOODED SEAL
Cystophora cristata
Location: North Atlantic to Arctic Ocean
Length: Up to 2.7 m (8¾ ft)

This seal lives on drifting sea ice around Greenland. The male has an inflatable black "hood" on his snout, and can also inflate a nasal membrane so it protrudes from one nostril like pink bubble gum. He uses these adornments to show off to rival males and to attract females.

Female hooded seal

Efficient flippers
As with all true seals, the leopard seal's hind flippers point backwards, enabling it to propel itself easily through the water.

BEARDED SEAL
Erignathus barbatus
Location: Arctic waters
Length: Up to 2.5 m (8¼ ft)

The bearded seal is a bulky animal that uses its luxuriant whiskers to search the sea bed for clams and similar prey. It breeds on drifting sea ice.

LEOPARD SEAL
Hydrurga leptonyx
Location: Antarctic waters
Length: Up to 3.4 m (11 ft)

Named for its ferocity as much as for the black spots on its hide, the leopard seal is a powerful predator that hunts other seals and penguins. It often lurks close to floating ice, where it can ambush prey that dives into the water. It also eats a lot of shrimp-like krill and fish when this is available.

Up to 78 per cent of crabeater seals have scars and injuries from failed **leopard seal attacks.**

CRABEATER SEAL
Lobodon carcinophaga
Location: Antarctic waters
Length: Up to 2.4 m (7¾ ft)

Millions of crabeater seals live on sea ice in the cold Southern Ocean. They feed almost exclusively on shrimp-like krill – straining them from the water with elaborate multi-lobed teeth that interlock to form a very efficient sieve.

SOUTHERN ELEPHANT SEAL
Mirounga leonina
Location: Antarctic waters
Length: Up to 5 m (16½ ft)

Male elephant seals are hulking giants, up to five times heavier than the relatively slim females. They fight each other for control of females on the breeding beaches of cold Southern Ocean islands, roaring loudly through their enlarged noses.

HARP SEAL
Pagophilus groenlandicus
Location: North Atlantic to Arctic Ocean
Length: Up to 1.7 m (5½ ft)

Harp seals breed in colonies on sea ice. They favour sites where the ice is too thin and unstable to carry the weight of a polar bear, hoping to keep their white-coated pups safe. But this does not protect them from human hunters, who kill many harp seals every year.

Harp-shaped marking

Sensitive whiskers
The seal's whiskers help it detect prey.

Seal pup

RIBBON SEAL
Histriophoca fasciata
Location: North Pacific, southern Arctic Ocean
Length: Up to 1.5 m (5 ft)

Most seals have drab coloration, but this one has a striking pattern of black with broad white bands. It breeds on drifting sea ice and each female ribbon seal raises her pup alone.

Seals

Specialized for hunting at sea, seals are marine carnivores. But unlike some ocean mammals, they cannot spend their entire lives at sea – they must return to land to breed.

Seals form a group known as the pinnipeds. There are three types – the eared seals, the walrus, and the true seals. Eared seals include the sea lions and fur seals. As well as the external ear flaps for which they are named, they have long front flippers and can move quite well on land. The walrus is similar but with long tusks. True seals have hind limbs specialized for swimming and move on land with difficulty.

A skunk's spray can be **smelt** by a human up to **1 km (½ mile) away**.

Striped skunk

Many animals are armed with defensive weapons to keep predators away, but few of these are as effective as a skunk's. Any predator that tries to attack it risks being drenched in a blast of foul-smelling chemicals.

Skunks are nocturnal, solitary carnivores that are similar to the badgers and weasels. But despite being technically a carnivore, the striped skunk eats a variety of foods – mostly insects, but also small mammals, carrion, and some fruit and other plant material. It can live in a variety of habitats, including woodlands, forests, agricultural land, and even towns. During the winter, the striped skunk spends most of its time in an underground den and can lose up to half its body weight.

Alarm signal
If the skunk is disturbed, its fur will stand on end.

Facing the enemy
When cornered, and while still facing the threat, a skunk can bend its rear around and direct the spray.

Narrow jaw
The jaws and teeth are adapted for eating insects and other small animals.

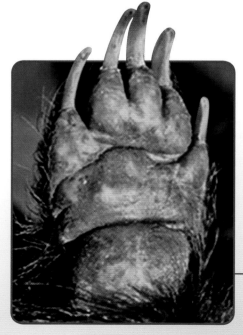

Digging claws
The skunk's front feet are equipped with five long, stout claws, which it uses to dig in the soil for food. A lot of its prey consists of juicy insect grubs that it digs out of the ground. It may also excavate its own den, although it often uses a ready-made burrow dug by another animal.

Flat feet
A skunk walks on the soles of its feet, like bears do.

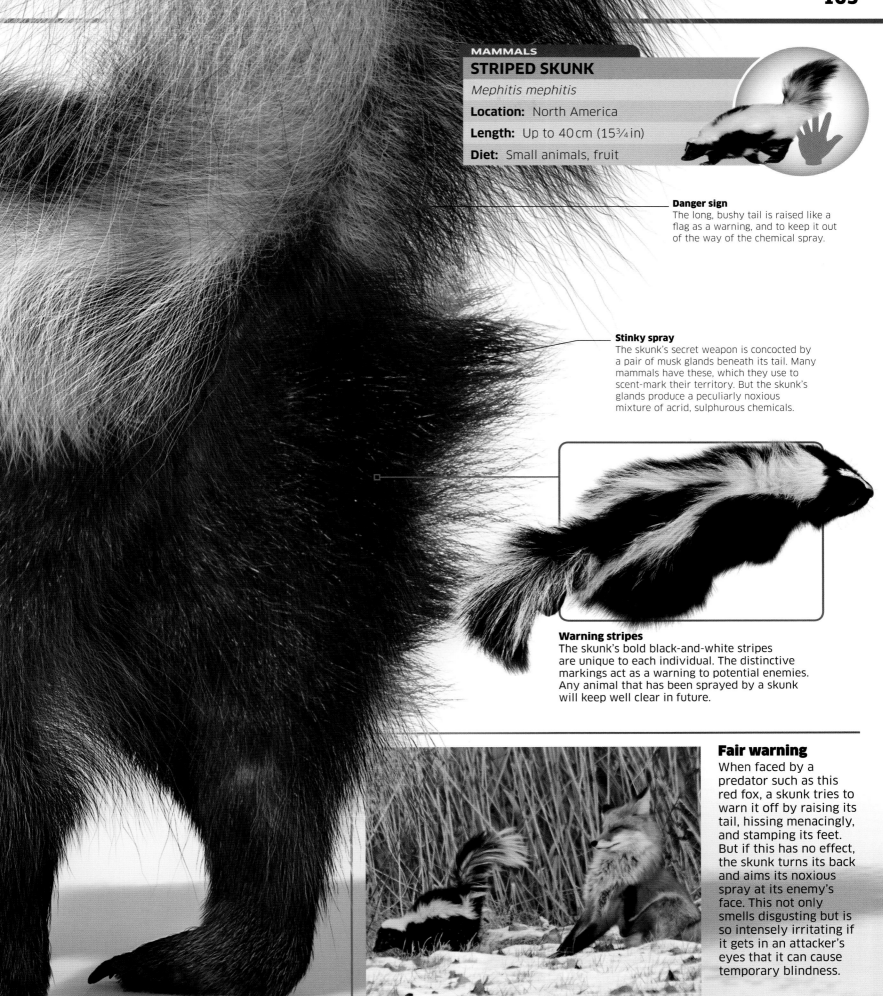

MAMMALS

STRIPED SKUNK

Mephitis mephitis

Location: North America

Length: Up to 40 cm (15¾ in)

Diet: Small animals, fruit

Danger sign
The long, bushy tail is raised like a flag as a warning, and to keep it out of the way of the chemical spray.

Stinky spray
The skunk's secret weapon is concocted by a pair of musk glands beneath its tail. Many mammals have these, which they use to scent-mark their territory. But the skunk's glands produce a peculiarly noxious mixture of acrid, sulphurous chemicals.

Warning stripes
The skunk's bold black-and-white stripes are unique to each individual. The distinctive markings act as a warning to potential enemies. Any animal that has been sprayed by a skunk will keep well clear in future.

Fair warning
When faced by a predator such as this red fox, a skunk tries to warn it off by raising its tail, hissing menacingly, and stamping its feet. But if this has no effect, the skunk turns its back and aims its noxious spray at its enemy's face. This not only smells disgusting but is so intensely irritating if it gets in an attacker's eyes that it can cause temporary blindness.

The **jaws and teeth** of a **wolverine** are **strong enough to crack the thigh bone** of a moose.

SEA OTTER
Enhydra lutris
Location: North Pacific shores
Length: Up to 1.2 m (4 ft)

Mustelids

Typical mustelids are sleek, sinuous, fiercely predatory land animals that often hunt and kill animals bigger than themselves. But some mustelids hunt in the water, and others are stocky omnivores.

The predators are the weasels, mink, and polecats – short-legged, low-slung hunters that are built for pursuing prey in underground burrows. Martens have a similar build, but are adapted for leaping through the trees, while otters are equipped for swimming and diving. The badgers, by contrast, are specialized for digging in search of small prey, and eat a very wide range of foods.

Prickly prey
The otter dives to gather sea urchins and eats them at the surface while floating on its back.

Webbed feet
Big hind feet have webbed toes for propulsion when swimming and diving.

One of the heaviest of the mustelids, this otter lives almost entirely at sea among the submerged kelp (seaweed) forests of north Pacific shores. An extremely dense coat of fur provides such good insulation that the otter can sleep on the water, anchored by kelp fronds to avoid being swept away by the current.

EURASIAN OTTER
Lutra lutra
Location: Eurasia, northwest Africa
Length: Up to 82 cm (32¼ in)

This elegant aquatic hunter has a tapering tail and dense, short fur that give it perfect streamlining underwater. It mainly hunts fish in rivers, lakes, and shallow coastal seas, locating them in cloudy water with its long, sensitive whiskers.

WOLVERINE
Gulo gulo
Location: Northern Eurasia, North America
Length: Up to 1.5 m (5 ft)

One of the biggest mustelids, the wolverine lives in the northern forests and Arctic tundra, where it hunts and scavenges for prey as large as reindeer. It has hugely powerful jaws for gnawing at frozen meat and crushing bones.

A least weasel is able to **kill a rabbit ten times its own weight**.

The sea otter's **fur is denser** than the **fur of any other animal**.

1.8 m (6 ft) – the length of the **longest mustelid**, the **giant otter**.

167

EUROPEAN PINE MARTEN
Martes martes

Location: Europe, western Asia
Length: Up to 58 cm (23 in)

Unlike other mustelids, martens regularly hunt in trees, and have sharp semi-retractable claws for climbing. The European pine marten is one of the best known; active mainly at night, it leaps from branch to branch with effortless grace to pursue squirrels. It also hunts on the ground for other small animals.

Furry tail
The marten's long, furry tail helps it keep its balance.

EUROPEAN BADGER
Meles meles

Location: Europe, western Asia
Length: Up to 90 cm (35½ in)

The European badger uses its sturdy clawed feet to create extensive burrow systems, and to dig up juicy roots, insect grubs, and other small animals, including entire wasps' nests. It feeds mainly on earthworms, but it may take ground-nesting birds, moles, hedgehogs, and similar prey. It also eats a lot of fruit and nuts.

LEAST WEASEL
Mustela nivalis

Location: Northern Eurasia, North America
Length: Up to 26 cm (10¼ in)

Although this is the smallest mustelid, it is a formidable hunter. Its slender, flexible body is primarily adapted for chasing mice and voles through their runs and burrows, but it can kill much larger prey. In the far north its fur turns pure white in winter.

White underside

Tiger

The largest of the big cats, the tiger is one of the most powerful predators on Earth. Relying on its enormous strength, it is specialized for hunting big prey.

Few predators regularly hunt alone for animals larger than themselves, but a tiger may take on a buffalo six times its own weight. Stealthily it creeps as close as possible, then charges and leaps on its victim from behind. Smaller animals may be killed with a bite to the top of the neck while larger animals are seized by the throat and throttled.

White flashes
Seen from the back, each ear is black with a central patch of pure white. During an aggressive encounter, the tiger flattens and twists its ears so that the spots are visible from the front. This suggests the flashes are mainly used as a warning.

Striped coat
A wild tiger is nearly always orange with black stripes, and is whiter below.

Long tail
The tiger uses its tail for balance during an attack.

Short, muscular neck

Leaping legs
Longer back legs help the tiger to jump.

Protective padding
Loose skin around the belly provides protection during tiger fights.

Muscle power
Powerful front legs help to bring down prey.

Big paws
The feet have broad, cushioned pads for silent stalking.

Camouflage

Whereas most big cats have plain or spotted coats, the tiger has unusual dark stripes. They act as very effective camouflage, especially among long grass where they mimic the vertical pattern of light and shade. The stripes break up the tiger's outline, allowing it to get very close to its target without being detected, as it stalks prey before launching an attack.

Retractable claws

The claws are adapted for seizing prey, rather than traction when running. Normally they are retracted into sheaths, which keeps their tips needle-sharp. But when the tiger leaps on a victim, its front legs straighten and the claws extend automatically to seize hold of its quarry.

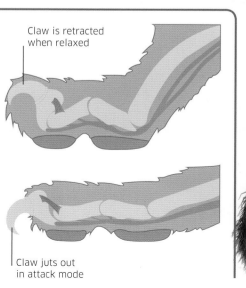

Claw is retracted when relaxed

Claw juts out in attack mode

50 kg (110 lb) – the **amount of meat a tiger can eat in a single meal.**

Tigers can run at **up to 65 km/h (40 mph)** in short sprints.

169

Touch sensitive
Long whiskers help the tiger feel its way in the dark.

Rounded ears
Although its ears are small, a tiger has excellent hearing.

Furry ruff
Males have a large ruff of fur around their necks.

Canine tooth

Carnassial teeth

Killing power
Like all cats, the tiger has big, meat-slicing carnassial teeth but no chewing teeth. This gives it a short jaw, which maximizes the pressure that its powerful jaw muscles exert on the huge, prey-killing canine teeth.

MAMMALS

TIGER

Panthera tigris

Location: S. and E. Asia

Length: Up to 2.9 m (9½ ft)

Diet: Mainly large hoofed mammals

Cheetah

No animal can run faster than a cheetah. This highly specialized cat is uniquely adapted for accelerating faster than most sports cars, and pursuing its prey over short distances at blistering speed. Only the swiftest, most agile of its quarry can hope to escape.

The cheetah is different from other cats, which rely on stealth, strength, and sharp claws for hunting. By contrast the cheetah is a sprinter, like a greyhound, with the same slender build, flexible spine, and long legs. But it must creep as close as possible before launching its attack, because it cannot keep up its speed for very long.

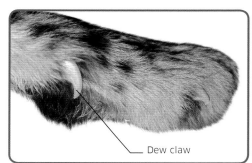

MAMMALS

CHEETAH

Acinonyx jubatus

Location: Africa, W. Asia

Length: Up to 1.4 m (4½ ft)

Diet: Small grazing animals

Vital tail
The long tail helps the cheetah balance when turning at speed.

Curved claw
Each foreleg has a sharp, curved dew claw on the inner side, just above the foot. The cheetah uses the claw to trip prey up when it is within range. Once it has its victim on the ground, the cat kills it with a suffocating throat bite.

— Dew claw

In for the kill
Cheetahs usually hunt small, fast gazelles, which are often agile enough to elude them by quicky changing direction. The cheetah's quick bursts of speed can cause it to overheat, and once it catches its prey and kills it, the cat may have to recover for up to 20 minutes before it is able to start eating.

Running claws
The main claws lack fleshy sheaths, so are always exposed. They provide grip like the spikes on running shoes.

Each chase lasts only **45 seconds** to **a minute** on average. Any longer than that and the cheetah will **give up**.

Cheetahs **frequently lose kills** to other **big cats** due to their **lack of stamina**.

40–50 per cent of **cheetah chases** end in a **kill**.

171

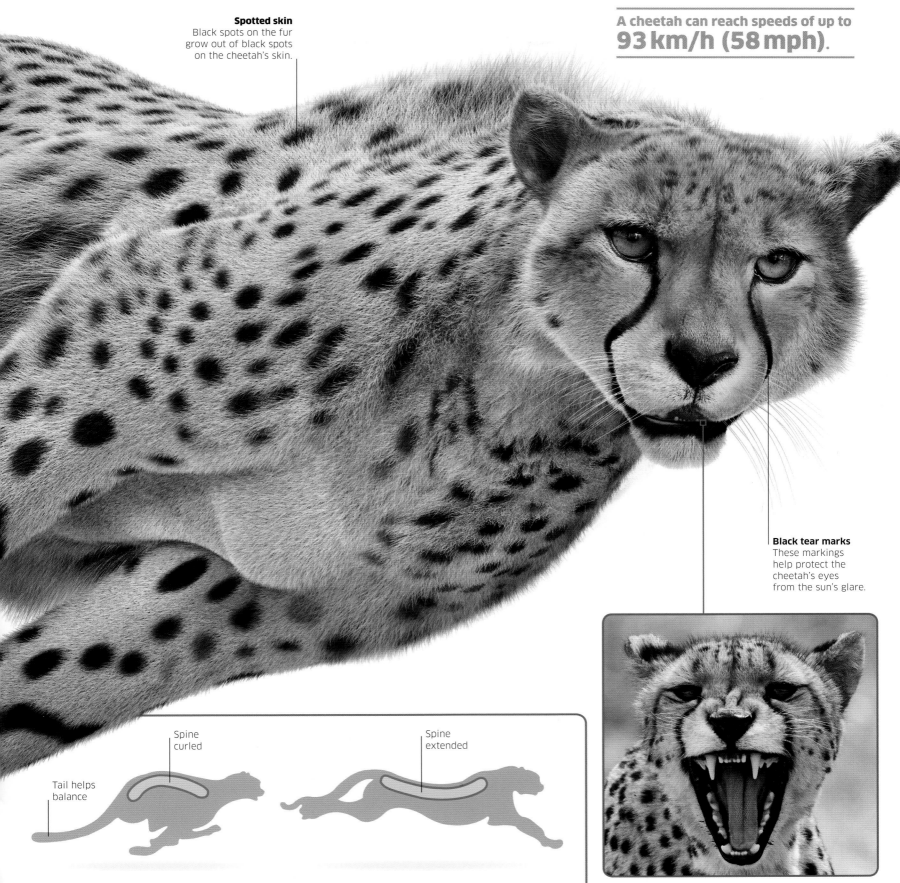

Spotted skin
Black spots on the fur grow out of black spots on the cheetah's skin.

A cheetah can reach speeds of up to
93 km/h (58 mph).

Black tear marks
These markings help protect the cheetah's eyes from the sun's glare.

Spine curled

Spine extended

Tail helps balance

Flexible spine

The cheetah owes its astonishing speed to its extremely long stride, which allows it to cover a lot of ground with each step. It has very long legs, and their effective length is increased by a flexible spine. When the cheetah is moving at full speed the spine curls up to allow the hind legs to reach forward, then straightens and extends in the opposite direction to allow them to push back further than usual.

Small teeth
Compared with typical big cats, the cheetah has small canine teeth. This is because it has extra-large nostrils to take in all the air it needs for a high-speed chase. The nostrils take up a lot of space in its skull, leaving no room for broad upper-canine tooth roots.

Family life
A lion pride varies in size according to location and the availability of prey. It consists of up to eight adult females, their young, and between one and three adult males, who defend the territory and protect the pride from rival males.

Lion

Almost as big as tigers, and with the same body adaptations for killing large prey, lions are the only big cats that live in groups, called prides. Males and females look different, reflecting their separate roles within the pride.

Female lions, or lionesses, are sleek, fast, and agile. They are effective hunters, either alone or in pairs and groups. Males are much bigger and more muscular. When they fight for control of prides, the biggest males nearly always win, so they get to mate with the most females and the cubs inherit their strength. Male lions are strong enough to kill large prey, but they usually leave hunting to the more athletic females.

Magnificent mane
Male lions' manes range in colour from golden to very dark, and tend to darken with age. The darker and thicker the mane, the more attractive the male is to females.

Hunting tactics
Lionesses are the main hunters for the pride. They stalk prey to within 30 m (98½ ft) before launching an attack, and often work together to surround an animal and cut off its escape.

An adult male lion's roar is so loud it can be heard up to 8 km (5 miles) away.

Tufty tail
Among cats, the tuft at the tip of the tail is unique to lions.

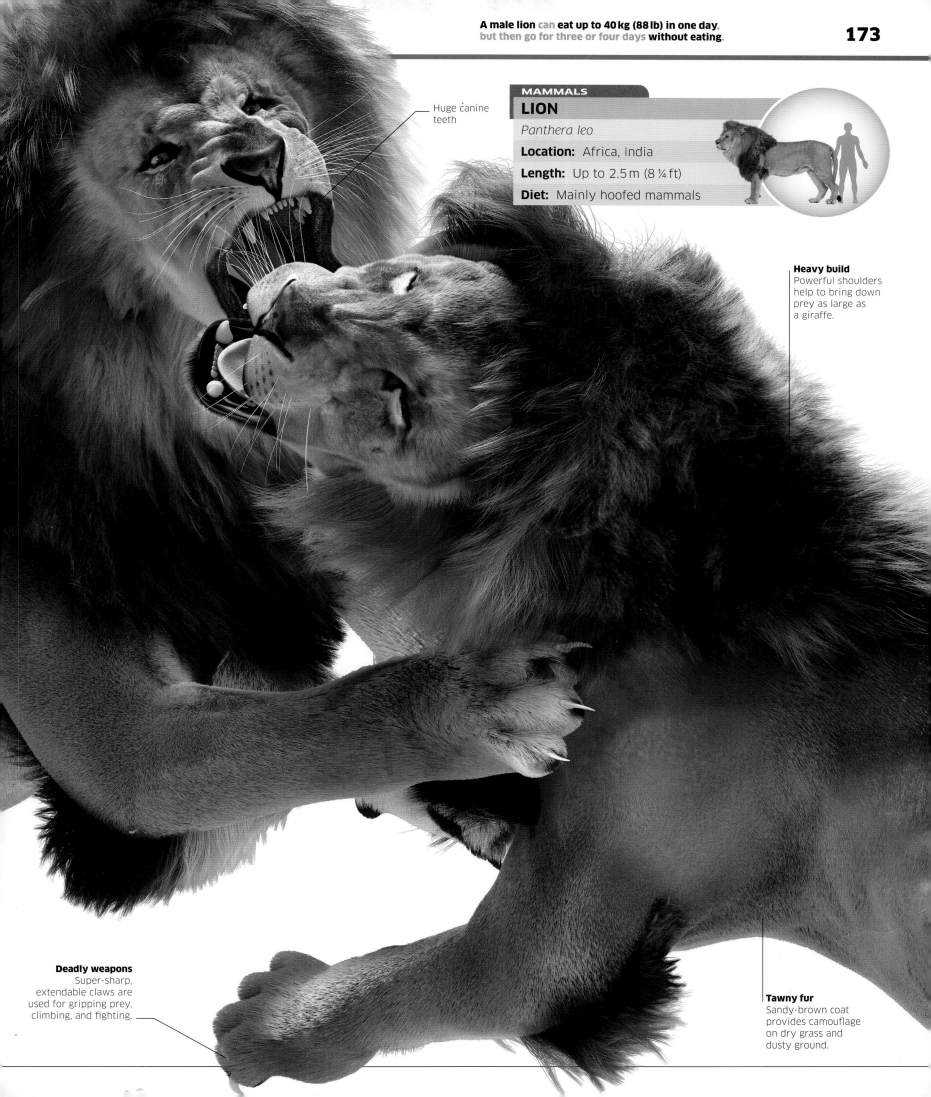

A male lion can eat up to 40 kg (88 lb) in one day, but then go for three or four days without eating.

173

Huge canine teeth

MAMMALS

LION

Panthera leo

Location: Africa, India

Length: Up to 2.5 m (8 ¼ ft)

Diet: Mainly hoofed mammals

Heavy build
Powerful shoulders help to bring down prey as large as a giraffe.

Deadly weapons
Super-sharp, extendable claws are used for gripping prey, climbing, and fighting.

Tawny fur
Sandy-brown coat provides camouflage on dry grass and dusty ground.

A snow leopard **kills** an average of **one large animal every two weeks**.

Snow leopards can hunt at **altitudes of 3,000–4,500 m** (9,840–14,760 ft).

Snow leopard

The most elusive of the big cats, the snow leopard is rarely seen due to its solitary nature and extreme habitat. It lives in some of the highest, coldest, most hostile mountain terrain on Earth and is uniquely adapted to survive in this harsh environment.

Native to the mountain ranges of Asia, including the Himalayas and the vast Tibetan plateau, the snow leopard is a solitary hunter that preys on a variety of animals ranging from ground squirrels to camels. Its main prey are ibex and wild sheep, which it pursues over steep, rocky slopes with astounding agility. Its large lungs ensure that it gathers enough oxygen from the thin mountain air, while its very thick fur keeps it warm.

MAMMALS
SNOW LEOPARD

Panthera uncia

Location: Central Asia

Length: Up to 1.25 m (4 ft)

Diet: Mammals and ground birds

Long fur
The snow leopard's long, thick fur gives it a stocky appearance. It can grow up to 12 cm (5 in) long in winter.

Small ears

Furry feet
The soles of a snow leopard's feet are unusually furry. This helps to prevent the cat losing heat through its feet, and may improve its grip on bare rock. The feet are also broader than those of most cats; they spread its weight across deep snow, helping to stop the animal from sinking in.

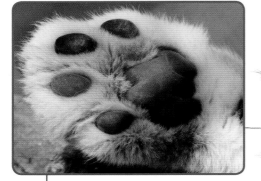

Deep breather
Big nasal cavities allow the snow leopard to inhale large amounts of air at a time.

Coat markings
Dark-grey and black spots provide camouflage

Retractable claws

6,500 The maximum number of **snow leopards thought to be left in the wild**. There may be **as few as 4,000.**

A snow leopard uses its **thick, very furry tail** like a duvet, **to keep warm** while it is asleep.

A snow leopard can kill prey
up to three times its own weight.

Short legs
The legs are relatively short, adapted for agility rather than speed.

Lean, muscular body

Balancing tail
The snow leopard's extra-long, bushy tail helps the animal to keep its balance when leaping from rock to rock in pursuit of prey. Snow leopards often chase fast-moving animals such as ibex down very steep slopes, gaining speed as they race downhill, but rarely missing their footing on the rocky terrain.

Hidden in plain view
A snow leopard prefers to ambush prey from above in the dim light of dawn or dusk. Using rocks and shrubs for cover, it relies on its superb camouflage to stay concealed from potential prey. Even in broad daylight it can be very difficult to pick out when crouching quietly on a boulder, the mottled pattern of its coat blending seamlessly with the patchwork of lichen and bare rock.

Rocky nursery
Typically solitary, male and female snow leopards meet to mate in late winter. Between one and five cubs are born just over three months later, in a rocky den. Initially blind and helpless, the cubs stay with their mother for at least 18 months before leaving to find their own hunting territories.

CARACAL
Caracal caracal

Location: Africa, Arabia, Southwest Asia

Length: Up to 1.1 m (3½ ft)

Also known as the desert lynx, this cat's most obvious feature is its long, lynx-like, black-tufted ears. The caracal is a nocturnal hunter, mainly of small mammals, birds, and reptiles, but it will also take on larger, faster animals, such as antelope.

Short tail

Wild cats

Dedicated predators, cats are adapted for eating meat and nothing else. They cannot chew, and their short jaws and big, stabbing canine teeth are specialized weapons for grabbing and killing prey.

The cat family is divided into two groups. The pantherines, most of which can roar, include most of the big cats. Non-pantherines cannot roar, and are usually smaller – although this group does include the cheetah and puma. Cats are almost all solitary hunters that rely on stealth to get close enough to prey to launch an attack.

SERVAL
Leptailurus serval

Location: Sub-Saharan Africa

Length: Up to 92 cm (36¼ in)

This tall African cat is adapted for stalking through long grass, listening for small prey with its huge, mobile ears. Compared to its overall body size, it has the longest legs of any cat species.

OCELOT
Leopardus pardalis

Location: Central and South America

Length: Up to 1 m (3¼ ft)

Feeling the way
Long, sensitive whiskers help the ocelot find its way at night.

EUROPEAN WILDCAT
Felis silvestris silvestris

Location: Europe

Length: Up to 66 cm (26 in)

Related to the ancestor of the domestic cat, the European wildcat looks similar to a pet tabby, but with a bushier tail. Rare and very shy, it is a ferocious hunter of small mammals. Other subspecies of the wildcat live in Africa and Asia.

The beautiful striped and spotted coat of the ocelot provides it with superb camouflage among the dappled shade of its tropical forest habitat. A lone, night-time hunter, it is a good climber and swimmer, preying on a variety of mammals, birds, reptiles, and even fish.

Highly territorial, ocelots sometimes
fight to the death
over disputed ground.

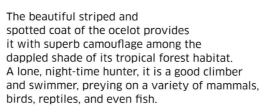

The **jaguar** has exceptionally **powerful jaws**, and can **bite clean through a turtle shell**.

Leopards often **drag their prey up trees** to stop other **predators stealing it**.

The puma is the **most widespread** of all **American land animals**.

177

EURASIAN LYNX
Lynx lynx
Location: Eastern Europe, Asia
Length: Up to 1.1 m (3½ ft)

Like all lynxes, this species has black-tufted ears and a short tail. It hunts mainly in cold, northern forests where its large, furry paws stop it from sinking into deep snow. It can kill animals up to four times its size, such as reindeer.

MARBLED CAT
Pardofelis marmorata
Location: Southeast Asia
Length: Up to 62 cm (24½ in)

Like many cats, this beautifully marked small cat is an excellent climber, but is unusual in that it spends much of its time in trees. High in the tropical forest canopy, it hunts birds, squirrels, lizards, and similar small prey, mostly at night.

PUMA
Puma concolor
Location: Americas
Length: Up to 1.6 m (5¼ ft)

Also known as the cougar, or mountain lion, the puma is one of the biggest non-pantherine cats, and is strong enough to kill a moose. Adaptable to different habitats, it has a vast range across the Americas, living in deserts, prairies, forests, and mountains.

PALLAS'S CAT
Otocolobus manul
Location: Central Asia
Length: Up to 65 cm (25½ in)

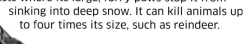

Its short legs and very thick fur give this cat an unusually stocky, bulky appearance. Its fur provides insulation against the bitter chill of the Himalayas and the Tibetan plateau.

FISHING CAT
Prionailurus viverrinus
Location: Southern Asia
Length: Up to 1.1 m (3½ ft)

This is the only cat that feeds mainly on fish. It usually scoops them out of the shallows along the banks of rivers, but it will also dive underwater and swim after particularly tempting prey.

JAGUAR
Panthera onca
Location: Central and South America
Length: Up to 1.7 m (5½ ft)

The biggest American cat, and the only New World pantherine, the jaguar is found in a variety of forest habitats and swampy grasslands. It preys on anything it can catch, from mice to crocodilians.

Spotted coat
The rosettes are usually larger than those of a leopard.

INDOCHINESE CLOUDED LEOPARD
Neofelis nebulosa
Location: Eastern Asia
Length: Up to 1.1 m (3½ ft)

A dramatically marked species, the clouded leopard has exceptionally long canine teeth that enable it to kill prey much larger than itself, such as deer and wild pigs. It is a very good climber, and has been seen running head-first down tree trunks and hanging upside-down from branches.

LEOPARD
Panthera pardus
Location: Africa, southern Asia
Length: Up to 1.9 m (6¼ ft)

The leopard is a stealthy hunter that can survive in many different habitats, from deserts to jungles and swamps. All leopards are marked all over with clusters of black spots – even black leopards, whose very dark fur masks their spotted pattern.

Rosette-like spots are visible in the dark fur

Sharp weapons
Retractable claws always stay sharp.

In Tanzania's **Ngorongoro Crater**, spotted hyenas obtain **90 per cent** of their food by **hunting**.

15 minutes – the time it can take a group of hyenas to **eat a zebra**.

Scavenging lions often **steal the kills** of less powerful hyenas.

Good hearing
Large rounded ears direct sound efficiently and mean that the hyena can hear and communicate very well.

Sharp eyes
Excellent vision allows the hyena to pinpoint its prey.

Laughing call
Spotted hyenas make a variety of calls to communicate with each other, some of which are known for sounding like human laughter.

Sharp canine tooth

MAMMALS

SPOTTED HYENA

Crocuta crocuta

Location: Sub-Saharan Africa

Length: Up to 1.6 m (5¼ ft)

Diet: Other mammals, carrion

60 km/h (37 mph) – the **speed** at which a **spotted hyena** can **chase its prey**.

14 kg (31 lb) – the amount of **meat** a spotted hyena can **eat at a sitting**.

179

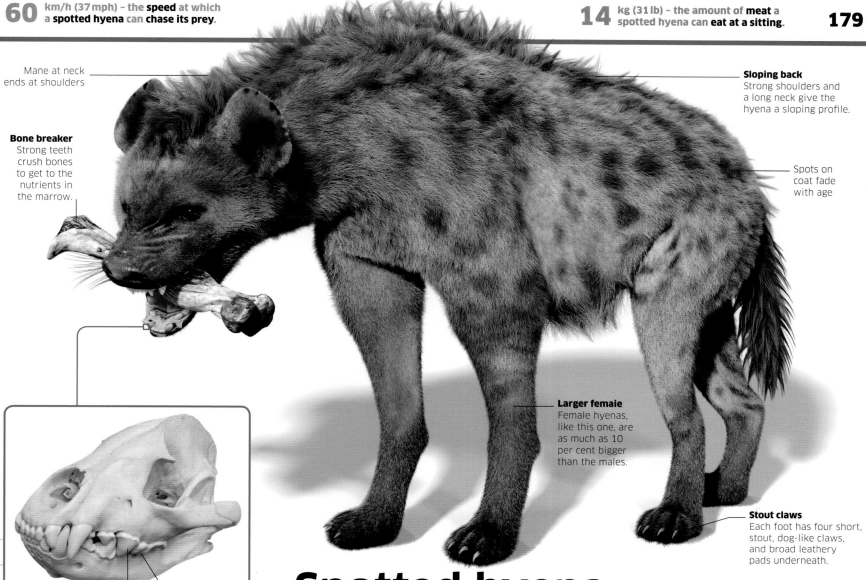

Mane at neck ends at shoulders

Bone breaker
Strong teeth crush bones to get to the nutrients in the marrow.

Sloping back
Strong shoulders and a long neck give the hyena a sloping profile.

Spots on coat fade with age

Larger female
Female hyenas, like this one, are as much as 10 per cent bigger than the males.

Stout claws
Each foot has four short, stout, dog-like claws, and broad leathery pads underneath.

Bone-crushing premolar   Carnassial

Bone-crushing teeth
The hyena's massively muscled jaws are armed with huge, conical premolar teeth that are strong enough to shatter the leg bones of a giraffe. These lie in front of sharp, blade-like carnassial teeth, similar to those of cats and dogs, for scissoring through tough hide, meat, and sinew.

Spotted hyena

Sometimes known as the laughing hyena because of its eerie cackling calls, this scavenger is also one of the most lethally effective predators on the African plains.

The spotted hyena is adapted for scavenging the remains of the dead, with hugely powerful jaws and teeth for cracking the bones that other carnivores discard, and a digestive system that can process every part of a carcass. Despite this it mainly kills live prey, often hunting in packs. Its combined talents have made it the most successful big carnivore in Africa.

Hyena society
Spotted hyenas live in female-dominated clans of up to 80 animals, although most clans are smaller. Young females stay in the clan, while young males leave to join neighbouring clans.

Hunting
Other hyena species are primarily scavengers, but in most parts of its range (the area where it lives) the spotted hyena is mainly a hunter. It tackles small prey alone, but hunts in packs for big prey such as zebras or even African buffalo. The hyenas wear down their victim by a long chase that can cover up to 5 km (3 miles), then launch a joint attack.

Closeable ears
The meerkat can close its small ears tightly to keep out sand and dust whilst digging.

High viewpoint
Standing upright on a rock, mound, or bush helps the meerkat spot potential danger as early as possible.

Digging claws
The very long claws on the meerkat's front paws are adapted for digging – both to make burrows and to dig for insects and small mammals. A meerkat can dig very quickly, shifting its own weight in sand in just a few seconds.

Meerkat

Its habit of standing up on its hind legs, either to watch for predators or bask in the morning sun, has made this slender desert mongoose one of the most instantly recognizable of African mammals.

The various species of mongoose are small, ground-dwelling carnivores. The meerkat is one of the most sociable, living in clans of around 20 in large networks of underground burrows, dug in the sandy soil of southern African deserts. These clans hunt insects and other small animals by daylight, while one meerkat stands guard. When it spots danger, it gives a warning bark or whistle. The other meerkats then run for safety to the nearest burrow entrance.

Slender feet
The hind legs have powerful thighs but small, slender feet.

Balancing tail
The dark-tipped tail helps the meerkat balance when standing upright.

Venomous prey
Meerkats often eat scorpions, and may have some immunity to the powerful venom. But the meerkat usually avoids being stung by grabbing the scorpion and biting off its tail, which carries the sting. The scorpion is then defenceless and makes an easy prey. A meerkat pup, such as the one pictured left, is taught to do this by adults in its clan.

Group sunbathing
Each meerkat clan is dominated by one breeding pair that produces most of the young. Other male and female adults in the clan help to care for the breeding pair's pups. Each morning, the whole clan may gather outside the burrow to warm up after the cold desert night. They either lie on their backs or stand upright, soaking up as much sunlight as possible.

One burrow can have up to 15 entrance holes and several different levels.

A meerkat can spot a bird of prey more than 300 m (984 ft) away.

181

MAMMALS

MEERKAT

Suricata suricatta

Location: Southern Africa

Length: Up to 29 cm (11½ in)

Diet: Insects and other small animals

Sensitive snout
The meerkat uses its excellent sense of smell to sniff out prey, and to identify other meerkats, either as clan members or enemies.

Anti-glare patches
Dark markings around the eyes improve the meerkat's vision by reducing glare from the sun.

A meerkat can make **different alarm calls** depending on whether it spots predators on the ground or in the air.

Heat-absorber
Dark skin beneath the fur warms up fast when the meerkat stands upright to soak in the sun.

Hunter's view
The eyes face forwards, giving binocular (two-eyed) vision, which enables the meerkat to see in 3D and judge distances accurately.

Desert camouflage
Grey-brown fur provides good camouflage in the scrubby, sandy deserts of southern Africa.

AFRICAN WILD ASS
Equus africanus
Location: Northeast Africa
Length: Up to 2 m (6¹/₂ ft)

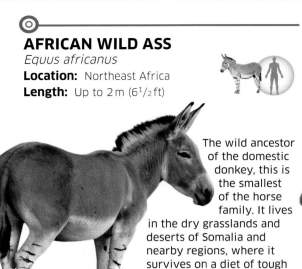

The wild ancestor of the domestic donkey, this is the smallest of the horse family. It lives in the dry grasslands and deserts of Somalia and nearby regions, where it survives on a diet of tough desert plants and can go without water for up to three days.

ONAGER
Equus hemionus
Location: Western and central Asia
Length: Up to 2.5 m (8¹/₄ ft)

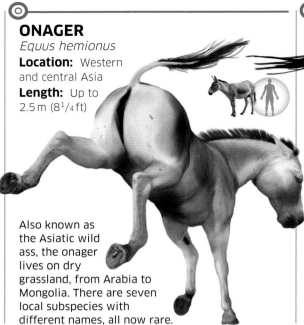

Also known as the Asiatic wild ass, the onager lives on dry grassland, from Arabia to Mongolia. There are seven local subspecies with different names, all now rare.

KIANG
Equus kiang
Location: Central Asia
Length: Up to 2.1 m (6³/₄ ft)

Closely related to the onager, but with a darker coat, the kiang lives on the high Tibetan plateau to the north of the Himalayas. It is the least threatened of the wild asses, and sometimes gathers in large herds of 100 or more.

PRZEWALSKI'S HORSE
Equus przewalskii
Location: Central Asia
Length: Up to 2.8 m (9¹/₄ ft)

This is the only surviving truly wild horse that is related to the ancestors of domestic horses. Discovered in Mongolia in the 1870s but almost wiped out in the 20th century, it has been reintroduced to its native range and appears to be slowly increasing in numbers.

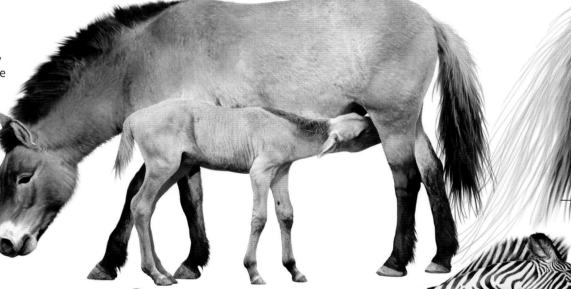

Fly whisk
Mobile tail has a tuft of long hair for brushing away biting flies.

MOUNTAIN ZEBRA
Equus zebra
Location: Southwest Africa
Length: Up to 2.6 m (8¹/₂ ft)

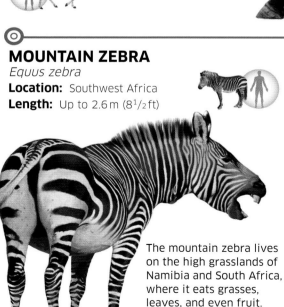

The mountain zebra lives on the high grasslands of Namibia and South Africa, where it eats grasses, leaves, and even fruit. It has narrow stripes with broad horizontal bands on its haunches.

GRÉVY'S ZEBRA
Equus grevyi
Location: East Africa
Length: Up to 2.7 m (8³/₄ ft)

The biggest and rarest of the zebras, Grévy's zebra has narrow stripes and a slender head. Restricted to a few dry grasslands in east Africa, it wanders nomadically in search of food and water. When breeding, males form groups which occupy and defend large territories.

Male rivalry
Territorial stallions may fight with rivals.

A **newborn Grévy's zebra** can stand after just six minutes, and **run away from predators within 45 minutes**.

Onagers are **among the fastest hoofed mammals**, able to **run at 70 km/h (43 mph)**.

183

Horses

Domestic horses are familiar worldwide, but most of their wild relatives are now very rare. Only the kiang and the plains zebra roam the grasslands in large herds, like the domestic horse's ancestors.

Horses are adapted for life on open plains, where there is no cover and the only defence against powerful predators is to outrun them. Long legs and specialized hooves give horses the speed they need, while their big teeth enable them to feed on coarse, abrasive grass.

Bristly mane
The striped mane is coarse and bristly, and stands upright.

Plains zebra
Beneath its stripes, the plains zebra has all the familiar features of horses – a long muzzle so it can graze while keeping watch for danger, big chewing teeth, long legs, and a single large hoof on each foot. The reason for its bold stripes is unknown, but theories include helping the herd to blend in as one, keeping the animal cool, and even warding off insect bites.

Toe bone

Bony hoof core

Hoof

Single hoof
The ancestors of zebras, horses, and asses had three or more toes. But after millions of years of evolution, now just one toe on each foot remains, capped by a strong hoof. The result is a strong, shock-absorbing foot ideal for running at speed.

MAMMALS
PLAINS ZEBRA

Equus quagga burchellii

Location: Eastern and southern Africa

Length: Up to 2.5 m (8¼ ft)

Diet: Grass, leaves, buds

Black rhinoceros

With its huge horned head and thick hide, the black rhinoceros is a survivor from a prehistoric age of giant herbivores. Now critically endangered by illegal hunting, it is restricted to a few wildlife reserves in eastern and southern Africa.

The black rhinoceros is a heavyweight browser – an animal that feeds by gathering the leaves and tender shoots of bushes and trees. These do not contain a lot of nutrients, but the rhino's great size enables it to eat them in bulk to get the nutrition it needs. Its horns can kill enemies such as lions, and are also used in fights between rivals, often inflicting lethal wounds.

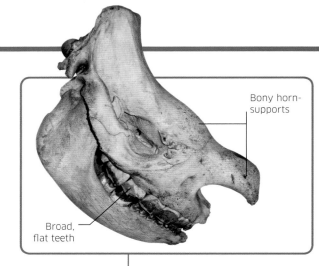

Bony horn-supports

Broad, flat teeth

Thick hide
The rhino's thick skin protects it from sharp thorns.

Neck hump

Massive skull
The black rhinoceros has a heavy skull and jaw, with large cheek teeth but no front teeth. Its horns rest on bony supports, with an extension of the skull supporting the larger front horn.

Ears fringed with hairs

Tufted tail

Horns
Black rhinos normally have two horns and the front horn is the longest.

Small eyes
A rhino has poor vision, and relies on its hearing and sense of smell.

Hoofed foot
The big, sturdy feet each have three hoofed toes.

Armed protection
In the late 20th century, the black rhinoceros was almost wiped out by poachers, who today still sell its horn for use in traditional Chinese medicine or for dagger handles. It is now strictly protected within fenced reserves, often by armed guards, but numbers are still low. This blind baby rhino is one of many that face continued threats to their survival.

BLACK RHINO

WHITE RHINO

Pointed or square?
While the foliage-browsing black rhino has a pointed, prehensile upper lip for grasping leaves, the African white rhino is a grazer, with a square lip for cropping grass at ground level.

1.3 m (4¼ ft) – the **length** of the **largest-known black rhino horn**.

There are only about **5,000** black rhinos **alive today**.

55 km/h (34 mph) – the **top speed of a black rhino**.

MAMMALS

BLACK RHINOCEROS

Diceros bicornis

Location: Africa

Length: Up to 3.8 m (12½ ft)

Diet: Leaves, twigs

Friend or foe?
The rhino is often attended by red-billed oxpeckers, which remove skin parasites such as bloodsucking ticks. But oxpeckers also pick at wounds to make them bleed, so they can drink the rhino's blood.

Horn structure
The horn is an outgrowth of the skin and is made of hair-like keratin fibres fused into a solid mass.

Wrinkled skin
To protect it from the sun's glare, rhinos coat their thick, rough skin in layers of mud.

Prehensile lip
The rhino uses its pointed, mobile upper lip to pluck stems and leaves.

Up to half of all male black rhinos die of injuries caused **by the horns of rival males**.

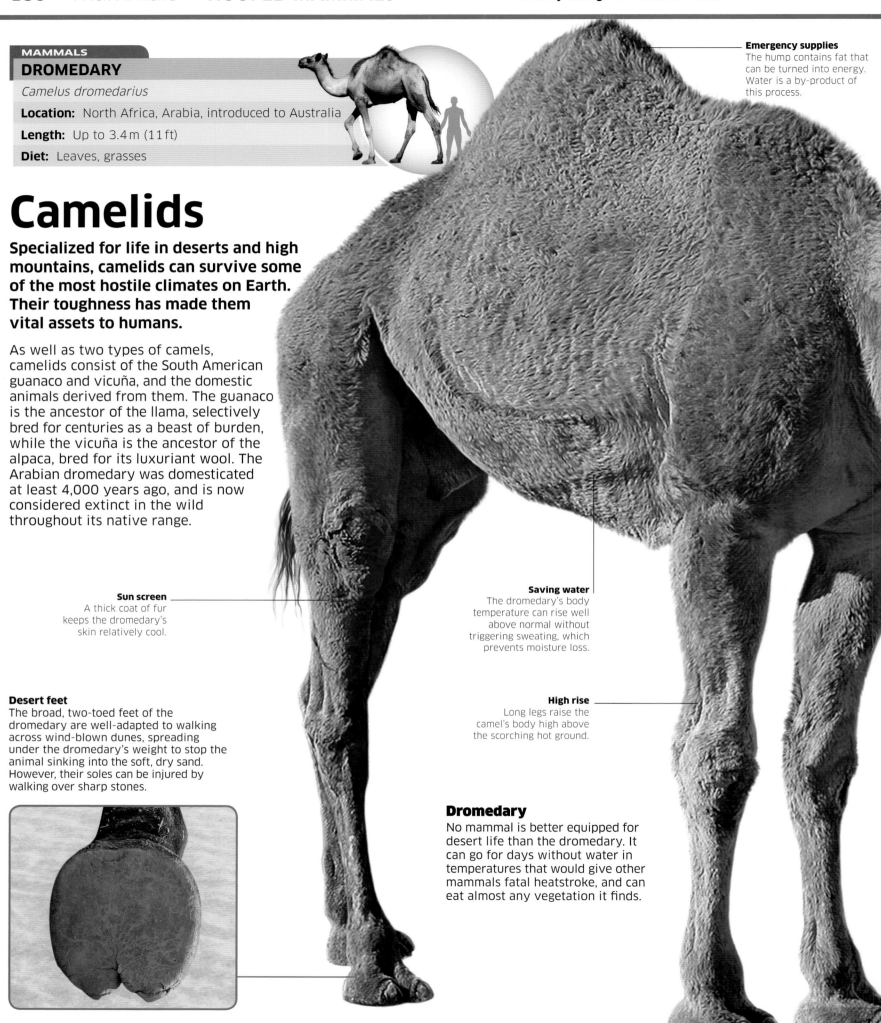

DROMEDARY

Camelus dromedarius

Location: North Africa, Arabia, introduced to Australia

Length: Up to 3.4 m (11 ft)

Diet: Leaves, grasses

Camelids

Specialized for life in deserts and high mountains, camelids can survive some of the most hostile climates on Earth. Their toughness has made them vital assets to humans.

As well as two types of camels, camelids consist of the South American guanaco and vicuña, and the domestic animals derived from them. The guanaco is the ancestor of the llama, selectively bred for centuries as a beast of burden, while the vicuña is the ancestor of the alpaca, bred for its luxuriant wool. The Arabian dromedary was domesticated at least 4,000 years ago, and is now considered extinct in the wild throughout its native range.

Emergency supplies
The hump contains fat that can be turned into energy. Water is a by-product of this process.

Sun screen
A thick coat of fur keeps the dromedary's skin relatively cool.

Saving water
The dromedary's body temperature can rise well above normal without triggering sweating, which prevents moisture loss.

Desert feet
The broad, two-toed feet of the dromedary are well-adapted to walking across wind-blown dunes, spreading under the dromedary's weight to stop the animal sinking into the soft, dry sand. However, their soles can be injured by walking over sharp stones.

High rise
Long legs raise the camel's body high above the scorching hot ground.

Dromedary
No mammal is better equipped for desert life than the dromedary. It can go for days without water in temperatures that would give other mammals fatal heatstroke, and can eat almost any vegetation it finds.

A thirsty dromedary can drink **130 litres (229 pints)** of water in just **13 minutes**.

187

Thornproof lips
Tough skin on its lips enables the dromedary to eat thorny desert shrubs.

Dust-proof
The dromedary has thick eyebrows and unusually dense, double-layered eyelashes that keep blinding dust out of its eyes during desert sandstorms. It can also close its nostrils to seal them against the dust and prevent choking.

Twin humps
The humps are small and conical.

VICUÑA
Vicugna vicugna

Location: Andes, South America
Length: Up to 1.9 m (6¼ft)

The graceful, lightly built vicuña lives in the rugged central Andes mountains, on high grassy plains, and in the Atacama Desert, where temperatures plunge to below freezing at night. It is kept warm by a dense coat of soft, fine wool that led to its domestication and the evolution of the thick-woolled alpaca.

BACTRIAN CAMEL
Camelus ferus

Location: Northwest China, Mongolia
Length: Up to 3.5 m (11½ ft)

Although it has the same adaptations for desert life as the Arabian dromedary, the two-humped Bactrian camel lives in the much colder deserts of Central Asia. Like the dromedary it was domesticated several thousand years ago, and the domestic type is now considered a different species.

GUANACO
Lama guanicoe

Location: South America
Length: Up to 2.1 m (7 ft)

The guanaco lives across South America, where it is well-adapted for cold, dry conditions. Its blood has a very high concentration of oxygen-carrying red cells which enable it to live in the thin, high-altitude air. It can even survive in the Atacama Desert – the driest hot desert on Earth.

Unlike most pigs, warthogs spend
the night in underground burrows.

The upper tusks of a male warthog
are up to 30 cm (11¾ in) long.

Sparse hair
The body is thinly covered
with bristly hair.

Cooling mud
Like most pigs, the warthog
enjoys wallowing in liquid
mud. It does this partly to
cool down in the tropical
African climate, because its
skin does not have sweat
glands. But the coating of
mud also helps protect the
skin from sunburn, and from
biting flies that could
carry disease.

Blunt upper
tusk

Common warthog

**Despite its huge tusks and strange, warty face, the warthog is a type
of wild pig. It is one of only two pig species that lives on grasslands
instead of in woodlands and forests, and it is adapted for eating the
most abundant food available in its habitat – grass.**

The warthog's spectacular upper tusks are used mainly for defence against
powerful predators such as lions and leopards. The lower pair is honed to a sharp
edge by grinding against the upper pair every time the animal closes its mouth.
These lower tusks can inflict serious injuries, but they are mostly used for
unearthing juicy roots to supplement the warthog's grassy diet.

Lethal blades
The lower tusks
are shorter and
much sharper than
the upper ones.

On bended knee

The warthog's ability to
eat grass is vital to its
survival on the African
savanna. Its short neck
and relatively long legs
make grazing tricky, so
it goes down on its
"knees", which are
actually modified wrist
joints. Thick skin pads
on the joints prevent
injury as the warthog
grazes, shuffling along
in its kneeling position.

Head to head

Mature males defend their territories from other males, ramming
each other with their blunt upper tusks. The warts on their faces
prevent serious injury and the fights are more like ritual combats
than bloody struggles.

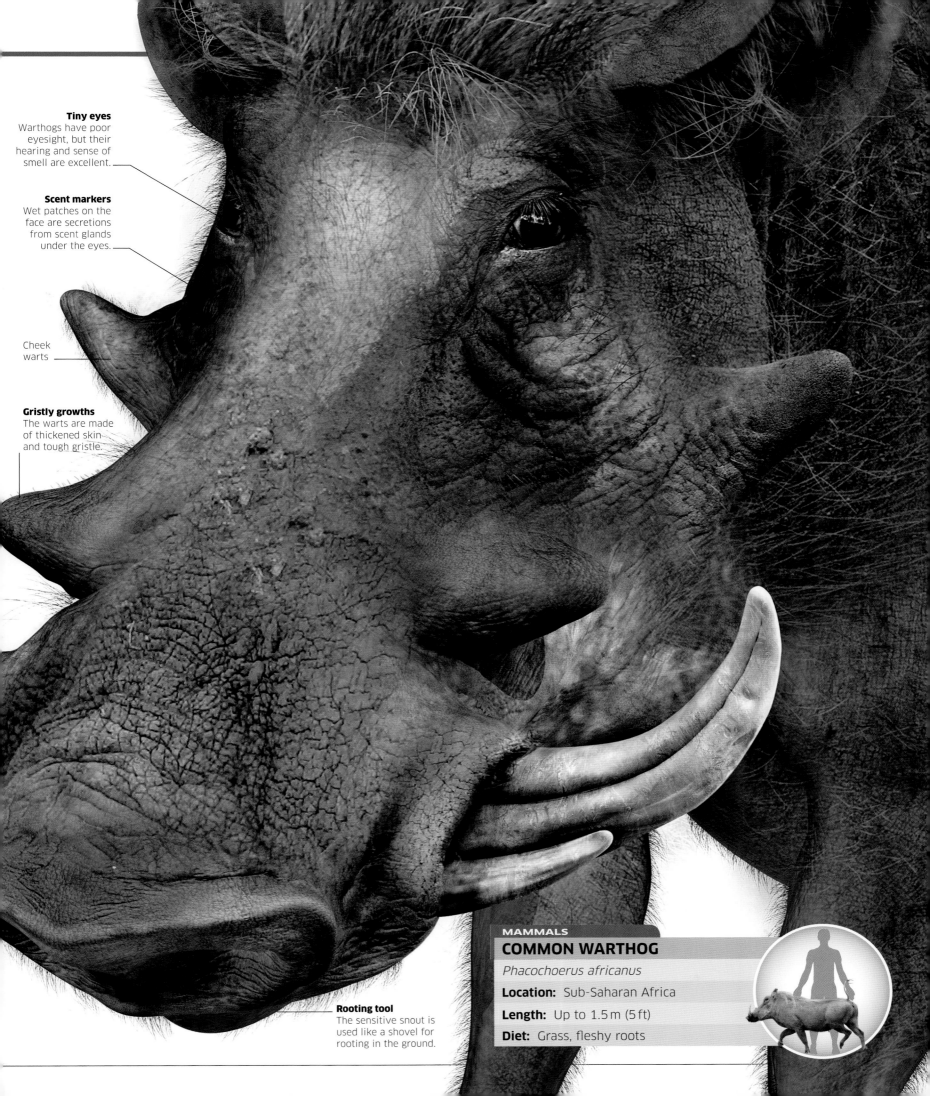

Tiny eyes
Warthogs have poor eyesight, but their hearing and sense of smell are excellent.

Scent markers
Wet patches on the face are secretions from scent glands under the eyes.

Cheek warts

Gristly growths
The warts are made of thickened skin and tough gristle.

Rooting tool
The sensitive snout is used like a shovel for rooting in the ground.

MAMMALS
COMMON WARTHOG
Phacochoerus africanus

Location: Sub-Saharan Africa

Length: Up to 1.5 m (5 ft)

Diet: Grass, fleshy roots

Western red deer

The spectacular antlers of the red deer stag are weapons, status symbols, and proof of his strength. Only the stags with the biggest antlers stand a good chance of seeing off their rivals and impressing breeding females.

The red deer is one of the biggest deer species and, as with most deer, only the male has antlers. These are shed and regrown each year, reaching full size in time for autumn when the strutting, roaring stags compete to control a harem of females to mate with. They only fight as a last resort, locking antlers and trying to push each other backwards until one gives way.

Locking horns
Competing stags have little time to eat during the breeding season, and may lose up to a fifth of their body weight.

Soft velvet
In spring the stag's antlers fall off and a new pair starts growing. A furry skin covering, called velvet, supplies them with oxygen-and nutrient-rich blood. When the antlers are fully grown, the velvet dries out and the stag rubs it off to reveal bare bone.

Built for speed
Long, slender legs provide the speed to escape predators.

Thickened mane
Stags develop a mane during the breeding season.

MAMMALS

WESTERN RED DEER

Cervus elaphus

Location: Europe to E. Asia

Length: Up to 2.05 m (6¾ ft)

Diet: Leaves, grass

2 cm (¾ in) a day – the **rate** at which **red deer antlers** grow.

During the **breeding season**, stags may even "fight" with **bushes or small trees**.

A successful stag **may mate with up to 20 females** during the breeding season.

191

Spotted young

Red deer are born with spotted coats that improve their camouflage in grass. They can stand within a few hours of birth, and are able to follow the adults by the time they are 3 or 4 weeks old. They must quickly learn to rely on speed to escape predators.

Male and female

Female red deer are smaller than the males, and have no antlers. This shows that the antlers are purely for impressing and fighting with other red deer. If they were needed for survival, females would have them too. In deer species that must compete for food, the females are more likely to have them.

Fighting is dangerous, and every year many stags are **injured or killed** by stronger rivals.

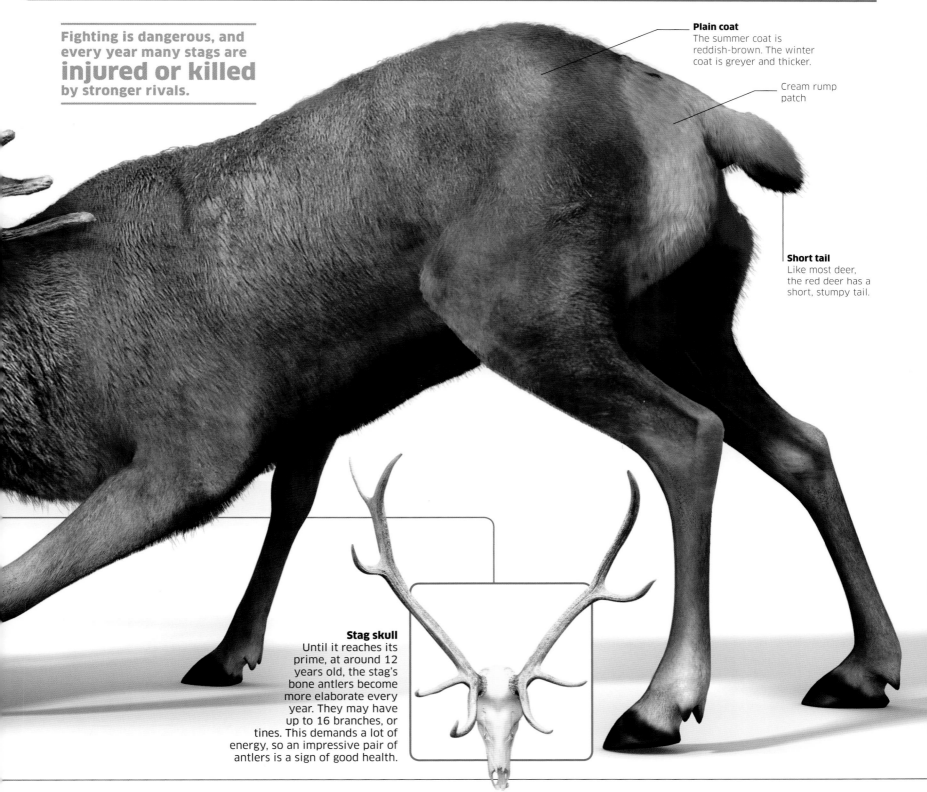

Plain coat
The summer coat is reddish-brown. The winter coat is greyer and thicker.

Cream rump patch

Short tail
Like most deer, the red deer has a short, stumpy tail.

Stag skull
Until it reaches its prime, at around 12 years old, the stag's bone antlers become more elaborate every year. They may have up to 16 branches, or tines. This demands a lot of energy, so an impressive pair of antlers is a sign of good health.

192 mammals ∘ **HOOFED MAMMALS**

1 m (3 ft) – the **length** of the **horns** of an **Alpine ibex**.

Dorsal crest

When a springbok is alarmed or excited, two folds of skin along its lower back open up to reveal a crest of white fur. The reason for this is unclear, but it certainly draws attention, alerting other springboks and warning them of possible danger.

Bovids

Ranging from elegant gazelles to hulking, heavyweight bison, the bovids are the most diverse of the hoofed animals. Many of them are distinguished by their spectacular horns.

The bovids are two-toed, hoofed animals similar to deer. Like deer they are adapted for eating leaves and grass, with complex, four-chambered stomachs for processing their bulky, fibrous food. Some are territorial animals that live in pairs or small family groups, but many more roam widely in large herds.

Cape springbok

The highly agile springbok gets its name from its habit of "pronking" – springing high off the ground. Mainly carried out by juveniles, often in response to danger, this behaviour may serve as a warning to other springbok, and to demonstrate fitness, encouraging any enemies to pick on a weaker victim.

Strong legs
Powerful muscles enable the springbok to leap high.

MAMMALS
CAPE SPRINGBOK
Antidorcas marsupialis

Location: Southwestern Africa

Length: Up to 1.1 m (3½ ft)

Diet: Grass, leaves

SERENGETI WHITE-BEARDED WILDEBEEST
Connochaetes mearnsi
Location: Eastern and southern Africa
Length: Up to 2.4 m (8 ft)

This chunky, heavy-headed antelope lives in big herds on the African savannas. It makes regular mass migrations around the grassy Serengeti plains, during which it risks falling prey to lions, wild dogs, spotted hyenas, and Nile crocodiles.

SOUTHERN GERENUK
Litocranius walleri
Location: Eastern Africa
Length: Up to 1.4 m (4½ ft)

Also called the giraffe-necked antelope, the gerenuk is an extremely slender, long-legged, agile animal that regularly stands on its hind legs to reach low tree foliage. It rarely drinks, because its food provides all the moisture it needs.

Standing tall
By balancing on its hind legs, the gerenuk can reach the juicy leaves of acacia trees.

Before 1800, up to 600 million bison roamed the prairies of North America. By 1900 there were fewer than 500 left alive.

An Arabian oryx can survive for weeks in the desert without drinking at all.

193

Ringed horns
Both sexes have horns, but the male's are much thicker and stronger.

AMERICAN BISON
Bison bison
Location: North America
Length: Up to 3.8 m (12¹/₂ ft)

The bison, or buffalo, once roamed the American prairies in vast herds, but was hunted to near-extinction in the 1800s. Bulls are colossal, with massive forequarters for fighting with rivals.

ALPINE IBEX
Capra ibex
Location: Southern Europe
Length: Up to 1.35 m (4¹/₂ ft)

The ibex is a wild goat, famous for its agility and sure-footedness in the steep, rocky terrain of its native mountains. Both sexes have horns though the male's are particularly spectacular. He uses them to spar with other males.

Gripping hooves
Split hooves with cushioned pads enable the ibex to cling to steep slopes and rocky terrain.

MUSK OX
Ovibos moschatus
Location: N. America, Greenland
Length: Up to 2.3 m (7¹/₂ ft)

A relative of sheep and goats, the musk ox is adapted for life on polar tundra, where it scrapes away snow to feed on grass, leaves, and lichens. It is often preyed upon by Arctic wolves.

ARABIAN ORYX
Oryx leucoryx
Location: Middle East
Length: Up to 2.3 m (7¹/₂ ft)

The striking-looking Arabian oryx was hunted to near-extinction by the 1970s, but has been saved by captive breeding and reintroduction. Specialized for desert life, it roams widely in search of grass that has grown in the wake of recent rainfall.

Ringed horns
Both sexes have spectacularly long horns. Males sometimes clash horns to establish dominance.

When **galloping** the giraffe can reach a **top speed** of **60 km/h (37 mph)**.

No two giraffes have exactly the **same coat pattern**.

Giraffe

The majestic giraffe is the tallest of all living animals. Its astonishing height enables it to browse high in the the treetops, where it has the pick of tender young leaves that shorter animals have no hope of reaching.

Being so tall creates problems. The giraffe has to have an unusually big heart to pump blood up to its brain, and a system for preventing fainting when it raises its head after lowering it to drink. The giraffe must also breathe fast to get enough air into its lungs. But its uniquely long neck and legs allow it to spot danger from a distance, and males use their necks to wrestle with rivals.

Muscular shoulders

Powerful legs
The giraffe's front legs can deliver a powerful kick to predators.

Tufted tail

Bony horns
This male has knobbly horns, or ossicones, which it uses when fighting other males. A female's horns are thinner and hairier.

MAMMALS

GIRAFFE

Giraffa camelopardalis

Location: Africa

Height: Up to 6 m (19¾ ft)

Diet: Leaves

Big eyes
Giraffes are able to see over long distances.

Flexible tongue
The giraffe often feeds on the tall acacia trees that dot the African savanna grasslands. But acacia twigs are very thorny, so it uses its long, mobile tongue to probe between the thorns and pull leaves into its mouth. It then uses its teeth to strip the leaves. The skin of the giraffe's tongue and lips is unusually thick, to stop the thorns piercing them.

Long muzzle

Long tongue
The tongue may be up to 45 cm (17¾ in) in length.

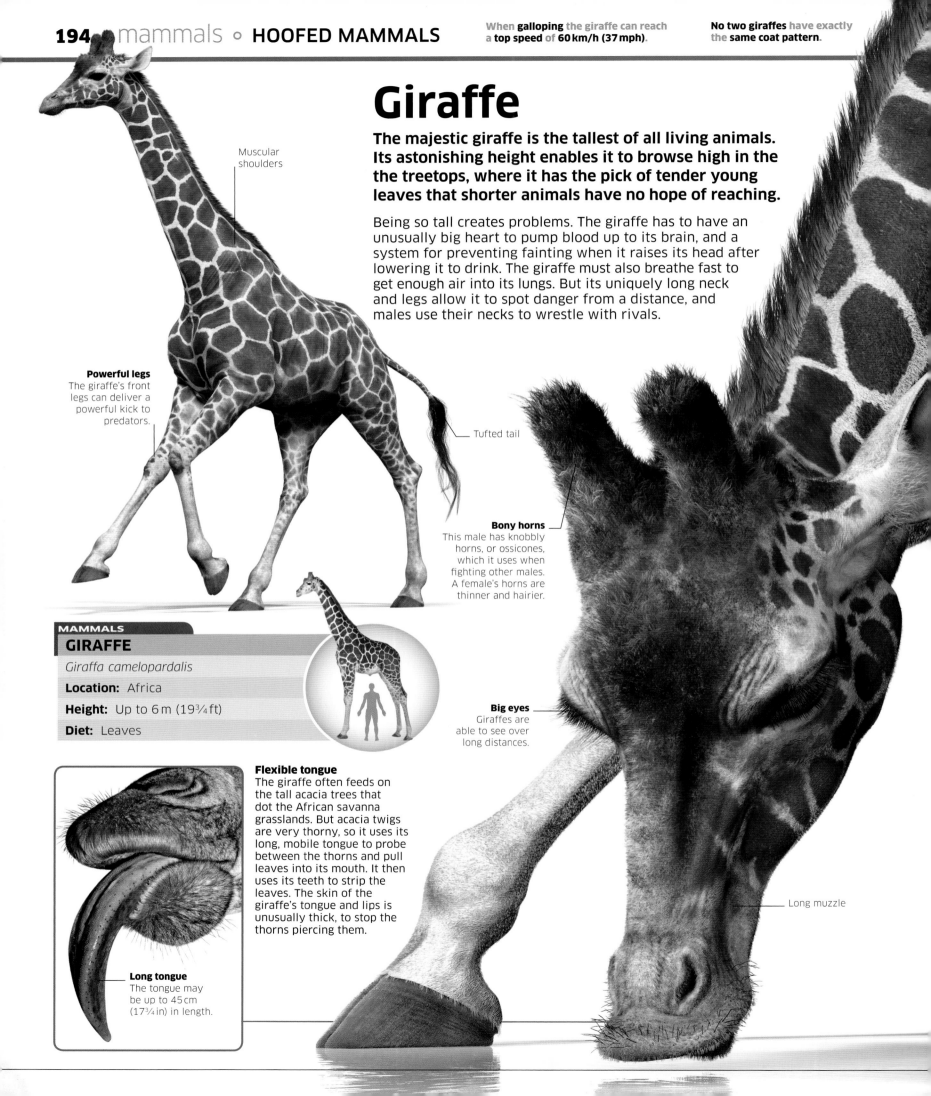

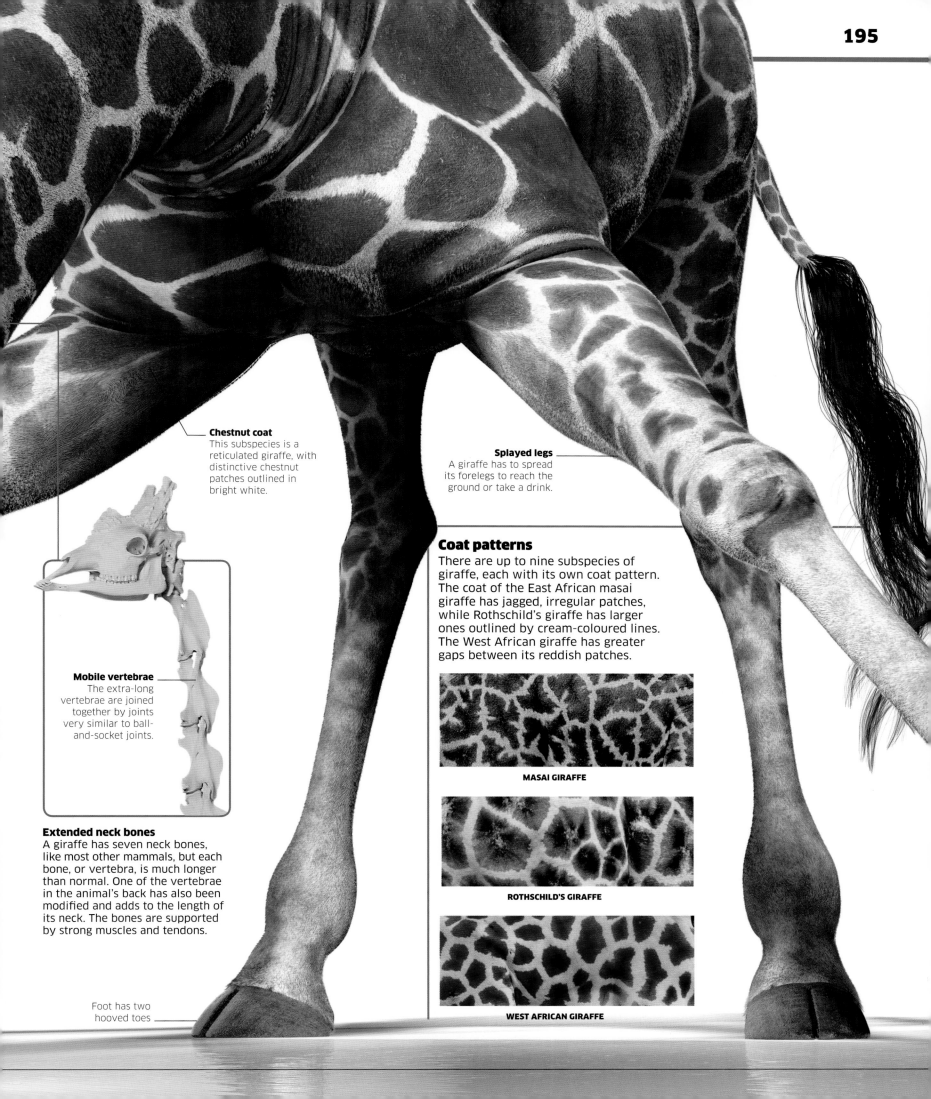

Chestnut coat
This subspecies is a reticulated giraffe, with distinctive chestnut patches outlined in bright white.

Splayed legs
A giraffe has to spread its forelegs to reach the ground or take a drink.

Mobile vertebrae
The extra-long vertebrae are joined together by joints very similar to ball-and-socket joints.

Extended neck bones

A giraffe has seven neck bones, like most other mammals, but each bone, or vertebra, is much longer than normal. One of the vertebrae in the animal's back has also been modified and adds to the length of its neck. The bones are supported by strong muscles and tendons.

Foot has two hooved toes

Coat patterns

There are up to nine subspecies of giraffe, each with its own coat pattern. The coat of the East African masai giraffe has jagged, irregular patches, while Rothschild's giraffe has larger ones outlined by cream-coloured lines. The West African giraffe has greater gaps between its reddish patches.

MASAI GIRAFFE

ROTHSCHILD'S GIRAFFE

WEST AFRICAN GIRAFFE

Hippopotamus

Despite its seemingly lazy lifestyle, the hippopotamus's unpredictable, aggressive nature makes it one of the most dangerous of African mammals.

There are only two kinds of hippo, and it has no other land-living relatives. In fact, DNA evidence shows that the hippo's closest relatives are whales, which is appropriate, as water plays a key role in a hippo's survival. By day, the hippo must escape the fierce African sun by submerging itself in water. At night, it emerges to graze on land for up to five hours, often travelling far from its daytime habitat.

Daily wallow
The hippo's skin is thick, but it dries out much faster than the skin of most mammals, so it spends much of its day wallowing in rivers or lakes. If a hippo stays out of the water for too long, its skin will be damaged by the sun and could even crack.

Natural sunblock
Glands within the hippo's skin secrete an oily fluid that turns reddish orange when exposed to the air. Pigments in the fluid act as a sunblock, absorbing the rays from the sun that cause sunburn. They also fight bacteria, helping wounds heal quickly.

Short, bristly tail

Webbed toes
Hippos walk on stout hooves with four webbed toes.

Heavyweight body
The huge, barrel-shaped body can hold a lot of bulky food.

30 km/h (19 mph) – the **speed** at which **a hippo can run**.

68 kg (150 lb) – the amount of **grass** a **hippo can eat** in one **feeding**.

197

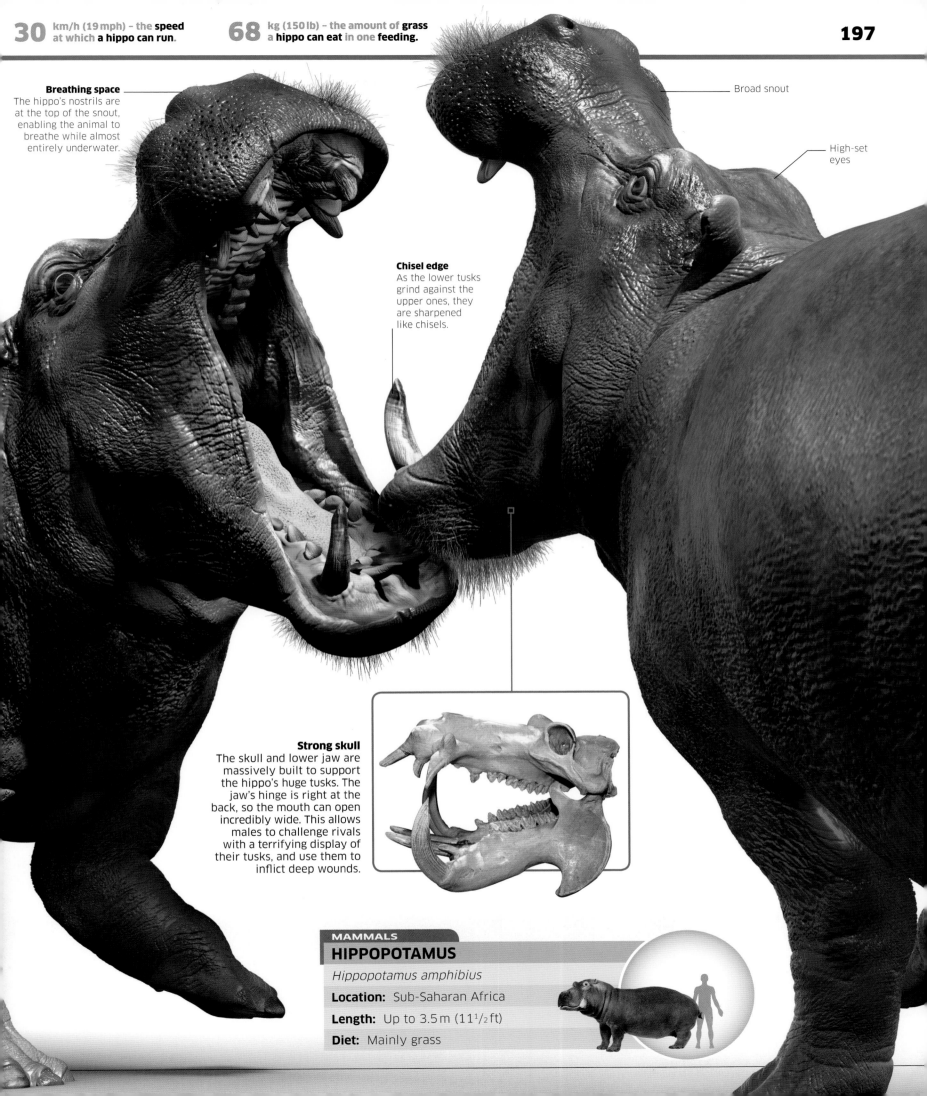

Breathing space
The hippo's nostrils are at the top of the snout, enabling the animal to breathe while almost entirely underwater.

Broad snout

High-set eyes

Chisel edge
As the lower tusks grind against the upper ones, they are sharpened like chisels.

Strong skull
The skull and lower jaw are massively built to support the hippo's huge tusks. The jaw's hinge is right at the back, so the mouth can open incredibly wide. This allows males to challenge rivals with a terrifying display of their tusks, and use them to inflict deep wounds.

MAMMALS

HIPPOPOTAMUS

Hippopotamus amphibius

Location: Sub-Saharan Africa

Length: Up to 3.5 m (11½ ft)

Diet: Mainly grass

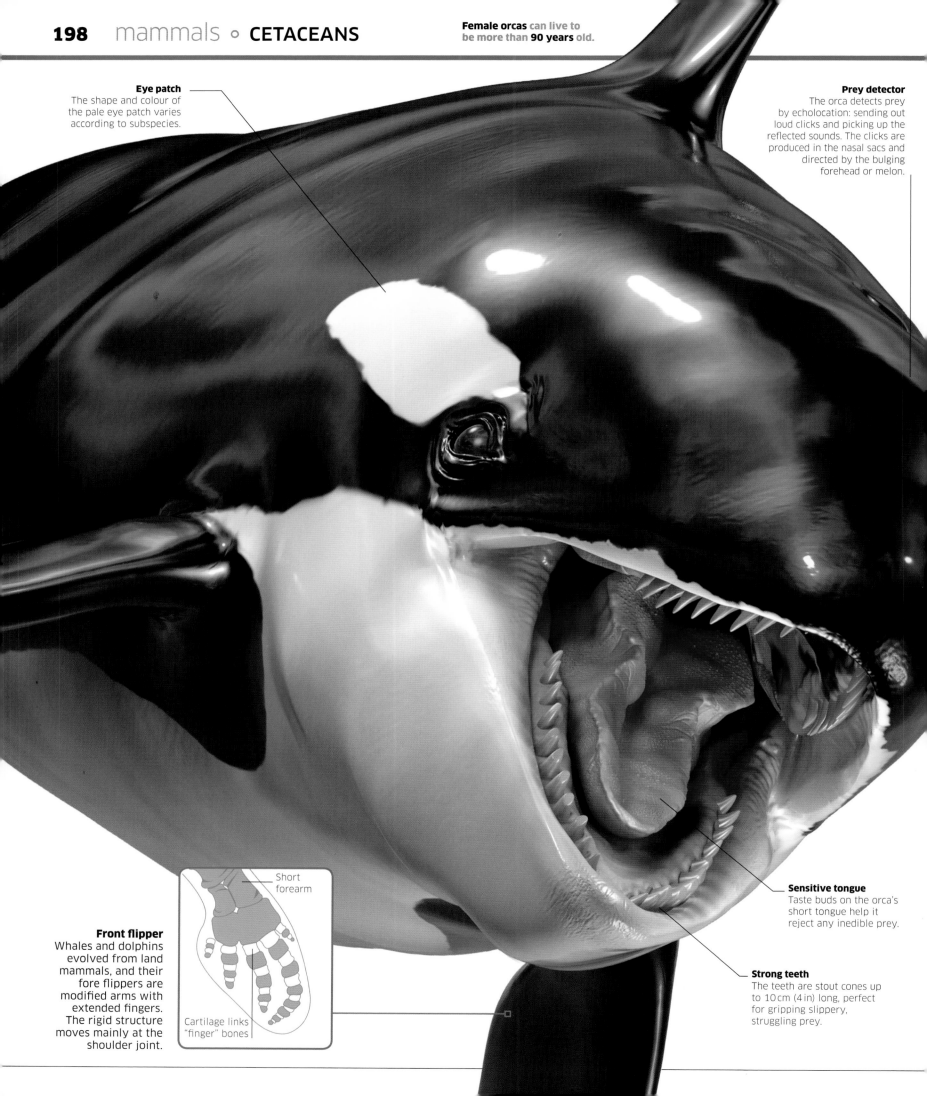

Female orcas can live to be more than **90 years** old.

Eye patch
The shape and colour of the pale eye patch varies according to subspecies.

Prey detector
The orca detects prey by echolocation: sending out loud clicks and picking up the reflected sounds. The clicks are produced in the nasal sacs and directed by the bulging forehead or melon.

Sensitive tongue
Taste buds on the orca's short tongue help it reject any inedible prey.

Strong teeth
The teeth are stout cones up to 10 cm (4 in) long, perfect for gripping slippery, struggling prey.

Front flipper
Whales and dolphins evolved from land mammals, and their fore flippers are modified arms with extended fingers. The rigid structure moves mainly at the shoulder joint.

Short forearm

Cartilage links "finger" bones

1.8 m (6 ft) – the height a
male's dorsal fin can reach.

Orcas are **highly social** and live in family
groups, or pods, of up to **40 individuals**.

An orca can swim at speeds
of up to **56 km/h (35 mph)**.

199

Dorsal fin
A female orca has a tall triangular
dorsal fin, but this is only half the
height of a male's. The shape of
the fin varies, and can be used to
identify individual orcas.

Blowhole
Like all mammals the
orca breathes air. Its nostril
is a hole in the top
of its head, which
remains closed
while the orca
is underwater.

Muscular tail
Powerful muscles
drive the orca
through the water
at high speed.

Tail flukes
The fish-like
tail has a pair
of horizontal
fin-like flukes.

Keeping close
An orca calf swims close
to its mother, and stays
with her for life, even
after reaching maturity.

Hunting together

Orcas are among the most intelligent of all animals.
They learn fast and can also pass on their knowledge
to others. This allows family groups to work together to
devise new, often ingenious ways of catching prey.

Tempting target
A "spyhopping" orca lifts its head from the water to
identify prey. Here, one has spotted a Weddell seal on
a drifting ice floe near Antarctica.

Joint action
Swimming in perfect formation, the orcas surge
towards the ice floe and dive beneath it. This pushes
up a wave that bears down on the floating ice.

Mission accomplished
The wave strikes the ice and washes over it in
a wall of water. The helpless seal is swept off the
floe and into the jaws of the waiting orcas.

MAMMALS

ORCA

Orcinus orca

Location: Worldwide

Length: Up to 9.8 m (32 ft)

Diet: Various marine animals

Orca

**Also known as the killer whale, the orca is actually a giant
dolphin that uses its intelligence and power to stalk and seize
prey ranging from small fish to sharks, seals, and even whales.**

One of the most powerful predators on the planet, the orca prowls the
world's oceans in family groups that specialize in hunting particular
types of prey. Some are experts at rounding up shoals of fish, using
a complex repertoire of sounds to coordinate their group tactics,
while others team up to outwit and ambush other marine mammals.

Every year, most humpbacks **migrate to breed** in warmer waters, covering more than **8,300 km (5,157 miles) each way**.

Tail behaviour
The whale uses its giant tail to make a loud cracking noise by slapping it against the surface of the water. This is called lobtailing and is thought to be a form of communication with other whales.

Driving force
The powerful tail propels the whale through the water.

Humpback whale

Renowned for its spectacular leaps right out of the water, the humpback is one of the baleen whales – ocean giants that feed by filtering seawater for small animals. It is one of the largest and heaviest living things on the planet.

The humpback is a type of whale known as a rorqual, which has a series of pleats extending beneath its body from its chin to its belly. When the whale is feeding, the pleats allow the throat to expand like a balloon and hold a huge volume of water. The whale uses its colossal tongue to force the water out of its mouth, through a mesh of bristly plates called baleen. The whale then swallows the fish and other small animals trapped by the baleen, before gulping another giant mouthful of water.

Black and white
Smooth skin is black above, and mottled white below.

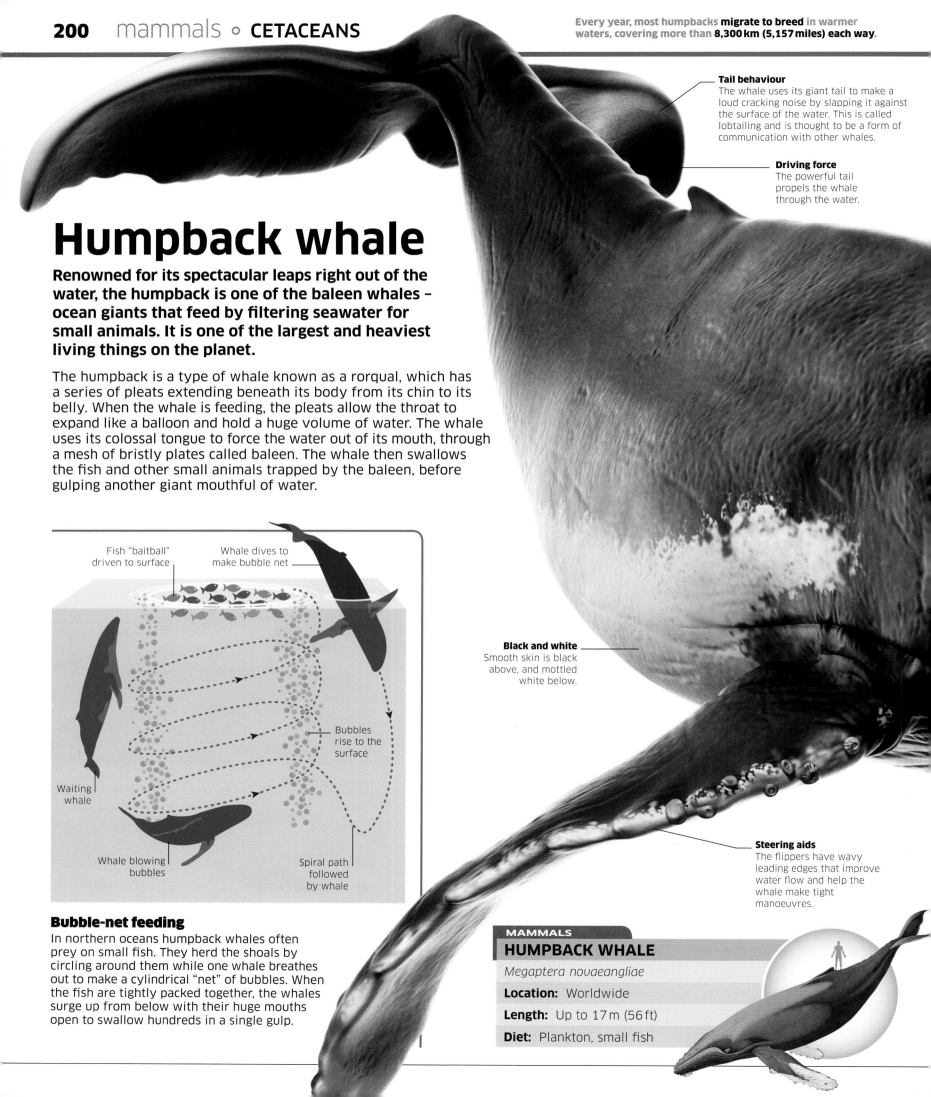

Fish "baitball" driven to surface

Whale dives to make bubble net

Bubbles rise to the surface

Waiting whale

Whale blowing bubbles

Spiral path followed by whale

Steering aids
The flippers have wavy leading edges that improve water flow and help the whale make tight manoeuvres.

Bubble-net feeding

In northern oceans humpback whales often prey on small fish. They herd the shoals by circling around them while one whale breathes out to make a cylindrical "net" of bubbles. When the fish are tightly packed together, the whales surge up from below with their huge mouths open to swallow hundreds in a single gulp.

MAMMALS

HUMPBACK WHALE

Megaptera novaeangliae

Location: Worldwide

Length: Up to 17 m (56 ft)

Diet: Plankton, small fish

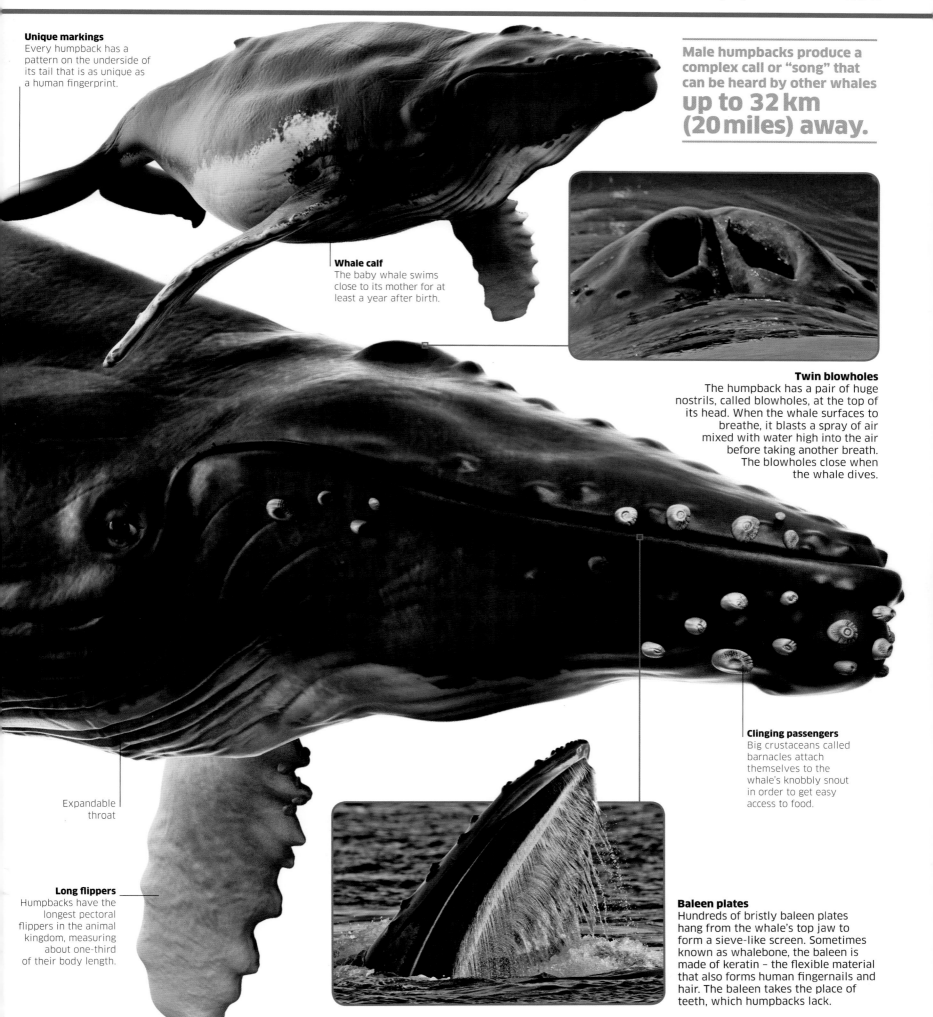

34 tonnes – the **weight of a humpback whale**, more than **three times** that of an adult **African savanna elephant**.

An **adult humpback** can eat **more than 1,000 kg (2,200 lb)** of **small fish and krill** every day.

201

Unique markings
Every humpback has a pattern on the underside of its tail that is as unique as a human fingerprint.

Male humpbacks produce a complex call or "song" that can be heard by other whales **up to 32 km (20 miles) away.**

Whale calf
The baby whale swims close to its mother for at least a year after birth.

Twin blowholes
The humpback has a pair of huge nostrils, called blowholes, at the top of its head. When the whale surfaces to breathe, it blasts a spray of air mixed with water high into the air before taking another breath. The blowholes close when the whale dives.

Expandable throat

Clinging passengers
Big crustaceans called barnacles attach themselves to the whale's knobbly snout in order to get easy access to food.

Long flippers
Humpbacks have the longest pectoral flippers in the animal kingdom, measuring about one-third of their body length.

Baleen plates
Hundreds of bristly baleen plates hang from the whale's top jaw to form a sieve-like screen. Sometimes known as whalebone, the baleen is made of keratin – the flexible material that also forms human fingernails and hair. The baleen takes the place of teeth, which humpbacks lack.

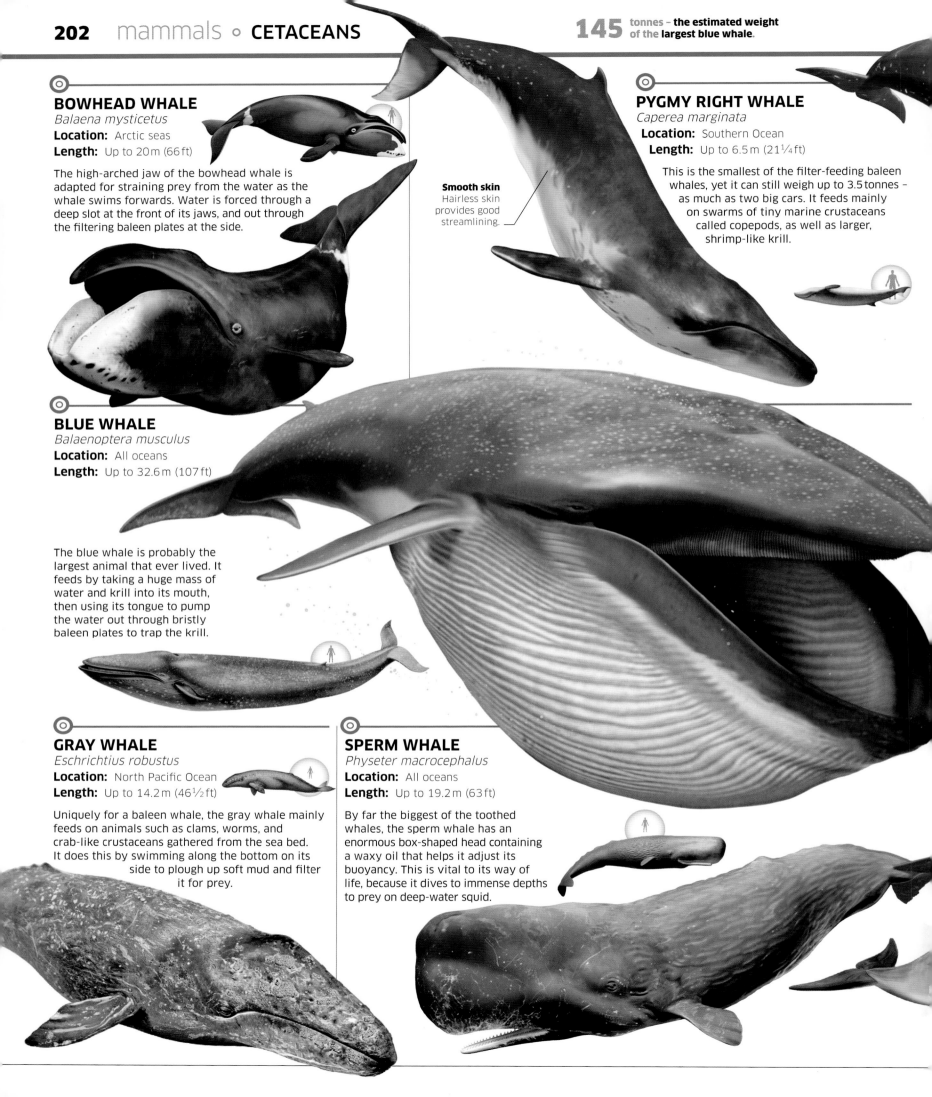

BOWHEAD WHALE
Balaena mysticetus
Location: Arctic seas
Length: Up to 20 m (66 ft)

The high-arched jaw of the bowhead whale is adapted for straining prey from the water as the whale swims forwards. Water is forced through a deep slot at the front of its jaws, and out through the filtering baleen plates at the side.

Smooth skin
Hairless skin provides good streamlining.

PYGMY RIGHT WHALE
Caperea marginata
Location: Southern Ocean
Length: Up to 6.5 m (21¼ ft)

This is the smallest of the filter-feeding baleen whales, yet it can still weigh up to 3.5 tonnes – as much as two big cars. It feeds mainly on swarms of tiny marine crustaceans called copepods, as well as larger, shrimp-like krill.

BLUE WHALE
Balaenoptera musculus
Location: All oceans
Length: Up to 32.6 m (107 ft)

The blue whale is probably the largest animal that ever lived. It feeds by taking a huge mass of water and krill into its mouth, then using its tongue to pump the water out through bristly baleen plates to trap the krill.

GRAY WHALE
Eschrichtius robustus
Location: North Pacific Ocean
Length: Up to 14.2 m (46½ ft)

Uniquely for a baleen whale, the gray whale mainly feeds on animals such as clams, worms, and crab-like crustaceans gathered from the sea bed. It does this by swimming along the bottom on its side to plough up soft mud and filter it for prey.

SPERM WHALE
Physeter macrocephalus
Location: All oceans
Length: Up to 19.2 m (63 ft)

By far the biggest of the toothed whales, the sperm whale has an enormous box-shaped head containing a waxy oil that helps it adjust its buoyancy. This is vital to its way of life, because it dives to immense depths to prey on deep-water squid.

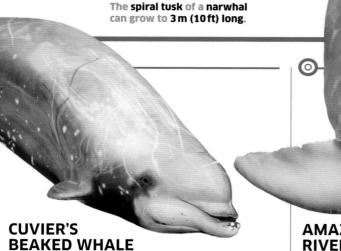

The **spiral tusk of a narwhal** can grow to **3 m (10 ft)** long.

In 2011, a **Cuvier's beaked whale** dived to a depth of **2,992 m (9,816 ft)** – the **deepest recorded dive** by any mammal.

203

NARWHAL
Monodon monoceros
Location: Arctic seas
Length: Up to 5 m (16½ ft)

The narwhal is remarkable for the spiral tusk that projects from the male's upper jaw. This is now thought to be a sensory organ, able to pick up changes in the narwhal's environment, but it is also used for fighting and attracting a mate.

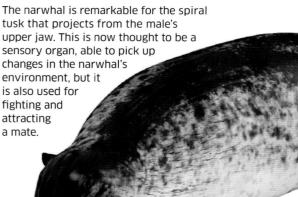

CUVIER'S BEAKED WHALE
Ziphius cavirostris
Location: All oceans except Arctic
Length: Up to 7 m (23 ft)

Named for their beak-like snouts, the mysterious beaked whales are rarely seen because they live in the open ocean. This is the most widespread of 22 species, and has a protruding lower jaw, which in mature males is adorned with large peg-like teeth.

AMAZON RIVER DOLPHIN
Inia geoffrensis
Location: Amazon river basin
Length: Up to 2.5 m (8¼ ft)

One of a small number of freshwater dolphins, this lives in muddy waters, where it hunts largely by underwater echolocation. Its long snout is lined with two types of teeth for dealing with different types of prey, including fish, crabs, and turtles.

Cetaceans

This group – the whales, dolphins, and porpoises – includes the biggest animals on the planet. The largest and most powerful marine predator, the orca (see pp.242–243), belongs to this group, as well as some of the most intelligent of all animals.

Cetaceans are the most highly specialized of all marine mammals, feeding and breeding at sea. There are two types – the giant baleen whales that filter small animals from the water, and the group of generally smaller toothed whales, including dolphins and porpoises, which prey on larger fish and squid.

Prominent bulge or "melon"

BELUGA
Delphinapterus leucas
Location: Arctic seas
Length: Up to 4.5 m (14¾ ft)

Closely related to the narwhal, the beluga is unique among whales for its all-white skin. Highly social, it lives in groups that gather in crowds of hundreds or even thousands during the summer birthing season.

VAQUITA
Phocoena sinus
Location: Gulf of California
Length: Up to 1.5 m (5 ft)

The smallest and rarest porpoise, the vaquita is found in very shallow waters and feeds on fish and squid. Because of its limited range it is the most seriously endangered of all marine mammals.

COMMON BOTTLENOSED DOLPHIN
Tursiops truncatus
Location: All warm oceans
Length: Up to 3.8 m (12½ ft)

Dolphins are small toothed whales adapted for fast swimming in pursuit of prey. This is the most well-known species – a highly social, very intelligent animal with a complex form of language and a remarkable ability to learn new skills.

LONG-FINNED PILOT WHALE
Globicephala melas
Location: North Atlantic and Southern Oceans
Length: Up to 6.7 m (22 ft)

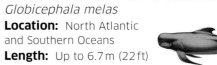

This is a large dolphin, but with an unusually bulbous forehead. This forehead swelling, or melon, contains a structure that – as with all toothed whales – focuses the animal's echolocation clicks, enabling it to detect prey in dark water.

Index

Acknowledgments

The publisher would like to thank the following people for their assistance in the preparation of this book: Sheila Collins, Kshitiz Dhobhal, Mik Gates, Pooja Pipil, Heena Sharma, and Jemma Westing for design assistance; Ann Baggaley, Carron Brown, Stella Caldwell, Agnibesh Das, Charlie Galbraith, and Deeksha Saikia for editorial assistance; Nishwan Rasool for additional picture research; Kealy Wilson and Ellen Nanney from the Smithsonian Institution; Hazel Beynon for proofreading; and Jackie Brind for the index.

Smithsonian Enterprises:
Kealy E. Gordon, Product Development Manager
Ellen Nanney, Licensing Manager
Brigid Ferraro, Vice President, Education and Consumer Products
Carol LeBlanc, Senior Vice President, Education and Consumer Products
Chris Liedel, President

Curator for the Smithsonian:
Dr. Don E. Wilson, Curator Emeritus of the Department of Vertebrate Zoology, National Museum of Natural History, Smithsonian

The publisher would like to thank the following for their kind permission to reproduce photographs:

(Key: a-above; b-below/bottom; c-centre; f-far; l-left; r-right; t-top)

123RF.com: tudor antonel adrian 13tc, Andreas Altenburger 124cl, Ivanov Arkady 84crb, belizar 185tl, bennymarty 192cr, Vladimir Blinov 193bl, Steve Byland 111cla, 114tc, Berangere Duforets 148cla, Абаджева Марина 81cb, 84clb, dirk ercken 68tc, Iakov Filimonov 91crb, 152clb (DHOLE), Teresa Gueck 6cb, 32tl, Irina Iglina 159ca, Eric Isselee 31crb, 85clb, 174tl, 114cl, 124bc, 132tc,217tr, 141tl, 165tr, 176tc, 177tr, 194c, Michal Kadleček 155bc (hunting salmon), Anan Kaewkhammul 177cr, kajornyot 106tr, Naveen Kalwa 46cr, Micha Klootwijk 81c, 111tc, 111crb, 166bl, Sommai Larkjit 125cra, Keith Levit 165tc, Peter Llewellyn 139br, Tracie Louise 114bl, Bruce MacQueen 101cra, Maurizio Giovanni Bersanelli 192bc, Andreas Meyer 49bc, moori 177c, Christian Musat 193cb, NewAge 107tl, Wannee Nimcharoen 115bl, Duncan Noakes 172c, 189br, coroiu octavian 115c, Alexandr Pakhnyushchyy 143crb, photoroad 146cl, Alex Popov 151tc, Eduardo Rivero 111clb, Ron Rowan 135bc, Andrei Samkov 150tc, Alexey Sokolov 111cra, Sergei Uriadnikov 147tr, Vasiliy Vishnevskiy 140cla, Allan Wallberg 114bc, wirojsid 147tc, wrangel 103cla, 104tc, 176clb, Teerayut Yukuntapornpong 14c, Michael Zysman 86ca; **Alamy Stock Photo:** David A. Northcott / Corbis 80clb, The Africa Image Library 188bc, age fotostock 15clb, Arco Images GmbH 155br, Arctic Images 158c, RIEGER Bertrand / hemis.fr 91bc, Juniors Bildarchiv / F260 63bc, Juniors Bildarchiv / F349 179br, Ger Bosma 20tc,20cl, Arco / C. Hütter 91clb, J & C Sohns / imageBROKER 81tl, Chris Godfrey Wildlife Photography 174cl, Hugh Clark / Nature Photographers Ltd 148br, JAMES D WATT / Stephen Frink Collection 201cra, Ethan Daniels 53br, Sarah Darnell / RGB Ventures / SuperStock 191tr, David R. Frazier Photolibrary, Inc. 143tl, Keith Douglas 155cr, dpa picture alliance archive 81tc, Arnold Drapkin / ZUMAPRESS.com 199tl, Mark Duffy 133cla, Val Duncan / Kenebec Images 175cr, Stuart Dyer 83cr, Jason Edwards / National Geographic Creative 120tl, Roger Eritja 24cl, 108bl, 122clb, 151cr, 151crb, Fve Media 90cla, John Gibbens / Design Pics Inc 162cla, André Gilden 168tc, Paul Gordon 186bl, Jonathan Hewitt 143br, Martha Holmes / Nature Picture Library 196cla, Christian Hütter20bc, imageBROKER 170bl, Jason O. Watson 77crb, David Keith Jones / Images of Africa Photobank 195c, blickwinkel / Koenig 89c, 134crb, Don Johnston_MA 175bl, Thomas Marent / Rolf Nussbaumer Photography 141clb, Michael Patrick O'Neill 45br, MichaelGrantWildlife 65crb, Mint Images Limited 90bl, Zeeshan Mirza / ephotocorp 89tl, MShieldsPhotos 131tc, William Mullins 112clb, National Geographic Creative 145cr, Natural History Museum, London 103cra, Naturepix 31cl, Norman Owen Tomalin / Bruce Coleman Inc. 123bc, Pink Sun Media 141cb, Sergio Pitamitz / Corbis 128cl, Radius Images 119br, robertharding 196tr, Willi Rolfes / Premium Stock Photography GmbH 191tc, Andreas Rose / imageBROKER 146cb, 160cl, Aditya "Dicky" Singh 146tr, Tom Soucek / Design Pics Inc 156tl, inga spence 157cr, 161bl, Walt Stearns / Stephen Frink Collection 57cr, tbkmedia.de 188br, Dave Watts 195bc, Terry Whittaker 177tc, WILDLIFE GmbH 28bl, 29cr, 162clb, Wildscotphotos 163cla, blickwinkel / Woike 112c, Bernd Zoller / imageBROKER 108bc; **Ardea:** Steve Downer 13cr, Adrian Warren 82tr, M. Watson 98clb, 127crb; **Australian Antarctic Division:** Tony Bojkovski 99tr; Fabrice Chanson 137c; **Corbis:** 102cla, Theo Allofs / Minden Pictures 114tr, Ingo Arndt / Minden Pictures 64tr, 154bl, FLPA / Bernd Rohrschneider 125ca, Jürgen & Christine Sohns / imageBROKER 152cl, Clouds Hill Imaging Ltd. 48br, Sylvain Cordier / Copyright : www.biosphoto.com / Biosphoto 190tr, Daniel J. Cox 163c, Stephen Dalton / Minden Pictures 89cr, 89bl, 148ca, Reinhard Dirscherl 6cb (Jellyfish), Suzi Eszterhas / Minden Pictures 137tr, Warren Faidley 92cr (SKY), Katherine Feng / Minden Pictures 157br, Gallo Images 172cl, Sergey Gorshkov / Minden Pictures 166crb, 199tr, Darrell Gulin 135tc, Martin Harvey 194bl, Huetter, C 143tc, Imaginechina 132cb, Mitsuhiko Imamori / Minden Pictures 16bl, Stephen J. Krasemann / All Canada Photos 130clb, Adam Jones / Visuals Unlimited 34clb, Frans Lanting 124tr, 195cb, Boden / Ledingham / Masterfile 165cr, Albert Lleal / Minden Pictures 28cb, 109cr, Thomas Marent / Minden Pictures 145br, ZSSD / Minden Pictures 34cla, Momatiuk - Eastcott 163ca, Nature Connect 37cl, Andrey Nekrasov / imageBROKER 12ca, Flip Nicklin / Minden Pictures 52c, 105tr, 137bc, D. Parer & E. Parer-Cook / Minden Pictures 10bl, 120bl, Norbert Probst / imagebroker 54tc, Fritz Rauschenbach 29cr, Mary Robbins / National Geographic My Shot / National Geographic Creative 184br, Zack Seckler 105cr, Roland Seitre / Minden Pictures 121cr, 124clb, 140cl, 148tr, 182clb (Kiang), Anup Shah / Minden Pictures 143tr, Paul Souders 162cb, Fotofeeling / Westend61 76cl, Terry Whittaker / FLPA 175br, Steve Winter / National Geographic Creative 172tl, Christian Ziegler / Minden Pictures 148c; **Dorling Kindersley:** Andy and Gill Swash 152cla, Blackpool Zoo 187tr, Blackpool Zoo, Lancashire, UK 133cb, 136tl, 182clb, British Wildlife Centre, Surrey, UK 167tr, 190bc, Cotswold Wildlife Park 132cra, Cotswold Wildlife Park & Gardens, Oxfordshire, UK 126tc, Peter Janzen 66crb, Twan Leenders 62cb, 67tc, 74clb, 78tr, 79tl, Liberty's Owl, Raptor and Reptile Centre, Hampshire, UK 35crb, 102cr, 103br, 109br, The National Birds of Prey Centre, Gloucestershire 102tc, Natural History Museum, London 15crb, 26tr, 26clb, 26cb, 27cla, 31clb, 48clb,77cr, 157tr, 202crb, 203cla, Dr. Peter M Forster 51cr, Linda Pitkin 51tc, John White 67cl, Wildlife Heritage Foundation, Kent, UK 170ca, 174tr, Jerry Young 67tl, 67clb, 91tr, 121crb, 149ca, 150bc; **Dr Don Hodgers:** 21bl; **Dreamstime.com:** 155bc, Aaskolnick 31cr, Guido Amrein 162br, Kushnirov Avraham 143cr, Mikhail Blajenov 91cr, 106cl, 159cla, Lukas Blazek 141cr, Canvaschameleons 80br, Neal Cooper 115cra, Kim Deadman 77tr, Jelle Dekker 7cr, Divehive 42cr, Geza Farkas 26crb, Simone Gatterwe 199cb, Hakoar 106ca, Hotshotsworldwide 139bc, Hungchungchih 156tr, Isselee 85br, 101clb, Junkii 101bc, Denise Kappa 154tr, Karin59 103cl, Brian Kushner 102ca, Lucasdm 171br, Ludek Lukac 132clb, Mgkuijpers 81crb, 106tl, 183bc, Mychadre77 6cl, PeterWaters 36tr, Photooasis 26tc, Pnwnature 14tl, Konstantin Pukhov 193crb, Rafael Benari 103cb, Paulo Resende 78tc, Jason P Ross 71cb, 77bc, Rqs 30tc, Scattoselvaggio 134br, Shijianying 31cb, Brandon Smith 159cr, Teo1000 130bc, Trubavin 141cl, Woravit Vijitpanya 84cra, Vincentstthomas 141tr, Vladvitek 106cb, Marion Wear 124tl; **Edith Smith / Shady Oak Butterfly Farm:** 27tr; **FLPA:** Samuel Blanc / Biosphoto 163crb, Bill Coster 98tr, Robin Hausmann / Imagebroker 186tc, Jurgen & Christine Sohns 126bl, 188tr, Michael & Patricia Fogden 84cb, Minden Pictures 179bl, Philip Perry 184bc, Photo Researchers 95tr, 70tl, Chris & Tilde Stuart 184tr; **Fotolia:** Chrispo 107clb, Eric Isselee 197br, Strezhnev Pavel 116cr, Stefan Zeitz / Lux 107bc; **Getty Images:** Jonathan Bird 51tr, Mark Carwardine 99cra, David Cayless 170cb, David Courtenay 161br, Stephen Dalton 46tr, Daniel.Candal 97tl David W. Macdonald 180bl, Martin Harvey 180tl, Richard Herrmann 39tr, Jared Hobbs 113cra, Don Johnston 201bc, Rene Krekels / NiS / Minden Pictures 68br, Kenny Lee 100tr, Paul Nicklen 99cr, Pal Teravagimov Photography 113c, Panoramic Images 145bl, Doug Perrine 56bl, David Tipling / Digital Vision 92c (snow), v_ac_md 166tl, Mark Webster 38cl, Steve Winter 168bc; **imagequestmarine.com:** 39tr; **Jeroen Kooijman:** 35bl; **Jocelyn Rastel Lafond:** 165bc; **naturepl.com:** Dave Bevan 113crb, 113br, Jane Burton 53tl, Georgette Douwma 11tl, Suzi Eszterhas 161cr, Tony Heald 192tc, Kathryn Jeffs 199crb, 199br, Klein & Hubert 180bc, Steve Knell 113bl, Mark MacEwen 129tr, Owen Newman 122tc, Fred Olivier 99br, Constantinos Petrinos 52tl, Michael Pitts 82c, Jeff Rotman 12clb, Roland Seitre 120bc, 135clb, Martin Camm (WAC) 202cra, 203clb, **Dick Newell:** 164bl; **Oceanwidelmages.com:** Gary Bell 48tc; **Photoshot:** Gerald Cubitt / NHPA 136cb, Paulo de Oliveira / NHPA 46tl, 47tr, Nigel Downer 72bl, D. Robert Franz 101cr, Martin Harvey / NHPA 184bl, Daniel Heuclin 199cb, Mel Longhurst / Bruce Coleman 197cb, Thorsten Negro / Imagebroker 85cra, Oceans Image 50cl, Kjell Sandved 187ca, David Slater / NHPA 68bc, Layer, W. / Picture Alliance 153cr; **Press Association Images:** Themba Hadebe / AP 185tc; **Professor John R. Hutchinson,The Royal Veterinary College, United Kingdom:** 138tl; **Reuters:** 19br, **Chris Schuster:** 22cla; **Science Photo Library:** 25bl, Andy Harmer 21crb, **SeaPics.com:** C & M Fallows 57tr, www.skullsunlimited.com:** 179cl, 195cl; **stevebloom.com:** Jany Sauvanet / Biosphoto 87cl; **SuperStock:** Animals Animals 154cl, Biosphoto 199cr, Minden Pictures 144br, Roland Seitre / Minden Pictures 123bl; **Jean-Christophe Theil:** 86bc; **Tom M. Fayle:** 18cl; **Skulls Unlimited International, inc./ www.SkullsUnlimited.com:** 191bc; **Karen Warkentin:** 65bl